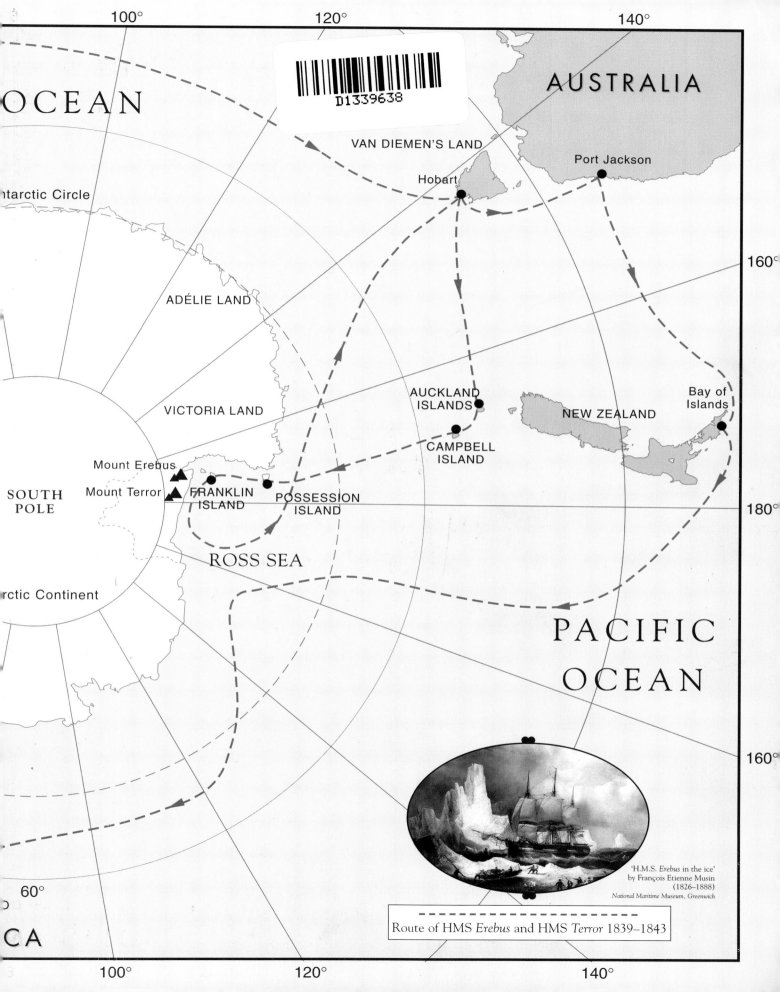

OCEAN

AUSTRALIA

VAN DIEMEN'S LAND

Port Jackson

Antarctic Circle

160°

ADÉLIE LAND

Hobart

AUCKLAND
ISLANDS

NEW ZEALAND

Bay of
Islands

VICTORIA LAND

CAMPBELL
ISLAND

180°

Mount Erebus

SOUTH
POLE

Mount Terror

FRANKLIN
ISLAND

POSSESSION
ISLAND

ROSS SEA

Arctic Continent

PACIFIC

60°

OCEAN

CA

100°   120°   140°

160°

'H.M.S. Erebus in the ice'
by François Etienne Musin
(1826–1888)
National Maritime Museum, Greenwich

Route of HMS Erebus and HMS Terror 1839–1843

SIR JOSEPH DALTON
HOOKER
TRAVELLER AND PLANT COLLECTOR

SIR JOSEPH DALTON
HOOKER

TRAVELLER AND PLANT COLLECTOR

RAY DESMOND

Preface by Sir Ghillean Prance

ANTIQUE COLLECTORS' CLUB
with
THE ROYAL BOTANIC GARDENS, KEW

DEDICATION

This book is dedicated to Viscount Eccles, who generously supported the restoration of Sir Joseph Hooker's portfolio of drawings from his Himalayan voyages and other book restoration projects of the Library of the Royal Botanic Gardens, Kew.

©1999 Ray Desmond
World copyright reserved
First published 1999

ISBN 1 85149 305 0

The right of Ray Desmond to be identified as author of this work has been asserted by him in accordance with the Copyright, Designs and Patents Act 1988

British Library Cataloguing-in-Publication Data
A catalogue record for this book is available from the British Library

Frontispiece: *The Lachoong (Lachung) valley in Sikkim which Hooker describes in his* Himalayan Journals. *(Photograph by Henry Noltie who botanised there in 1996.)*

Printed in England
by the Antique Collectors' Club Ltd., Woodbridge, Suffolk on Consort Royal Satin paper
supplied by the Donside Paper Company, Aberdeen, Scotland

CONTENTS

PREFACE

I have long been an admirer of my distant predecessor Sir Joseph Dalton Hooker and so it is a special pleasure to introduce this book. My own interest in Hooker began through use of the Bentham and Hooker *Handbook of the British Flora*. Later when working on my doctoral thesis I found that it was Joseph Hooker who wrote the treatment of the Chrysobalanaceae, which I was studying, for the Martius *Flora Brasiliensis*. Still later as I began a phase of extensive fieldwork in the Amazon region I became even more fascinated by the travels of Joseph Hooker. In this new book we can learn so much more about them than from Leonard Huxley's *Life and Letters of Sir Joseph Hooker.*

Soon after my arrival at Kew, as its eleventh Director, I was shown the wonderful portfolio of Hooker's drawings made on his travels in India. I was delighted that these precious documents were to be restored, thanks to the generous support of Viscount Eccles, the father of the then Chairman of our Board of Trustees, John Eccles. I was immediately convinced, not only of the importance of the restoration and preservation of the Hooker drawings, but also of the need to publish them together with an accompanying text.

Having read the fascinating manuscript submitted to me by Ray Desmond I am absolutely delighted that he persuaded us that there was a need for a broader work that covered much more of the travels of this nineteenth century traveller, explorer, taxonomist and phytogeographer. Desmond has produced yet another thoroughly researched and thoroughly readable book. Once I started reading it was hard to put the manuscript down. Desmond has certainly done justice to the travels of one of the great botanists and explorers of the last century.

Hooker's journeys to the remote and unexplored parts of the planet were not for adventure, but for the purpose of finding out more about plants and why and how they got to the different places where they occur. We are fortunate that Hooker wrote down so much about his observations and his interpretation of the facts which he gathered.

Today we take cameras on expeditions to record the plants and places we visit. It is perhaps fortunate that a talented artist like Hooker travelled before the days of compact portable cameras and so developed greater artistic skills which are amply portrayed in this book. I can only wonder why this book was not done sooner.

Sir Ghillean Prance FRS
Director
Royal Botanic Gardens, Kew

INTRODUCTION

When I was asked by the Royal Botanic Gardens at Kew to write an accompanying text to a selection of Sir Joseph Hooker's Indian topographical drawings, it occurred to me that it was also an opportunity to present a general overview of his travels in the southern hemisphere, the Middle East, Morocco and the United States as well as in India. They were all very productive excursions – he sketched, kept a journal, collected specimens for herbaria, and plants and seeds for British gardens – yet his reputation as a distinguished traveller has been overshadowed by his achievements as a plant taxonomist and geographer, although his expertise in these disciplines had been shaped and refined by his explorations.

Nicolas Bentley, discussing travel literature, believed that 'what counts is not the geography or the climate or the flora, it is the traveller's attitude of mind'. Hooker's 'attitude of mind' was one of infinite curiosity, a natural inquisitiveness about many subjects: fauna as well as flora, landscape and buildings, other cultures. His narrative skills were stimulated by exotic or primitive peoples such as the Maoris in New Zealand, the Lepchas in Sikkim, and the Indians in Tierra del Fuego. He had an eye for colourful or striking characters. In a few sentences he could deftly sketch the mien of a Rajah of Sikkim, a governor in Morocco, or a Buddhist monk.

He once told Darwin that he had always wanted 'to make a creditable journey in a new country'. As a young man he abhorred predictable routine and cosy domesticity. The conclusion of one expedition was soon followed by a restless urge to plan another. During his first year in India a tour in Borneo was still a possibility but, as he informed his father, 'I wish to see the Andes & every other part of the world as much & I shall no more be satisfied as a traveller by Borneo than I was by the Antarctic Expedition or even by the Himalayas'.

In his autobiography Darwin wrote that 'the voyage of the *Beagle* has been by far the most important event in my life and has determined my whole career'. It could be argued that the Antarctic voyage did the same for Hooker. It confirmed his preference for botanical research; it taught him the need for patient observation and for maintaining meticulous records; it gave him an appetite for further travel. 'I shall never regret having joined this expedition', he wrote to his father from H.M.S. *Erebus*. 'We must, along with Capt. Ross, fail completely, so as never to try it again, or succeed. No future botanist will probably ever visit the countries whither I am going – & that is a great attraction'. In all his travels he wanted to be the first scientist to land on a remote oceanic island, or to explore the eastern Himalayas, or to climb to the summit of the Atlas Mountains.

He was proud to be a member of an historic voyage to Antarctica, and in order that his parents might share this unique experience, he wrote them long letters which, contrary to Admiralty instructions, incorporated data from his official journal. His mother and compliant relations laboriously copied them for circulation among intimate friends. His father received the fullest details of his scientific progress; his mother, fiancée and aunts enjoyed the lighter moments in his nautical life. But from all he considerately concealed some of the perils of the voyage; nowhere in this copious correspondence have I found any mention of the incident when he came close to drowning. It was only when he was on the last stage of the homeward voyage that he admitted to his father that he would never undertake such a journey again. These letters are an invaluable account of a memorable voyage which lasted four years; they are, moreover, an insight into Hooker's aspirations.

By the time of his next expedition he had a much larger circle of friends to entertain with news of treks in the Himalayas and Assam. After his father, Charles Darwin was his most valued correspondent. In their letters, then and later, they speculated on matters of mutual interest, Darwin with his insatiable appetite for facts, usually being the interrogator. 'For years & years you have been my public & my judge', wrote Darwin in 1861. 'I care more for your opinion in Nat. History, than for all the rest of the world'. I do not know whether Hooker responded as frankly but he praised his friend fulsomely in a letter to Brian Hodgson in 1849. 'Darwin is one of the most amiable & pleasing men I ever met, a gentleman by birth & education, happily one of fortune & in all other respects & having travelled over the same countries (he as a man, I as a boy), I naturally accept his interpretations of my many difficulties'. I have frequently quoted from their letters their comments on plant geography, a subject central to much of their research.

During his travels Hooker often encountered plant species from other parts of the world. How did they get there? Why did Australia have more European plants than did South America? He was astonished to find similarities in the vegetation of Tierra del Fuego and land thousands of miles to the east. He and Darwin sought answers but sometimes failed to agree about possible solutions.

As well as botanising in Sikkim, Hooker also surveyed and mapped the country, at times working at altitudes above 14,000 feet. He calculated the height of its mountains and discovered that some of its great rivers rose in Tibet.

Someone once observed that 'Hooker the traveller prepared the way for Hooker the philosopher'. Interpreting the vegetation of the places that he had visited became his consolation in middle age when younger men went abroad collecting plants for Kew while he was confined to the Director's office. Many of his publications listed in the bibliography at the end of this book owe their existence to the evidence he had collected on his travels.

His travels made him an imperialist who ensured that Kew played an important role in the development of colonial agriculture. He was consulted about the organisation of several scientific voyages and, as the doyen of Antarctic exploration, advised Robert Falcon Scott on preparations for his polar expeditions. Hooker never lost his affection for India. His Indian researches were eventually recognised by his being made a Knight Commander of the Order of the Star of India, an honour – and there were many – which gave him the most satisfaction. While he was in India he confided to Brian Hodgson that his ambitions for the future were limited to his 'standing as a Naturalist & Traveller'. Posterity has chosen to recognise the former while overlooking the latter.

Few people seem to know that he was also a competent artist who obsessively filled many small notebooks with topographical sketches. His flower drawings, usually confined to delineating distinguishing characteristics, were executed on larger sheets of paper, and subsequently metamorphosed by W.H. Fitch into bold plant portraits. The drawings which have been selected are from Kew's collections unless otherwise stated. I am most grateful to Mrs Julie Hooker and her children, Jane, Charles and Andrew Hooker, for allowing me to reproduce a number in their possession. Some scientific drawings are reproduced by permission of the Natural History Museum, South Kensington. The National Maritime Museum and the Scott Polar Research Institute have allowed me to include drawings in their possession.

I have quoted extensively from Hooker's letters and his *Himalayan Travels* (the pagination of all extracts comes from the 1891 reprint) in order to give the reader some impression of his style. There appears to be little consistency in the spelling of Sikkimese place-names, even modern guide-books differ. I have, therefore, decided to use Hooker's spellings but to give modern variants, when known, in parentheses after the first mention of the name.

I am indebted to Leonard Huxley's *Life and Letters of Sir Joseph Hooker* (1918) in two volumes which still remains the definitive biography. I also wish to acknowledge the immense help I have received from the multi-volume *Correspondence of Charles Darwin*, currently being published by Cambridge University Press. I am grateful to the Syndics of Cambridge University Library for permission to quote from the Darwin letters in their possession.

I am grateful to Mrs Rachel Lambert Mellon, Roy Lancaster and Henry Noltie for the loan of transparencies, and to Mrs Selden for some photographs.

I appreciate the assistance I have received from the staff at Kew: the Keeper of the Herbarium, Professor Simon Owens; the Librarian, Miss Sylvia FitzGerald and her staff; and individual botanists – Dr P. Cribb, D. Field, L. Forman, Professor D. Pegler; the Head of Information Services Department, Mrs Alyson Prior. Other institutions whose facilities I have used are the Royal Geographical Society and the libraries of the Linnean Society, the Natural History Museum, the Indian Office Library and Records (British Library), and the Zoological Society of London.

Sir William Jackson Hooker (1785–1865). Crayon drawing by Sir Daniel Macnee. Hooker sat for this portrait shortly before he left Glasgow University for Kew Gardens in 1841.

Chapter I

FORMATIVE YEARS

William Jackson Hooker was born in Norwich in 1785, the son of a merchant's clerk. His father's devotion to gardening and his mother's artistic talents doubtless influenced their son's chosen career as a botanist who also illustrated his own works. After leaving the local grammar school, his first job was in the estate office at Starston Hall where he stayed for two years. An active member of a flourishing community of Norwich botanists, he discovered, when only twenty, a moss, *Buxbaumia aphylla*, new to the British Isles. Diffidently, he took it to James Edward Smith, a local doctor who had recently purchased the herbarium, library and papers of the Swedish naturalist, Carolus Linnaeus. Smith advised him to show it to Dawson Turner, a

(Opposite) Painting by Marianne North of the celebrated view from Darjeeling which was Hooker's base during his exploration of Sikkim.

Yarmouth banker and the county's leading authority on non-flowering plants. Turner who supported Hooker's application for fellowship of the Linnean Society of London became his mentor and also his financial adviser when Hooker came into his inheritance in 1806. Smith acknowledged Hooker's growing competence as a botanist when he dedicated *Hookeria*, a new genus of moss, to him in 1808.

At the instigation of the President of the Royal Society, Sir Joseph Banks, who also advised the King on the management of his royal garden at Kew, Hooker went botanising in Iceland in 1809, heedless of Dawson Turner's admonition that he should first finish his research on liverworts. Although his Icelandic collections were lost when the ship bringing him back was destroyed by fire, he published his journal of the trip in 1811, and with a resilience and versatility so characteristic of the man, returned to studying liverworts. His *British Jungermanniae*, published in parts between 1812 and 1816, and illustrated by the author, was dedicated to Dawson Turner, now his father-in-law. Dawson Turner had persuaded Hooker to invest part of his inheritance in his brewery at Halesworth, a small country town in Suffolk.

There his second son, born on 30 June 1817, was christened Joseph after his paternal grandfather, and Dalton after his godfather, the Reverend James Dalton, a collector of lichens and mosses. Almost instinctively, Joseph Hooker absorbed the enthusiasm for natural history shared by his father and friends. In a speech at a Royal Society anniversary dinner in 1887, he wryly saw himself as 'the puppet of natural selection'. He recalled that at the age of five or six he had precociously informed his mother that he had identified a moss growing on a Glasgow wall as *Bryum argenteum*. Visits to Dawson Turner's home introduced him to the pleasures of a well-stocked library.

> . . . my great delight was to sit on my grandfather's knee and look at the pictures in Cook's 'Voyages'. The one that took my fancy most was the plate of Christmas Harbour, Kerguelen Land, with the arched rock standing out to sea, and the sailors killing penguins; and I thought I should be the happiest boy alive if ever I would see that wonderful arched rock, and knock penguins on the head.[1]

His father's passion for mosses and ferns inevitably focused his attention on cryptogams. From his mother he acquired a love of art, music and literature.

The birth of William Hooker's third child, his profligate purchase of books, and the uncertain future of the Halesworth brewery forced him to write to supplement an inadequate income. By 1820 he had published four botanical works and thought himself eligible for an academic post. With Sir Joseph Banks's backing, he was appointed in 1820 to the newly-created chair of botany at Glasgow University to teach botany to medical students and to manage a small botanic garden.

Joseph Hooker attended the local grammar school and frequent excursions

1. Address at the anniversary dinner of the Royal Society, 30 November 1887.

with his father in the Highlands sharpened his powers of observation. One wonders if he ever sensed that his brother, William, was his mother's favourite. When her sons were seven and eight respectively, she told her father, Dawson Turner, that 'I think that Joseph would be the child to please you in his learning. He is extremely industrious, though not very clever. Willy *can* learn the faster if he chooses, but while his elder brother sets his very heart against his lessons, Joseph bends all his soul and spirit to the task before him'.[2]

Less censorious, his father discerned in his son at the age of thirteen the promise of 'becoming a zealous botanist', and at fifteen judged him to be 'contented and happy at home, and studying Orchideae most zealously'. He noted approvingly that he could remember plant names without any effort. Another of Joseph's diversions was insects, especially beetles, which he collected obsessively. His stamina and energy – desirable attributes for a future plant collector – are confirmed in an anecdote Lady Hooker (her husband had been knighted in 1836) related to her father. 'A fortnight ago, Joseph walked 24 miles – from Helensburgh to Glasgow – rather than wait for the steamer next morning, by which delay he would have missed a lecture'.[3] Sir William Hooker singled out his son's diligence for praise. 'He has worked at plants with a degree of steadiness and ardour that has been most gratifying, and it appears that his industry is likely to meet with its reward'.[4]

This 'reward' was the prospect of joining a voyage to Antarctica. Sir William had met its commander, James Clark Ross, in the autumn of 1838 at a friend's house. Never missing an opportunity to advance Joseph's interests, Sir William suggested that he might be enlisted as a naturalist. Ross cautiously agreed provided his son first qualified as a doctor and entered the medical services of the Royal Navy. To prepare himself for the eventuality of overseas travel,

This engraving of the *Resolution* and *Adventure*, commanded by Captain James Cook, 1772–1775, at anchor off Kerguelen's Land, had inspired a very youthful Joseph Hooker that he, too, would like to travel.

2. L. Huxley. *Life and Letters…* vol. 1, 1918, 22.
3. Lady Hooker to D. Turner. 7 May 1836. Ibid., p. 27.
4. W. Hooker to D. Turner. 9 January 1839. Ibid., p. 32.

Joseph Hooker in 1837 had enrolled in the astronomy class at Glasgow University where, as he told his grandfather, he had

> . . . gained the requisite knowledge, practical & theoretical, of working the different problems for time, longitude & latitude, nor will this be useless to me in after life for travelling abroad as I hope I may in a few years. I can by means of a chronometer & sextant lay down bearings, etc. with much accuracy.[5]

His mapping of Sikkim in the late 1840s was made easier by his familiarity with such instruments.

Confident that he would be selected, Hooker concentrated on qualifying for his M.D., giving any spare time to reading about the flora of Van Diemen's Land (Tasmania), one of the destinations of the voyage. When the nature of his duties had not been clarified, he sought an interview in April 1839 with Ross who told him that the surgeon, Robert McCormick, would be the zoologist on the voyage and Joseph assistant surgeon and botanist, an arrangement not to the young man's liking. Hooker asked him candidly 'whether he would take a Naturalist with him and give him accommodation, provided Government would sanction or send him'.[6] Ross replied evasively that such a person had to be an all-round naturalist as Darwin had been on the *Beagle*. Hooker retorted that Darwin had possessed untested knowledge and was unknown at the outset of the voyage which had subsequently made his reputation. He, too, hoped to benefit in a similar manner from this Antarctic venture. Assured, however, by Ross that he would be given 'every opportunity of collecting that he could grant', Hooker somewhat reluctantly accepted the rank of assistant surgeon on H.M.S. *Erebus*, one of the two ships being fitted for the voyage.

At that time the rudiments of botany were taught to medical students as an introduction to materia medica, so that as doctors they would be able, if necessary, to prepare their own drugs. So it often fell to ships' surgeons to take on any natural history duties during voyages of survey and discovery. The surgeon, Alexander Brown, voluntarily collected plants for British botanists during his voyages in the late 1690s. William Anderson, Captain Cook's surgeon on his third voyage, was also a competent naturalist. The Admiralty usually chose naval surgeons for botanical and zoological investigations. John Richardson served as naturalist on two of Franklin's expeditions to the North Pole. T.H. Huxley enlisted as surgeon-naturalist on H.M.S. *Rattlesnake*'s survey of Australia's eastern seaboard and New Guinea. R.H. Hinds added botanical investigations to his medical duties on H.M.S. *Sulphur*'s exploration of the Pacific coast of America.

From about the middle of the eighteenth century, voyages of discovery involved scientific as well as colonial and commercial objectives. Sometimes qualified scientists usurped the natural history functions of ships' surgeons. Eventually, botanists, zoologists and geologists took their place and

5. Hooker to D. Turner. 14 January 1837. *Letters from J.D. Hooker, 1839-87*, vol. 13, f. 283.
6. Hooker to his father. 27 April 1839. Ibid., f. 87.

professional artists drew their collections. Louis-Antoine de Bougainville had a botanist, Philibert Commerson, on board during his voyage around the world in 1766–69. In 1768 Captain James Cook left England in H.M.S. *Endeavour* on his first circumnavigation. Joseph Banks, a young man of independent means, paid for the privilege of joining the ship with his companions who included two naturalists and a botanical artist. 'No people ever went to sea better fitted out for the purpose of Natural History, nor more elegantly', John Ellis informed Linnaeus. They had equipment for catching and preserving insects, a variety of nets, trawls and hooks to catch marine life, bottles to preserve small creatures in spirits, 'a telescope by which, put into the water, you can see to the bottom to a great depth, where it is clear', and a fine library of books on natural history and travel.

Fourteen months after his return in August 1771, Cook commanded two ships on a second voyage. The German scientist, Johann Reinhold Forster, the first officially paid naturalist on a British voyage, and his son Johann Georg, replaced Banks. Cook's poor relations with the irascible, dogmatic and dour Forster may have occasioned his outburst. 'Curse the scientists', he is alleged to have said, 'and all science into the bargain'. For his third voyage he fell back on to the services of his surgeon, W. Anderson. The French responded to Cook's exploits by mounting an expedition under the aegis of their Academy of Sciences; among the experts recruited for *La Pérouse* were a mineralogist, a naturalist, a botanist, a gardener and a botanical artist. Gradually it became routine practice to have scientists on major expeditions. But nothing matched the staffing of Nicolas Baudin's survey of the Australian coast in 1800. Napoleon himself was involved in the selection of twenty-four scientists, several for each discipline in order to have replacements at hand in the event of death. This impressive French initiative showed up the lack of resources of a British survey in the same region in 1801 under Captain Flinders who had to make do with a naturalist, a mineralogist and a gardener.

When H.M.S. *Beagle* was commissioned in 1831 to complete an earlier survey of the coast of South America, the Admiralty made no provision for any scientific research apart from some equipment for the preservation of any specimens that might be collected. It was a whim of its commander, Robert FitzRoy, who wanted a congenial companion to share his scientific interests, that brought a naturalist on board. The Reverend J.S. Henslow, Professor of Botany at Cambridge, asked to nominate a suitable candidate, proposed his young friend Charles Darwin. 'I have stated that I consider you to be the best qualified person I know of who also is likely to undertake such a situation', he told Darwin. 'I state this is not on the supposition of y^r being a *finished* naturalist, but as amply qualified for collecting, observing, & noting anything new to be noted in natural history'.[7] He did not add that querulous FitzRoy needed someone with Darwin's equable temperament. Darwin's father paid for his son's clothing and some scientific equipment.

7. *Correspondence of Charles Darwin*, vol. 1, 1985, pp. 128–29.

Joseph Hooker found himself in the same predicament of parental dependency when he joined H.M.S. *Erebus*. The Admiralty supplied two vasculums for collecting plants, twenty-five reams of 'blotting, cartridge and brown' paper for drying them, and two Wardian cases for housing and transporting live plants. Nothing else. His father paid for his outfit, his microscopes and some basic reference books, and his grandfather presented him with a travelling thermometer. Many years later Hooker recalled that 'it is a fact that not a single glass bottle was supplied for collecting purposes, empty pickle bottles were all we had, and rum as a preservative from the ship's stores'.[8]

The expedition which Hooker now joined had its genesis in a resolution of a meeting of the British Association for the Advancement of Science at Dublin in 1835. This urged the Government to determine the exact location of the South Magnetic Pole and, at the same time, to carry out scientific research in geography, hydrography, natural history and terrestrial magnetism. The matter was raised again at the British Association's meeting at Newcastle in 1838, approved by the Government, and supported by the Royal Society which was asked by the Admiralty to prepare a programme of scientific projects.

Ross requested Hooker to attend the Royal Society's deliberations on the botanical requirements of the programme. After the first meeting in July 1839, Hooker complained to his grandfather that he had been 'very shabbily treated'. The Royal Society submitted a report of 100 pages[9] which expounded the recommendations of the various committees it had convened. As botanist, Hooker had to make herbaria of representative vegetation of all the places the ships visited: 'however sterile and uninviting a place may appear to be, it is most desirable to know exactly what plants those regions produce'. His attention was drawn in particular to the little-known flora of Kerguelen's Land. At St Helena whatever survived of the endemic flora had to be recorded. Tree-ferns on that island and in Tasmania were to be investigated and their fibres examined: 'substitutes for hemp are very desirable'. Plants that might be of potential use in medicine and manufacture or as food were high on his list of priorities. It was, for instance, suggested that some Antarctic lichens might be used as dyes. Whenever possible, he was to send home seeds and bulbs of 'useful and ornamental plants'. Nor was he to overlook fungi and algae 'and all those minute species of cryptogamous plants which are parasites'. Any duplicate plants were to be sent to Calcutta for distribution among India's botanic gardens.

James Clark Ross was a seasoned Arctic explorer who had served under his uncle, Sir John Ross, and under Sir William Edward Parry in several attempts to find the elusive North West Passage between the Atlantic and the Pacific. In June 1831 he became the first to reach the North Magnetic Pole. An interest in natural history gained him the fellowship of the Linnean Society of London. Between 1834 and 1838 he carried out a magnetic survey of Great Britain and Ireland for the Admiralty. He was an obvious choice for leader of

8. L. Huxley, *Life and Letters...*, vol. 1, 1918, pp. 47-48.
9. *Report of the President and Council of the Royal Society on the Instructions to be prepared for the Scientific Expedition to the Antarctic Regions*, 1839.

Sir James Clark Ross (1800-1862). This oil painting by John R. Wildman amply endorses his reputation as being 'the handsomest man in the Navy'. He participated in nine expeditions in the North and South Poles. His scientific expertise gained him the fellowship of the Royal Society, the Linnean Society and the Royal Astronomical Society. *(National Maritime Museum, London.)*

an expedition to determine the position of the South Magnetic Pole, and to conduct a series of magnetic observations in the southern hemisphere.

A suggestion to use a steamboat for the expedition was rejected in favour of adapting two three-masted bomb ships which had been designed to fire heavy mortars. H.M.S. *Erebus* of 372 tons and H.M.S. *Terror* of 326 tons, already sturdily built, were further strengthened with layers of oak planks and sheets of double-thickness copper. Their bows were reinforced with oak and African teak bound together with iron braces. No other ships at that time had been so thoroughly converted to withstand the pressures of ice-laden seas. A stove in the capacious hold circulated hot air through pipes running along each side of the ship. Ice-saws, up to eighteen feet in length, were provided to cut passages through the ice; ice anchors would enable the ships to be fastened securely to ice floes. Both ships rolled and pitched alarmingly in rough seas but without any strain. The *Erebus* proved to be faster and often during the voyage had to heave-to in order to let its companion catch up.

The ships were well-stocked with tinned food expected to last the duration of the voyage: boiled, roasted and seasoned mutton, beef and veal, soup and concentrated gravy; tons of vegetables; 'medical comforts' such as pickled walnuts, onions, mustard, pepper, and gallons of lime juice. Only one case of scurvy occurred during the entire voyage and that sailor was already infected when he enlisted. Ross, on his return, recommended that all naval vessels should be stocked with canned provisions, a suggestion the Admiralty

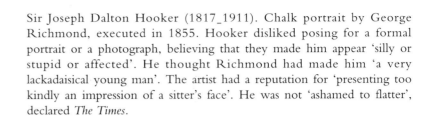

Sir Joseph Dalton Hooker (1817_1911). Chalk portrait by George Richmond, executed in 1855. Hooker disliked posing for a formal portrait or a photograph, believing that they made him appear 'silly or stupid or affected'. He thought Richmond had made him 'a very lackadaisical young man'. The artist had a reputation for 'presenting too kindly an impression of a sitter's face'. He was not 'ashamed to flatter', declared *The Times*.

implemented in 1847. All the crew were issued with snow boots, fishermen's boots and three suits of warm jackets, trousers and shirts. Each ship was well equipped with meteorological and magnetic instruments. Hooker claimed that they had photographic equipment for producing daguerreotypes but no photographs of the expedition are known to have survived.

The crews of both ships, in total 128 men, were all volunteers, and Hooker was the youngest. Ross chose as his second-in-command and as captain of the *Terror*, Francis R.M. Crozier who had been on three of Parry's Arctic expeditions. John Robertson, the *Terror's* surgeon, had additional responsibilities for geological and zoological research; his assistant surgeon, David Lyall, dealt with botanical matters. Robert McCormick, surgeon on the *Erebus* who was to collect zoological and geological specimens (ornithology was his real interest), had been assistant on Parry's 1827 journey. He had joined H.M.S. *Beagle* as surgeon/naturalist and consequently considered Darwin an interloper. When the *Beagle* reached America his application to be discharged on grounds of ill-health was granted, but it has been said that his jealousy of Darwin was the real cause of his departure. Hooker experienced no hostility from McCormick who never interfered with his botanising. Indeed he wrote to his father from the Cape that 'McCormick and I are exceedingly good friends'. Shortly before the ships sailed McCormick introduced Hooker to Charles Darwin whom they had accidentally met in Trafalgar Square. Years later Hooker still remembered that casual meeting. 'I was impressed by his animated expression, heavy beetle brow, mellow voice, and delightfully frank and cordial greeting to his former shipmate'.[10] At the time he never revealed to Darwin that as a medical student he had seen a set of proof sheets of Darwin's *Journal* of the *Beagle* voyage, lent to him by one of his father's friends. He had kept them under his pillow in order to read them as soon as he woke. 'They impressed me profoundly, I may say despairingly, with the genius of the writer, the variety of his acquirements, the keenness of his powers of observation, and the lucidity of his descriptions. To follow in his footsteps, at however great a distance, seemed to be a hopeless aspiration; nevertheless they quickened my enthusiasm in the desire to travel and observe'.[11]

10. *Nature*, 22 June 1899, p. 187.
11. Ibid.

Chapter 2

Antarctic Exploration and the Start of Hooker's Travels

The Greeks called the constellation above the North Pole 'Arktos' (the bear) from which the word 'Arctic' comes. The opposite end of the globe (Aristotle believed the world to be spherical) became known as anti-arctic or Antarctic. With their love of symmetry, the Greeks reasoned that the land mass in the extreme north must be counterbalanced by a similar mass in the south, and later the medieval church vigorously debated the existence of a southern continent. Only when Magellen sailed round the world in 1519 was it actually proved to be a sphere. Cartographers added the mythical continent – 'Terra Australis' (southern land) – to their maps, and navigators and adventurers searched the southern hemisphere for it and its rumoured wealth of 'Brazil wood, elephants and gold'.

Quite by accident Francis Drake discovered the southern seas beyond Cape Horn when the *Golden Hind* was blown off course during a gale, the first European penetration of the outer limits of Antarctica. An obscure London merchant, Antonio de la Roché, may have sailed close to South Georgia in 1675. The astronomer and pioneer investigator of terrestrial magnetism, Edmond Halley, commanded a naval ship in 1698 to determine latitude and longitude in the Atlantic; a secondary mission was the location of *terra incognita*. He described his first icebergs as: 'great islands of ice, of so incredible a hight[*sic*] and magnitude, that I scarce dare write my thoughts of it'. He calculated them to be no less than 200 feet high, and one at least five miles long. Thus having briefly experienced the Antarctic seas, he prudently withdrew north when dense fog and encircling ice threatened the safety of his ship.

Jean Bouvet de Lozier commanded two French vessels with instructions to seek 'the southern lands formerly known to de Gonneville proceeding if needs be as far as 55 degrees South'. He met his first icebergs in December 1738 but neither they nor fog deterred him. Eventually he sighted land at 48° latitude but the weather and limited visibility prevented a landing. Although he did not know it he had discovered a lonely volcanic island. Cook who tried in vain to find it during his second voyage assumed that Bouvet had seen 'nothing but mountains of ice surrounded by a field of ice'. It also eluded Ross and it was not until 1898 that a German expedition rediscovered it and called it Bouvet Island. Bouvet had reached 54° South before pack ice compelled him to turn east. He skirted the impenetrable ice for well over a thousand miles looking for land. Rock and sand on some of the icebergs and colonies of penguins and seals convinced him of its presence. Alexander Dalrymple, an English astronomer, was equally convinced that somewhere beyond those inhospitable seas stretched a huge continent populated by more than 50 million people.

Its existence had fired the imagination of geographers and encouraged further exploration. Thirty-three years after Bouvet's abortive attempt, Yves-Joseph de Kerguélen-Trémarec led another French expedition with the same mission. The land he discovered in February 1772 he named 'La France Australe' believing it to be the fabled continent. Indifferent to the appalling weather and the grim terrain, he confidently reported that precious stones would be found there. A gullible French government equipped another expedition in 1774 to enable a more thorough exploration of their new territorial acquisition. Kerguélen found neither minerals nor timber nor any other useful commodities. Disenchanted with 'La France Australe' and appalled by its bleakness, he renamed it 'Land of Desolation'. He suffered a further humiliation when Captain Cook later sailed south of this new land, thus proving they were islands and not part of 'Terra Australis'.

The success of Cook's voyage around the world in the *Endeavour* made the Admiralty receptive to his desire to find the southern continent. He persuaded the Admiralty that even if he failed the voyage could still be justified by his exploration of oceanic islands. Even his request for two ships was sanctioned. His orders stated 'you are to discover and take possession in the name of King George of convenient situations in the South Lands'. This enterprise signalled a resolute beginning to Antarctic exploration. Joseph Banks who had sailed on the *Endeavour* now conceived an ambition to stand on the exact spot of the South Pole. He petulantly withdrew from the project, however, when the Admiralty refused to allocate sufficient space on the ship for the large party he wanted to take with him.

The first of Cook's three sorties into Antarctica lasted four months (December 1772 to March 1773) in the Atlantic-Indian Oceans sector. 'Ice islands' – one of his names for icebergs – many 200 feet high, increased the hazards of sailing in these dangerous waters. He subscribed to the current belief that such large floes indicated the presence of land, and also held the view that seabirds and penguins were harbingers of it. Some strands of drifting seaweed raised his hopes that land was close. He followed the edge of a mass of ice seeking an opening to the south. Just before noon on 17 January 1773 the *Resolution* and *Adventure* crossed the Antarctic Circle for a distance of four and half miles, the first ships ever to do so. When impenetrable ice frustrated any further progress, he turned towards New Zealand to warmer winter quarters. He never knew that at one point he had been only about seventy-five miles from the southern continental land.

Shortly after encountering some large icebergs on 9 January 1773, Captain Cook briefly crossed the Antarctic Circle.

His second exploratory cruise, between November 1773 and February 1774, concentrated on the southern Pacific. Barely a month after leaving New Zealand, he crossed the Antarctic Circle for the second time. He tacked between clusters of large bergs, noting *en passant* one 'not less than three miles in circuit', and recrossed the Antarctic Circle, having reached as far south as latitude 71°10′. The atrocious weather never abated. Sleet and snow froze to the rigging. 'Our ropes were like wires, sails like board or plates of metal . . . the cold so intense as hardly to be endured'. In one immense ice-field 'ninety seven ice hills or mountains, many of them vastly large' were counted. Cook admitted defeat and headed for the tropics. 'I will not say it was impossible any where to get farther to the South, but the attempting of it would be a dangerous and rash enterprise'.

His last venture took place in the western part of the Atlantic sector during the months of January and February 1775. He found South Georgia where Antonio de la Roche may have been a century earlier. There he spent eleven days surveying its islands. Not a tree or a shrub could be seen but his naturalist, J.R. Forster, collected the greater burnet (*Acaena ascendens*), a grass, possibly *Poa flabellata*, and a flowering plant, *Colobanthus crassifolius*. Cook wrote in his journal that he 'was now tired of these high southern latitudes where nothing was to be found but ice and thick fog'. He reckoned that land which he had named in February 1775 after Lord Sandwich was 'either a group of islands or else a point of the Continent'. They were, in fact, the South Sandwich Islands which Forster doubted could support any plant life.

He now believed that much of this legendary continent must lie within the Antarctic Circle, but he was certain that no-one

> . . . will ever venture farther than I have done and that the lands which may lie to the South will never be explored. Thick fogs, snow storms, intense cold and every other thing that can render navigation dangerous one has to encounter and these difficulties are greatly heightened by an unexpressable horrid aspect of the country, a country doomed by nature never once to feel the warmth of the Sun's rays, but to lie for ever buried under everlasting snow and ice.

Turning northwards with a relief shared by the crews of both ships, he brought his mission to a close. He correctly surmised that 'there is a tract of land near the Pole, which is the source of most of the ice which is spread over this vast Southern Ocean'.

Cook's pessimism may have deterred other explorers but such comments in his published journal as seals 'in such numbers that if you could not get out of their way you would be run over' and 'whales in particular were exceeding numerous' attracted the attention of British whalers and American sealers whose indiscriminate slaughter has practically eliminated stocks in the northern hemisphere. In 1786 Thomas Delano left London for South Georgia where Cook had reported that 'Seals or Sea Bears were pretty numerous'. During their pursuit of oil and skins these hunters discovered land. William Smith, a British sealer, found the South Shetland Islands in 1819. The following year, Edward Bransfield on board a British frigate, took possession of them for the Crown. Bransfield also sighted part of the Antarctic Peninsula without realising its significance. Nathaniel Palmer, an American sealer, who found some islands below the South Shetlands, saw distant mountains in 1821. He and a British sealer, George Powell, discovered the South Orkney Islands. Another American sealer, John Davis, landed on unknown territory in February 1821 and noted laconically in his log, 'I think this southern land to be a continent'. Few sealers cared about exploration but one of them, the Scot, James Weddell, recounted his discoveries in *A Voyage towards the South Pole* (1825). In 1823 he had reached open water in the pack ice in what is now known as the Weddell Sea. The discoveries in 1831–32 of John Biscoe, a British sealing captain, of Enderby Land and parts of the west coast of the Antarctic Peninsula – Adelaide Island and Graham Land – positively confirming the existence of large stretches of land at the Pole, earned him a royal premium from the Royal Geographical Society.

After Cook no official survey of the region was mounted until the Russian Government sent Captain Thaddeus Fabian von Bellingshausen of the Imperial Russian Navy to 'approach as close as possible to the South Pole and to search diligently for land'. His two ships left Kronstadt in 1819, explored the South Shetland Islands, South Georgia, and the Sandwich Islands, and circumnavigated the Antarctic continent. The absence of a naturalist on board was regrettable but this remarkable voyage south of Cook's route which discovered Alexander Land only forty miles from the continent, was the first to report active volcanoes, and estimated fairly closely the location of the South Magnetic Pole.

French scientific voyages were concentrating on the Pacific. Louis C.D. de Freycinet took the ship *L'Uranie* there in 1817–20; L.L. Duperrey followed in *La Coquille* in 1822–25; his second-in-command, Jules-Sébastien-César Dumond d'Urville, was also charged with botanical and entomological investigations. D'Urville sailed as commander on the *Astrolabe* (formerly *La Coquille*) on another circumnavigation in 1826–29. France had not participated in any Antarctic exploration so when another expedition to the Pacific was organised, a detour to the South Pole was included. The *Astrolabe* and a smaller vessel, the *Zelée*, were requisitioned and d'Urville appointed commander. Not strong enough to withstand severe ice pressure, the ships failed to break through the pack-ice in the Weddell Sea. Only by the crew laboriously breaking the ice and towing the ships did they finally escape. On a subsequent visit in 1840 he succeeded in sailing to within a few miles of the Antarctic continent. He named its long coastline after his wife Adélie. Erratic readings on all compasses convinced him that he was close to the South Magnetic Pole. He returned to France with a large collection of drawings and specimens which were illustrated in his multi-volume account of the voyage.

While in Antarctic waters, d'Urville's ships passed an American vessel belonging to the United States Exploring Expedition. In the 1820s American merchants connected with the country's sealing and whaling industry urged Congress to send a scientific expedition to the South Seas. Known officially as the United States South Seas Exploring Expedition (usually abbreviated to the Exploring Expedition), it did not get organised for another decade or more. Charles Wilkes, its commander, had six unsuitable ships but his complement included two naturalists, a botanist, a gardener, a taxidermist, a scientific instrument maker and an artist. The voyage lasted four years of which only three months were spent in Antarctica. With Tierra del Fuego as a base, Wilkes explored the Antarctic waters in February 1839. Like d'Urville he was faced by an impassable wall of ice in the Weddell Sea. A blur of distant mountains sighted on a second cruise in January 1840 was never recorded in the ship's log. The French claim to have been the first to have seen the Antarctic continent was disputed by the Americans. Wilkes's assertion that he had sailed along 1,500 miles of the Antarctic coast was rejected by Ross who challenged the accuracy of his charts. For Wilkes and d'Urville, Antarctica was an episode in a global itinerary; for Ross it was a major objective. When he sailed there in 1839 the configuration of the southern polar regions was being more precisely defined but many blank areas still remained to be filled in.

The Admiralty instructions regarding Ross's duties and route were explicit. At Madeira the sea rates of the ships' chronometers were to be checked; observations were to be made at St Paul Rocks – in fact magnetic observations were to be carried out wherever possible; magnetic observatories were to be set up at St Helena, and the Cape of Good Hope. The islands of St Paul and

Pencil drawing by Hooker of the *Erebus* and *Terror* off the Isle of Wight. Hooker started drawing and writing his journal from the very beginning of the voyage. (*Family of the late R.A. Hooker.*)

Amsterdam might be inspected *en route* to Tasmania, the site of a third observatory. The ships could be refitted in New Zealand before their exploration of Antarctica 'to determine the position of the magnetic pole' and 'to correct the positions of Graham Land and Enderby Land, and other places which have been seen only at a distance'. Surveys of the South Shetland or the South Orkney Islands, perhaps also the Sandwich Islands, and finally the Falklands might conclude their programme. The Admiralty left the detailed interpretation of these instructions to Ross.

On 30 September 1839 the *Erebus* and *Terror* left England on a voyage which was to last four years. Passing through the English Channel Hooker was surprised to spot a wren and sand martin so far from land. Porpoises were seen in the Bay of Biscay, and a drifting log of wood which was attracting the attention of inquisitive fish, when hauled on board, was found to be covered in barnacles and inhabited by small crabs.

On their arrival at Madeira on 20 October, Hooker notified his father that he had started a journal which, unfortunately, would have to be surrendered to the Admiralty at the end of the voyage. He had promised not to keep a duplicate copy but 'this I intend to evade by sending you as a letter the original journal which contains everything I can think of'.[1] He also hoped to be able to send duplicate dried plants to his father as his official collection was at the Captain's disposal.

While chronometers were being rated and barometers checked, Hooker did some sightseeing. The smell of heliotropes and daturas pervaded the town of Funchal. Occasionally he heard guitars being played. He admired the gardens of some English residents who organised a trip for him to the Curral, about

1. Hooker to his father. 20 October 1839. *J.D. Hooker. Correspondence, 1839-45 from Antarctic Expedition,* f. 9.

Pencil drawing by Hooker of Teneriffe, 3 November 1839. 'Teneriffe presents a very fine appearance from the sea, tops of the mountains are broken into most remarkable spiculae and from them the valleys run straight down into the sea, they are green with verdure. The rocks and precipices of which there are very many, are quite black and very desolate, spotted here and there with the *Euphorbia* [*canariensis*] which was the largest vegetable we could see'. (Hooker. *Journal*.) (*Family of the late R.A. Hooker*.)

3,500 feet up the mountain, 'one of the most romantic spots on the island'. They rode on ponies up a winding road whose banks were covered with China roses and fuchsias 'growing as profusely as bramble bushes in Scotland'. Trellises supported daturas, lantanas and hibiscus. Two thirds of the way up, situated in a thick chestnut wood, stood the country residence of the former British consul who now tended a plantation of 300–400 tea bushes. At the top of the valley they reached a precipice with spectacular views towards distant Funchal. Cautiously Hooker climbed a few feet down the precipice to break off a piece of *Ocotea foetens*. The absence of any alpines disappointed him.

Threatening storm clouds hastened the ships' departure on 31 October. Two days later seasoned sailors recognised the familiar triangular silhouette of Teneriffe's prominent peak on the horizon. With a glass Hooker could see *Euphorbia canariensis* growing everywhere. The hills were marked with the parallel lines of vine trellises. On their summits he believed he could identify *Pinus canariensis*. A quick visit allowed only a superficial examination of the volcanic rock shoreline where he found an attractive small seaweed in pools, tentatively identified some species of *Senecio* and *Plocama*, and collected about a dozen plants. There was no time to travel the twenty-eight miles from Santa Cruz to Orotava to see the venerable dragon's blood tree, *Dracaena draco*, reputed to be several thousand years old. Baron von Humboldt had made a pilgrimage to the site in 1799. Darwin had also admired it. When it was blown down in 1868 it had reached seventy feet in height and forty-five feet in girth.

Pencil drawing by Hooker of *Euphorbia canariensis* and *Plocama pendula* on Teneriffe near 'an immense jet of water, cast up to the height of about 20 feet from a hole in the rocks ... I need not add the jet was of sea water, forced by the impetus of an occasional large wave through subterranean cavities in the rock. We afterwards saw many holes through which the air rushed with great violence ... A beautiful rainbow crossed the spray'. (Hooker. *Journal*). (*Family of the late R.A. Hooker.*)

On 13 November they anchored at Porto Praya on St Jago, the main island in the Cape Verde archipelago well within the tropics. All the islands had distinguishing features: San Antonio was thickly wooded, and Sal a salt plain; Fogo boasted an active volcano, and Quail Island was flat-topped with precipitous sides; St Jago was a desert with a fertile mountainous interior. In just under a week for the crew to make observations, check chronometers, replenish supplies of fruit, vegetables and water, Hooker had time only to explore St Jago and Quail Island, and to collect about 110 species of plants. He wrote to the botanist Robert Brown that it was here that 'I first saw tropical vegetation & I need not tell you how much it delighted me, though it is confined to mere oases, in those sandy plains of which St Jago is composed'.[2] He compared its vegetation with that of the African desert. Plants on a peak in the valley of San Domingo reminded him of those in southern Europe. In making such familial connections he was beginning an investigation that was to be an abiding interest – the geographical distribution of plants.

Darwin had seen St Jago during the *Beagle* voyage and wherever their paths crossed, Hooker consulted Darwin's *Journal*. He sought the coastal cliff with its prominent white band, a stratum of sand and shells, which Darwin had described. On an excursion to the centre of the island he was struck, as Darwin had been, by the extraordinary sight of about 200 stunted acacias, bent at right angles in one direction half way up their trunks by the prevailing wind.

2. August 1840. *J.D. Hooker. Correspondence, 1839-45 from Antarctic Expedition*, f. 9.

Pencil drawing by Hooker of St Jago, Cape Verde archipelago, November 1839. Hooker discovered the island's flora 'to be purely African and Arabo-Saharan in character, but on ascending the mountains, I met with a few plants very characteristic of the Canaries and Madeira'. (Hooker. *Insular Floras.*) (*Family of the late R.A. Hooker.*)

St Jago. Watercolour by Fitch after a sketch by Hooker. '... the country for many miles consists of successive arid flats covered by yellow withered grass, and here and there rises a short conical hill from 4–800 feet high, sometimes covered to the summit with withered herbage, and others, composed altogether of red volcanic scoria'. (Hooker. *Journal.*) (*Family of the late R.A. Hooker.*)

> One tree particularly attracted my attention; its trunk grew horizontally from the side of a steep little valley, itself in the direction of the trade [wind], & I was puzzled to conceive why the branches were all twisted in a cork-screw manner, & were much stunted. A little consideration soon solved the mystery; the strength and vigour of the trunk had enabled it to resist the force of the wind, this is the case with all; as soon however as a branch was thrown out from the summit, it was immediately bent, the increase of twigs on it then enabled it to resume its original direction by breaking the current, until it overtopped these defending twigs, when it was again bent. A repetition of these causes soon made the corkscrew.[3]

Another trip to the valley of San Domingo was done on ponies 'as rough as bears, unshod, and having the most languishing eyes' but stubborn, and only vigorous kicking persuaded the obstinate creatures to move. During their descent the vegetation became more varied: a species of Anonaceae grew to twenty feet; there were genera from Leguminosae and Compositae; a striking Ascepliad had umbels of large flowers with purple-streaked petals. An unusual fungus disintegrated in a cloud of brown powder on being touched. Hooker had to leave behind his plant box and lichen hammer before attempting a difficult climb up a cliff face. One member of the party soon gave up. The volcanic rock provided holes for hands and feet with Hooker filling his pockets with plants at every step. He was rewarded at the top with an orange-red composite and a blue campanula. On the equally perilous descent Hooker paused to pluck a fern with soft green foliage. 'Encumbered as I already was I could not help stuffing every pocket of my shooting coat with the various treasures I encountered; a hammer would have secured 5 or 6 lichens besides'.[4] Safely at the bottom he emptied his pockets into his travelling plant portfolio which he valued as 'an indispensable addition to the vasculum'. They returned home by a different route, a narrow path leading out of the valley. By the time they reached the top the moon was up. In the darkness Hooker grabbed a few more plants to add to his haul.

As well as botanising, he had to see the famous Baobab tree, *Adansonia digitata*. This native of Africa, grotesquely shaped, had probably been brought to the Cape Verde Islands by the Portuguese. McCormick who had inspected it with Darwin in 1832 had climbed the swollen trunk to carve on it the year of their visit. On his second visit in the *Erebus* he added '1839' to his earlier graffiti. Hooker calculated it was about sixty feet tall with a trunk thirty-eight feet in circumference. He collected a bud and a single flower, all that he could find. The bud survived the journey back to the ship where it opened, a blossom about six inches across, pinkish in colour and smelling like 'current bushes with a sickly flavour'.

A week's sailing after leaving the Cape Verde Islands on 20 November brought them to St Paul Rocks, an isolated cluster of eight to ten rocks, the highest no more than seventy feet above sea level, some 500 or so miles east of America. All were splashed with guano hardened into a nacreous film. With great difficulty a landing was made in a cove where McCormick collected

3. *J.D. Hooker. Letters and Journal, 1839-43,* f. 35.
4. Ibid. f. 42.

Baobab tree, *Adansonia digitata*, drawn by R. McCormick and lithographed in his *Voyages of Discovery in the Arctic and Antarctic,* vol. 1, 1884. McCormick, who visited St Jago twice, carved his initials and dates on its trunk.

Pen and ink sketch by Hooker of the trunk of the Baobab tree, November 1839. 'The tree itself is not striking ... At a distance it somewhat reminded me of an English oak'. (Hooker. *Journal.*)

rock specimens and a seaweed, the only vegetation he could find. When a member of the landing party fell into the sea, and momentarily it was feared he might be attacked by sharks, Ross decided against a second landing which Hooker was to have joined. He had to make do with the 'admirable description' in Darwin's *Journal.*

Pencil drawing by Hooker of the solitary Atlantic island of Trinidade about 600 miles from Brazil. Its most prominent feature is the Nine-pin Rock on the right. Hooker was the first botanist to inspect its flora. (*Family of the late R.A. Hooker.*)

He endured the customary initiation ceremony when the *Erebus* crossed the Equator on its way to the small island of Trinidade or South Trinidad off the Brazilian coast. Almost as inhospitable as St Paul Rocks, and between four and six miles long, it had two prominent landmarks: Sugar Loaf Hill and Nine-pin Rock, the latter 'the most remarkable phenomenon I ever beheld'. Its thick column of greenstone, soaring to over 700 feet, reminded him of a lighthouse. Perpendicular cliffs thwarted a landing, but eventually he and some of the crew crawled on their knees along a submerged narrow ledge, precariously carrying the scientific equipment for routine magnetic readings. Hooker picked up 'a flat fronded brown seaweed' and examined the blanched trunks of dead trees. 'They lay in different directions, and except the introduction of goats has, by eating up all the young trees and leaving the old ones to perish, destroyed the vegetation, as was the case at St Helena (see Darwin), I am at a loss to conceive how they have so universally disappeared'.[5]

The party climbed the steep slopes above them, lichen-covered scree beneath their feet, with the intention of reaching the other side of the island. At about 700 feet a formidable barrier of cliffs barred their way. Hooker collected all he could see – a grass, a fern and a cyperaceous plant. In an attempt to land in another bay he was nearly swept away by the surf. He had wanted to climb a high hill, about 2,000 feet up to identify some trees which looked like tree-ferns on the skyline. On his return to the ship he lost part of his meagre collection in the surf. Before the ships departed, Captain Ross left two hens and a cock to multiply or to perish.

On 31 January 1840 Ross anchored off St Helena where the first permanent observatory was to be set up. This remote island of about forty-seven square miles, lay directly on the main shipping route between the Cape Verde Islands

5. L. Huxley. *Life and Letters ...,* vol. 1, 1918, p. 95.

and the Cape of Good Hope, about 1,200 miles from Africa, 1,800 miles from America and 700 miles from Ascension Island, its nearest neighbour. Portuguese mariners in the sixteenth century had used it for rest and reprovisioning but it lost its importance for them as their empire grew and ports were built on the West African coast. So they never opposed the Dutch who took possession of it in 1645. They, too, valued it less after they had colonised the Cape of Good Hope. The British East India Company moved in to make it a base for their eastern trade, and in 1658 resolved 'to fortify the Island of St Helena, whereon (it is believed) many good plantations may in tyme be made'. The island's flora had suffered severely during these successive occupations. The goats and pigs introduced by the Portuguese as a source of fresh meat for their passing ships had eaten much of it. In 1588 a Captain Cavendish reported seeing flocks of goats numbering thousands; single flocks could stretch for a mile. Trees had been felled for building materials and firewood. Invasive fruit orchards and vegetable gardens competed for space with native plants, many of them unique to the island. Redwood (*Trochetiopsis erythroxylon*), for instance, still grew abundantly when the British arrived; fifty years later it had been almost wiped out.

Joseph Banks on board Captain Cook's *Endeavour* botanised there for four days in May 1771. He had to penetrate its interior to find any large populations of wild plants. Cabbage trees (*Senecio redivivus* and *Melanodendron integrifolium*) still grew on the highest ridges and Gumwood (*Commidendron robustum*) clothed the lower ones. But he reported that the Ebony Tree (*Trochetiopsis melanoxylon*), used in tanning, had been brought almost to extinction. 'Other species of trees and plants which seem to have been originally natives of the Island are few in number'.[6] Although clearly aware of this disappearance of endemic plants he, nevertheless, proposed that the fertile soil 'might produce most if not all [of] the vegetables of Europe together with the fruits of the Indies'. His conviction that many crops could be cultivated 'and brought to at least a great degree of perfection' persuaded the Governor to form a small botanic garden in 1787. Ever since the 1760s St Helena had been a casual convalescent home for sick plants in transit between Britain and India and beyond. Now the new botanic garden organised this service more efficiently and both Banks and the royal gardens at Kew benefited. The Governor invited Banks to send Kew's plant collector, Francis Masson, 'to explore our Cabbage Tree lands (as we call them). I think he may find some plants worthy of notice'. In 1791 Banks received 'four more chests of trees and plants . . . they are mostly natives of the island and reared in the manner you directed'.

William Burchell, the island's schoolmaster and acting botanist between 1805 and 1810, listed 198 vascular plants in the wild. He deplored 'the decayed remains of trees and shrubs which must formerly have covered all these hills . . . the soldiers and inhabitants have been suffered barbarian-like to cut down the trees with a wanton waste'.

6. J.C. Beaglehole, editor. Endeavour *Journal of Joseph Banks*, vol. 2, 1962, p. 269.

William Roxburgh, the Superintendent of Calcutta's botanic garden, convalesced on St Helena during 1813 and 1814. A sick man, he still managed to identify 363 species of flowering plants and twenty-five ferns, of which only thirty-three were native species.

The East India Company was relieved of its control of the island in 1834 by the British Crown. Darwin had a chance to examine its geology and flora when the *Beagle* stopped there in July 1836. He was struck by the English character of the vegetation: Scots pines on the hills, thickets of gorse, weeping willows, and blackberry hedges.

> When we consider the proportional numbers of indigenous plants being 52, to 424 imported species, of which latter so many come from England, we see the cause of their resemblance in character. These numerous species, which have been so recently introduced, can hardly have failed to have destroyed some of the native kinds.[7]

Hooker's first impressions of the island were disappointing. Barren black rock hemmed in the settlement at Jamestown. Except for opuntias and mesembryanthemums from the Cape he could see little vegetation. This sterile landscape persisted for the first 700 feet of a short climb; higher up he found a mixture of larch, oak and Scotch fir with paths lined with *Buddleja*, *Hibiscus* and *Gossypium*. On his second day there he and McCormick rode up a winding road out of Jamestown. Furze, blackberries and mists made him think nostalgically of Scotland.

> Diana's Peak presents a long rugged wall covered to its summit with a soft foliage that descended even over the precipes, and clothes the whole hill with the richest green; lower down, the cliffs and slopes were covered with fir plantations among which the white houses, chiefly of retired officers, were romantically situated. [8]

Two days later his destination was the very top of the central ridge, Diana's Peak. During this ascent he passed two tall Norfolk Pines and a couple of *Araucarias*. At about 2,000 feet he came across relics of the original vegetation. The summit, 'a long irregular broken narrow wall', had Cabbage Trees, ferns and a solitary lobelia. There he also saw his first tree-fern (*Dicksonia arborea*), standing in bold relief against the sky, its trunk thick with moss 'and parasitical ferns of a rich brown colour bore at its summit a crown of magnificent large waving fronds'.

His last excursion took him over Flagstaff Hill, and across Sandy Bay valley, to Mr Wilde's garden where he climbed a Brazilian *Araucaria* to collect cones which he hung as trophies in his ship's cabin. During this visit and again in 1843 on the return voyage of *Erebus*, he assiduously sought the timber trees and shrubs that had once blanketed the island. All he found were a few weather-eroded and blackened trunks, absolutely dead, on some barren sea cliffs.

His own observations supplemented by Roxburgh's list enabled him to

7. N. Barlow, editor. *Charles Darwin's Diary*, 1933, pp. 410–11.
8. *J.D. Hooker. Letters and Journal, 1839-43*, f. 55.

Diana's Peak on St Helena about 1912. 'The summit of the Peak is a long irregular broken narrow wall, covered on all sides with these cabbage trees, ferns and a lobelia. Much delighted I was at finding a tree fern, the first I had ever seen. They are generally very small, and nestle amongst the other trees, one or two, however, stood out in bold relief against the sky'. (Hooker. *Journal*.) (*Royal Geographical Society, London*.)

calculate that the island once had about forty-five endemic species; of the 110 naturalised plants, no fewer than fifty were of European origin.[9] He asserted that most of the endemics had affinities with Africa. Later botanists have pointed out that a few genera were more closely related to South America; the Cabbage trees, for example, resembled the American woody Senecioneae. Other naturalists have detected similarities between the island's insects and snails and those of South America.

Three days after their arrival in St Helena Hooker wrote a long letter to his father.[10] Ross, he had realised, 'knows a good deal of the lower orders of animals, and between him and the invaluable books you gave me, I am picking up a knowledge of them'. The Captain generously made room in his cabin for Hooker to work in reasonable comfort: a table under the stern windows, a cabinet for his plants, a locker for his papers, and a drawer for his microscope. He was even allowed to use Ross's compound microscope and reciprocated these many kindnesses by routine reading of the hygrometer, preparing meteorological tables and, under Ross's supervision, drawing marine life caught in the tow nets.

9. *J.D. Hooker. Indian, Moroccan and Syrian Journals*, f. 665.
10. *J.D. Hooker. Letters and Journal, 1839-43*, ff. 89-101.

On board ship Hooker drew practically every day. He had already accumulated drawings of nearly a hundred microscopic crustacea and mollusca; 'some of them are very badly done, but I think that practice is improving me, and as I go on, I hope that some will be useful on my return'. He had similar reservations about other subjects he had drawn. 'My sketches are characteristic of the different places visited, but miserably done; they are not designed for any one but you to see. I have examined some of the plants, & shall send home part of the sketches with them'.

He hoped to despatch dried specimens of 200 plant species but, aware of contravening Admiralty instructions, warned his father that they were not to be made public until his return. 'Some are good specimens, others are only sent as mementoes'. Rather smugly, he wrote that 'McCormick has collected nothing but geological specimens, and pays no attention to the sea animals brought up in the towing nets, and they are therefore brought to me at once'. Ross encouraged Hooker by his genuine interest in his collections. He told his father that

> It would have amused you to come into the cabin and seen the Captain and myself with our sleeves tucked up picking seaweed roots, and depositing the treasures to be drawn, in salt water, in basins, quietly popping the others into spirits. Some of the sea weeds he lays out for himself, often sitting at one end of the table, laying them out with infinite pains, whilst I am drawing at the other end till 12 and 1 in the morning, at which times he is very agreeable and my hours pass quickly and pleasantly.

This agreeable existence in no way lessened his resolve to leave the Royal Navy at the end of the voyage. While he appreciated the opportunity to extend his range as an all-round naturalist, he, nevertheless, wished to concentrate on botany. 'Gaiety of any kind has still less charms for me', he informed his father. 'If ever, on my return, I am enabled to follow up botany ashore, I shall live the life of a hermit, as far as Society is concerned'.

After a week at St Helena the *Erebus* and *Terror* sailed for South Africa, all the time taking deep-sea soundings with a hemp line almost 20,000 feet long with a seventy-six pound lead weight. Ross lost some of his thermometers while making deep-sea temperature measurements. Drift bottles were regularly cast overboard. By such experiments he helped to pioneer the new science of oceanography.

About sixty miles north of the Cape, the crew sighted floating seaweed, 'a submarine forest' of *Laminaria*. The largest pieces hauled on board were twenty-four feet long, colonised by crustacea, mollusca, worms and other marine life. On arrival at the Cape on 17 March a permanent magnetic observatory was positioned next to the Cape Observatory. No doubt glad to be ashore again, Hooker busied himself with collecting 300 plants in the neighbourhood of the Cape itself and on Table Mountain. Their departure on 6 April 1840 marked the true beginning of the expedition, the first stage of their journey into Antarctica.

Chapter 3

VOYAGE INTO ANTARCTICA

While he was enjoying shore leave in South Africa, Hooker mused on the 'peculiar emotions attending the seeing new countries for the first time, which are quite indescribable'.

> I never felt as I did on drawing near Madeira and probably never shall again. Every knot that the ship approached called up new subjects of enquiry, and so it is with every new land or even every barren rock. It was the same on approaching the Cape and viewing Table Mountain. I could have, and did, sit for hours wondering whether this knoll was covered with heaths or Rutaceae, whether this rill produced the *Wardia*, or that rock the *Andraea*.[1]

For a fortnight after the ships left Africa, he was mainly occupied in drawing the contents of the tow nets, joining the crew in catching albatrosses with hook and line, or watching the floating masses of the gigantic seaweed, *Macrocystis pyrifera*. The thermometer fell as they sailed south, the wind became keen and cutting, and the ocean an inhospitable grey. Marion Island was sighted on 21 April, mountainous with black and red ridges, its terraces covered with greenish-brown grass. Hooker thought he spied some very small shrubs. They saw penguins for the first time, parading like soldiers on the beach. Ross had intended landing there or on the nearby Prince Edward Island but with a heavy swell and the threat of a gale he reluctantly gave up the attempt and set course for the Crozet Islands. 'These were the first Antarctic Islands we had seen and few of us will forget the feelings to which their desolate aspect gave rise'.[2]

The Crozet Islands are volcanic, rocky and usually obscured by fog. The *Erebus* passed Penguin Island, home of many colonies of these birds, also known as Inaccessible Island through the difficulty in landing there. Pig Island, so-called from the feral pigs which now overran it, appeared to the north. Ross had undertaken to deliver a chest of tea and some bags of coffee to eleven sealers hunting the sea elephant on Possession Island, the most eastern of this group of islands. When he anchored there, a rowing boat put out from the shore and six men came on board looking, according to Ross, 'more like Esquimaux than civilised beings'. Their clothes reeked of seal oil and they all wore boots made of penguin skins with the feathers turned inwards. Their leader impressed McCormick as 'an ideal Robinson Crusoe in costume'; Hooker somewhat romantically saw him as 'some African prince, pre-eminently filthy and without

1. Hooker to his father. No date. *J.D. Hooker. Letters and Journal, 1839-43,* ff. 105-06.
2. J.D. Hooker. *Flora Antarctica,* vol. 2, 1845, p. 218.

a most independent gentleman'. Quite oblivious of their disreputable appearance, they had no desire to return to the Cape despite eight months on the island. Food was no problem. They kept goats, ducks were an easy prey on an inland lake, fish and birds' eggs were plentiful, and the tongue and flippers of the elephant seal added a much appreciated delicacy. All they lacked were vegetables. Hooker could see no edible plant, just a long coarse grass and a kind of scurvy grass.

A quantity of *Macrocystis pyrifera* was hauled on board. Hooker discovered that its roots housed four other species of seaweed. Before the voyage was over there would be numerous opportunities to examine this giant kelp, which floated in the oceans from the North Pacific to South Georgia in the Atlantic and around the southern shores of Australia and New Zealand. 'If you see beds of weede, take heed of them and keep off from them', cautioned a sixteenth-century nautical guide. Joseph Banks on the *Endeavour* who found a specimen 126 feet in length, called it *Fucus giganteus*. Hooker discovered that specimens measuring between 100 and 200 feet were not uncommon. In the middle of Christmas Harbour on Kerguelen's Land he found that some pieces exceeded 300 feet.

Two days after leaving Possession Island, the crew of the *Erebus* saw their first iceberg, only twenty feet high and fast melting. So accurate were Captain Cook's charts that Ross had no difficulty in finding Bligh's Gap, a conical rock which the navigator had discovered and named. Their immediate task was to carry out magnetic and astronomical observations on Kerguelen's Land on 29 and 30 May to coincide with similar observations by other observatories all over the world.

Kerguelen's Land, an archipelago of more than 300 small islands in the South Indian Ocean, lay 700 miles east of the Crozet Islands, that is about half way between South Africa and Australia. After their discovery by Kerguélen-Trémarec in 1772, Cook was instructed by the Admiralty to survey them. When he arrived there on Christmas Day in 1776, he appropriately called his anchorage Christmas Harbour. An apparently barren landscape faced him except for masses of Joseph Banks's seaweed; one bay absolutely choked with it was dubbed Bay of Fucus giganteus. William Anderson, the expedition's surgeon and naturalist, inspected the meagre flora. Large spreading tufts, not unlike a saxifrage, provided some colour (later identified as *Azorella selago*). A plant looking rather like a cabbage invited culinary experiments. Its flavour which reminded the sailors of New Zealand scurvy grass was not to everybody's taste. Two other plants growing near streams and on marshy

(Opposite) Hand-coloured lithograph of *Macrocystis luxurians* and *Lessonia fuscescens* by Fitch. (Hooker. *Flora Antarctica,* vol. 2, 1847, plate clxxi). The *Erebus* and *Terror* frequently passed close to floating masses of gigantic seaweeds.

Plate CLXXI.

Fitch. del et lith.

Reeve imp.

C. Lessonia ovata
D. ———— fuscescens.

A.&B. Macrocystis luxurians.

Observatory Bay, Kerguelen's Land in 1929-31. 'The island presents a black and rugged mass of sterile mountains, rising by parallel steppes one above another in alternate slopes and precipices, terminating in frightful naked and frowning cliffs, which dip perpendicularly into the sea' (Hooker. *Flora Antarctica*, vol. 2, 1847, p. 219). (*Royal Geographical Society, London.*)

ground were served as a salad, 'the one almost like garden cresses, but very fiery, and the other altogether mild'. Anderson examined some grasses, a moss, and 'a beautiful species of lichen' (*Neuropogon taylori*), and calculated that the flora did not amount to more than sixteen to eighteen species. When Hooker first scanned Kerguelen's Land from the *Erebus* the greens on the flat land and the browns and yellows on the hills suggested ground rich in mosses. 'Surely, I thought, this cannot be such a land of desolation as Cook has painted it, containing only eighteen species of plants'.[3]

The *Erebus* came close to shore on 8 May but gales blew it far to leeward. Four days later both ships succeeded in anchoring in Christmas Harbour, flanked by its extraordinarily-shaped Arched Rock. Cliffs and headlands rose as high as 800 feet, terraced with horizontal ledges on which snow lay looking like a series of white stripes or bands. The weather matched these grim surroundings. Gales raged during forty-five of the sixty-eight days they stayed there, and only three days were clear of either snow or rain. Yet Hooker was delighted to be there, the realisation of a childish ambition after browsing through a copy of Cook's voyages in his grandfather's library.

3. Hooker to his father. 16 August 1840. *J.D. Hooker. Letters and Journal, 1839-43,* f. 120.

Lithograph of painting by J.E. Davis of Christmas Harbour, Kerguelen's Land. (J.C. Ross. *A Voyage of Discovery and Research,* vol. 1, 1847). 'I landed on a black rock to the right of the harbour, and walking round to the head of it, came to the beach of black sand described by [Captain] Cook, where there were a few penguins, droll-looking creatures with black backs and white breasts like pinafores, their flippers hanging down like swords from their sides; they were easily caught, being naturally slow in their motions when on land, toddling like a young child rather than running'. (Hooker. *Journal.*)

The ubiquitous *Macrocystis* girdled the shore with a green belt some eight to twenty yards across, sometimes its density making it impossible to pull a boat through it. Long strands of *Laminaria,* another seaweed, draped the rocks, constantly moving in the violent surf. The first terrestrial plants to catch Hooker's eye when he landed were a long grass, an *Agrostis,* a small *Ranunculus,* and the springy cushions of *Azorella selago* flecked with minute flowers, 'often so soft that the traveller plunges into or through them up to the middle'.

The cabbage that Anderson had cautiously recommended was everywhere, extending thick rhizomes up to two or three feet along the ground. Large cabbages on long, leafy stems sprouted at their extremities. Sealers and whalers had acquired a liking for the leaves and rhizomes, boiled and served in the fat of salt pork, generously peppered. Hooker compared the flavour of the rhizome to mild horse radish, and the hearts (eaten raw) to garden mustard; the seeds reminded him of those of cress, and the leaves which resembled cabbage when boiled were slightly bitter. The cooks on the *Erebus* and *Terror* invariably added it to beef and pork and pea soup. In the absence of fresh vegetables it was a godsend but Hooker could never stomach its stale cabbage

(Above) Pringlea antiscorbutica on Kerguelen's Land. Hooker found it in large clumps at the bottom of cliffs and on the slopes above. 'The *Pringlea* is exceedingly abundant over all parts of the island, ascending the hills up to 1,400 feet but only attaining its usually large size close to the sea, where it is invariably the first plant to greet the voyager'. (Hooker. *Flora Antarctica*, vol. 2, 1847, p. 240.)

(Opposite) Hand-coloured lithograph of *Pringlea antiscorbutica* by Fitch. (Hooker. *Flora Antarctica*, vol. 2, 1847, plates xc–xci). 'It was not in flower, but in a fine state of fruit, ... its thick root projecting horizontally, sometimes two or three feet long, and 1½ inches in diameter, and bearing at its extremity a tuft of leaves like the common cabbage; from the side of which a tall leafy spike is thrown out'. (Hooker. *Journal.*)

flavour. Because antiscorbutic properties were attributed to it, it was named after Sir John Pringle, the author of a book on scurvy. Hooker rated it . . .

> . . . the most interesting plant procured during the whole voyage . . . The contemplation of a vegetable very unlike any other in botanical affinity and in general appearance, so eminently fitted for the food of man, and yet inhabiting one of the most desolate and inhospitable spots on the surface of the globe, must equally fill the mind of the scientific explorer and common observer with wonder.[4]

Later botanists identified it as a survivor of the Pleistocene climate on Kerguelen's Land. Sir William Hooker, anxious to have it at Kew, repeatedly

4. J.D. Hooker. *Flora Antarctica*, vol. 2, 1845, p. 239.

Plate XC-XCI.

Pringlea antiscorbutica, *Hook fil.*

Fitch, del. et. lith.

Printed by Reeve. Brothers.

asked his son to send seed. Its failure to germinate in the Botanic Gardens naturally disappointed Sir William and irritated his son.

> I do not understand your not getting the Kerguelen's Land cabbage to grow. I have had fifty plants of it from seed. I had it growing in a bottle! (hanging to the after rigging), on a tuft of *Leptostomum* during all our second cruise in the ice, and brought it alive to Falklands. It was sprouting before the Cape Horn plants went home, from seeds I scattered under the little trees [in the Wardian case][5]

He assured his father that it would grow 'in a cool place, very wet and shaded, in a black vegetable mould like peat'. But neither Kew nor any other garden could ever coax it beyond a few inches growth before it succumbed to heat and parasitic fungus.

The little *Ranunculus* which he assumed was the one Cook's crew ate as a cress, he rejected as inedible but some of the crew were prepared to try anything as a change from their ship's provisions. He once saw the Scottish gunner sitting on a rock, his feet dangling in the surf, nonchalantly chewing large quantities of seaweed.

Two grasses were found to be highly nutritious fodder for the goats, sheep and pigs they released on the island, transforming them into plump carcasses for the pot. The black and very rich flesh of penguins introduced a distinctive pungency to stews, pies and curries.

Following his father's advice, Hooker paid especial attention to cryptogams – non-flowering plants – and conscientiously collected mosses and lichens. Those on hill tops, always frozen with snow and ice, were the hardest to remove – 'many of my best lichens and mosses were obtained by hammering at the icy tufts, or sitting on them till they thawed'.[6] Lichens predominated from the shore to the summit, but it is 'at the tops of the hills that they assume the appearance of a miniature forest on the flat rocks'. Stones were stained with delicate lilac tufts; bright yellow patches stood out against black cliffs; caves were smeared with light red ones. One of his favourite lichens was the inconspicuous *Neuropogen taylori*, a combination of black and sulphur yellow.

Although he never found any woody plants, fossil tree trunks covered by a layer of shale, and rich deposits of coal indicated that the land had once been forested and warmer.

He rediscovered all Anderson's plants and many more, of which eighteen were flowering plants, thirty-five mosses and liverworts, twenty-five lichens and fifty-one algae.

Whenever the weather hindered his botanical rambles, he stayed on board ship describing and drawing the specimens he had collected. 'There is some danger, however, that inaccuracies may have crept into my work, for the rolling of the ship often obliged me to hold on, while thus employed, and to have my microscope lashed to the table, which renders dissection under the glass particularly difficult'.[7] Despite the paucity of plants, he regretted leaving this desolate spot which had yielded so much valuable data. 'I took with me

5. L. Huxley, *Life and Letters ...*, vol. 1, 1918, p. 77.
6. Hooker to his father, 16 August 1840. *J.D. Hooker. Letters and Journal, 1839-43,* f. 120.
7. Hooker to his father. 27 October 1840. *J.D. Hooker. Correspondence, 1839-5, from Antarctic Expedition,* f. 41.

one of Ward's cases containing all the flowering plants I had found on the islands. It is put under the stern window in the captain's cabin. Some cabbage seeds are sown among them'.[8]

Kerguelen's Land, his first introduction to the flora of sub-Antarctica, had raised questions about the floristic relations between oceanic islands and continents. A letter to his father, written on 17 March, had set out his preliminary thoughts on a projected book on the Antarctic flora. He assumed that the evidence he would collect on this long voyage would form the bedrock of his theories on the geographical distribution of plants. He had been advised by Robert Brown, the botanist at the British Museum to collect everything, never to reject anything. George Walker Arnott at Glasgow University had also urged him 'to collect abundantly and make accurate observation', and consequently gently admonished Hooker for collecting fewer plants on St Helena than had Hugh Cuming who had been on the island for only a few hours.[9]

His father's dearest wish was to have his son in 'a climate & in a country where you may do something in botany'.[10] In another letter his father suggested he should employ an assistant collector to free himself for the task of identifying his collections. He was pleased his son had definitely made up his mind about botany as a career. 'I need not say how gratifying it will be to me to be assured that my collections & my library will be inherited by one who will make good use of them'.[11] Apropos of Joseph's rejection of conviviality, he added, 'I am neither surprised nor sorry that you have no taste for the gaieties of life but neither do I wish you to turn "hermit"'.

Hooker had not yet received a black-edged letter from his father, addressed to 'My very dear and only son', telling him of the death of William in Jamaica. Understandably Sir William was now extremely concerned about the health and safety of his surviving son. In some anxiety he informed Captain Ross that he had learned that Joseph had been in 'a very delicate state of health' and, in the opinion of one of the officers on the *Erebus*, 'quite unfit to undergo the fatigues of such a voyage as he had embarked on'.[12] His son's letter, despatched from Teneriffe had made him apprehensive about his health. 'Should it be such as to unfit him for the voyage, I am sure you will kindly desire him to return or allow him to remain in Van Diemen's Land [Tasmania] or New Zealand where he can be useful & not exposed to difficulties & privations for which his constitution is unsuited'. Ross reassured him that his son was perfectly well. A persistent cough in his childhood had led to Joseph being called 'croaky Joe' by his parents, and as a young man he had suffered from 'a nervous irritability of the heart', so his father was naturally over-protective. He had also checked with McCormick about his son's well-being which was soon to be tested by the rigours of severe gales of hurricane strength.

The *Erebus* and *Terror* left Kerguelen's Land on 20 July in choppy seas. Soon the first of many beds of drifting seaweed, some more than a mile across, passed them. At night the two ships kept in touch by firing guns and burning

8. *Antarctic Journal* (typescript), f. 103.
9. 17 June 1840. *J.D. Hooker. Correspondence received 1839-45*, f. 2.
10. 2 February 1840. Ibid., f. 97.
11. 13 February 1840. Ibid. f. 100.
12. 23 March 1840. *Letters from W.J. Hooker to J.D. Hooker*, f. 12.

Watercolour of icebergs, probably by Hooker. Note the creases in the paper suggesting that the drawing was folded to be enclosed in a letter home.

blue lights. When the *Terror* never answered these signals during a gale on 29 July, Ross gave up hope of seeing her again until they reached Hobart. The next day the boatswain was hit by the top mast stay sail, pitched into the sea, and drowned. Waves swamped a boat sent to pick him up, and four sailors washed overboard were rescued just in time before they succumbed to the freezing water. The presence of an iceberg called for extra vigilance. Never a day passed without snow, sleet or rain, and one morning large, curiously cone-shaped hailstones fell. Not far from Tasmania a hurricane stripped the ship of all its sails, the ship's boats were smashed, and Hooker's Wardian cases were badly damaged. But the ship survived. 'She rides like a duck over the waves & when a sea does break into her & sweeps the decks fore & aft, she seems to stagger a little, till a port is knocked out to let an immense body of water to escape'.[13]

On 16 August a pilot took the ship up the Derwent River past eucalyptus trees whose white trunks were starkly prominent on low undulating hills. As they approached Hobart Town the settlers' cottages came into view around the harbour and up the flank of Mount Wellington. After they had anchored, they learned that the *Terror* had arrived a day earlier. Tasmania was still called Van Diemen's Land at the time of Hooker's visit. Abel Tasman, its discoverer in 1642, had named it after his patron, Anthony van Diemen, the Governor-General of the Dutch East India Company. The British who had occupied it in 1803 to forestall the French, promptly used it as a dumping ground for transported convicts, and ruthlessly persecuted its small aboriginal population. Hooker had been informed that 'an old, a middle-aged man and a child . . . very savage but seldom seen' were the only survivors of the original inhabitants.

Captain Ross was welcomed by the Governor, Sir John Franklin, a celebrated Arctic explorer and an old friend. Convicts erected the third observatory of the voyage in nine days. During their three months' stay, both ships were caulked and painted, their rigging refitted, and gale damage repaired. Ross read –

13. Hooker to his father. 16 August 1840. J.D. Hooker. *Letters and Journal, 1839-43,* f. 120.

44

Rosebank Observatory, Tasmania, erected for use by Ross's crew. (J.C. Ross. *A Voyage of Discovery and Research*, vol. 1, 1847, p. 95.)

perhaps with dismay – in the local newspaper of the exploits of d'Urville's French expedition in Antarctica. In January the French commander had discovered snow-covered land devoid of any vegetation which he named Terre Adélie after his wife, and sailed for 150 miles along its coast convinced that he had found the actual continent. He then traced a wall of ice, well over 100 feet high, westwards for about sixty miles. This, too, he believed had land beneath its white canopy. Sickness amongst his crew forced him to abandon any further exploration and to return to Hobart. Fired by patriotic zeal to beat the British and the Americans in the search for the South magnetic Pole, d'Urville had deliberately ignored his government's orders. There was no news in the local press of the American expedition which had obeyed instructions not to divulge anything of its activities to the public. Nevertheless its commander, Lieutenant Wilkes, confidentially wrote to Ross not only suggesting more accessible routes to follow but also enclosing a chart of his own course and his territorial discoveries. Both expeditions had forestalled Ross by choosing a direct approach to the Pole. Piqued, he decided to ignore this friendly advice, and resolved to reach the Pole by a more easterly route. National pride demanded that the British party should not 'follow in the footsteps of the expedition of any other nation'.[14] But possibly the claims of sealers that open waters lay to the east also influenced his decision.

The earliest serious plant collector in Tasmania was probably the settler Robert William Lawrence who had botanised in the northern regions of the island around 1826. Until his death, some six years later, he sent plants to William Hooker in Glasgow. His friend Ronald Campbell Gunn, also became one of William Hooker's correspondents. An ex-army officer, he had served in Tasmania successively as superintendent of convicts, police magistrate, clerk

14. J.C. Ross. *A Voyage of Discovery*, vol. 1, 1847, p. 117.

Mount Wellington, Tasmania, drawn by R. McCormick and lithographed in his *Voyages of Discovery in the Arctic and Antarctic*, vol. 1, 1884. Hooker was delighted to find on its slopes the moss *Hookeria pennata* (i.e. *Cyathophorum bulbosum*) which had been named after his father by J.E. Smith.

to the Executive and Legislative Councils and as private secretary to Sir John Franklin. Joseph Hooker could not have had a better guide to the local flora. Gunn introduced him to the 'cider tree', so-called because of the potable liquid it yielded. To see it, Hooker travelled through a depressing forest of gum trees blackened by fires to a plateau in the centre of the island. He named the tall 'cider tree' *Eucalyptus gunnii* after his hospitable companion. Hooker visited the concentration of fossil vegetation in a quarry mentioned in Darwin's *Journal*. He contributed a note on a fossilised tree trunk, a six foot agate-coloured shaft embedded in a lava stream, to the *Tasmanian Journal of Natural Science*, founded by the Governor and Gunn.[15] His confidence grew with his botanical competence. 'My collections, I think, improve as I go on', he told his father; 'at least the collecting comes with greater facility to me'.[16] He ignored his father's offer to pay for 'a good, zealous collector' to assist him.

Lady Franklin who had founded a natural history society enrolled Hooker as an honorary member and also as a reluctant guest at several of her soirées. She disapproved of his sneaking out after one Sunday service to collect plants but he got a good haul of 500 specimens during that illicit foray. While he appreciated Lady Franklin's good intentions, she intimidated him. 'Old Sir John is a most kind-hearted fellow but *she* is the Governor'.[17] On the day the *Erebus* and *Terror* left, Gunn wrote to Sir William Hooker lauding his son's botanical expertise, his acute powers of observation and his industry which commendably left little time for frivolous dinners and balls. Shortly after midday on 12 November the

15. 'On the Examination of some Fossil Wood from Macquarie Plains'. *Tasmanian Journal of Natural Science*, vol. 1, 1842, p. 24.
16. 9 November 1840. *J.D. Hooker. Correspondence, 1839-45, from Antarctic Expedition*, f. 45.
17. Ibid.

Pen and ink sketch by Hooker on adjoining pages of his small notebook of a Tasmanian tree-fern, presumably *Dicksonia antarctica*.

A fossil tree trunk on Macquarie Plains, Tasmania, drawn by R. McCormick. (*Voyages of Discovery in the Arctic and Antarctic, 1884*). 'One of the most beautiful objects I saw there connecting Botany & Geology, was a beautiful trunk, standing erect & completely embedded in a stream of lava; the woody tissue is preserved in a most singular manner & is of a puce white color. The external portion of the wood & bark is converted into a hard & beautiful Agate'. (Hooker to C. Lyell, 1 June 1842.)

ships cleared the Derwent River to reach the open sea. Their destination, the Lord Auckland Islands, lay about 200 miles to the south west.

A week later they approached the islands which had been discovered by Captain Bristow in 1806, who returned the following year and thoughtfully left some pigs on the largest island (about 345 square miles). A comparatively lush landscape and a number of safe anchorages had convinced Ross of their potential as a penal settlement, a recommendation never taken up by the Colonial Office. A landing party came back with unexpected trophies: two boards recording the arrival of the U.S. brig *Porpoise* and d'Urville's *L'Astrolabe*

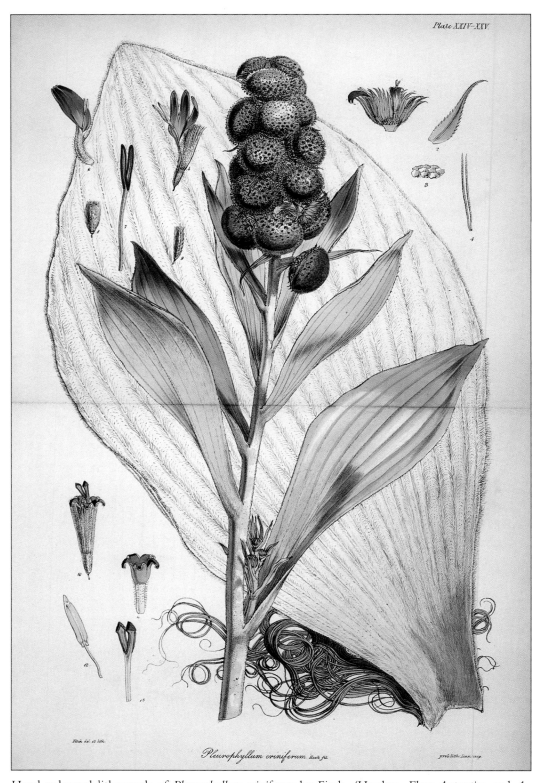

Hand-coloured lithograph of *Pleurophyllum criniferum* by Fitch. (Hooker. *Flora Antarctica,* vol. 1, 1844-45, plates xxiv-xxv). 'A very common and striking plant, often covering a great extent of ground, and forming the larger proportion of the food of the hogs which now run wild upon the islands of Lord Auckland's group ... The leaves are exceedingly handsome, generally two feet long and one or a little more in breadth'.

48

and *La Zélee* some eight months earlier. Their rivals had paused here on their way to New Zealand.

With no patients on board to treat, Hooker explored an island and its hinterland and distinguished five successive vegetational zones. The beach of pebbles and black sand and its fringe of rocks formed a maritime zone. The shoreline was emphasised by a belt of *Macrocystis*, and *Laminaria* clung to the rocks. He collected few plants here: some grasses, *Cardamine*, *Ranunculus* and a creeping *Coprosma*. Dense thickets stretching from the coast for about a quarter of a mile announced a woody zone where *Metrosiderus umbellata* was the dominant species. Mosses, liverworts, lichens and a vigorous community of ferns sheltered beneath a canopy of interlaced branches. He admired *Polystichum vestitum* for 'the beautiful symmetry of the crowns, with its velvety crosier-formed young leaves in the centre'. A shrubby zone had smaller forms of the trees in the woody zone, ascending the hill to about 800 or 900 feet gradually thinning out on grassy slopes. The upland and sub-alpine zone was open country covered with *Bromus* 'in large close tussocks from 2 – 3 feet high of a light straw colour'. He found some curious lichens on bare black ground. The alpine zone was confined to the tops of hills where some of his best finds were made. At about a thousand feet in a swamp *Stilbocarpa polaris* grew with 'clusters of green waxy flowers as large as a child's head . . . round and wrinkled leaves of the deepest green . . . a foot and a half across'. Its succulent roots and those of *Pleurophyllum criniferum* sustained the ravenous population of the descendants of Bristow's pigs. This latter plant, one of a trio Hooker claimed to be spectacularly beautiful, he described as an 'extremely handsome and showy species with copious large purple flowers'. He included *Celmisia vernicosa* for 'the delicacy of the rays tipped with a faint rose-colour' contrasting with 'the dark purple eye and the glossy varnished deep green foliage'. The tall spikes of golden-yellow flowers of *Chrysobactron rossii* (now *Bulbinella rossii*) could be seen from far off. He named it after Captain Ross who had found a splendid specimen on Campbell Island with 'no less than seven racemes of flowers'. He thought *Hebe benthamii* with flowers of a deep ultra-marine blue one of the prettiest ornaments of the barren hills. He was surprised to find tree-ferns so far south, two to four feet tall, with fronds four to five feet long, and struggled back to the ship clutching one.

He declared the eighty-two flowering plants he saw to be 'more remarkable for their beauty and novelty than the flora of any other country'.[18] But most of the plants he collected were non-flowering – lichens, ferns, fungi, seaweed and numerous mosses. His fear that the French and American expeditions may have done better was ill-founded. Indeed he had collected almost two-thirds of the known flora.

Before their departure on 12 December Hooker sowed seeds from Tasmania and planted some soft fruit trees. Ross enlarged the island's livestock with two rams, four ewes, some poultry and rabbits.

18. J.C. Ross. *A Voyage of Discovery*, vol. 1, 1847, p. 147.

Hand-coloured lithograph of *Celmisia vernicosa* by Fitch. (Hooker. *Flora Antarctica,* vol. 1, 1844-45, plates xxvi-xxvii). '... a very handsome plant ... one of the specimens gathered on Campbell Island measuring nearly a span across the leaves. Like many other Antarctic plants, it varies considerably in size, some of our specimens being scarcely an inch and a half across the leaves, which lie densely compacted'. It was one of the plants chosen to decorate his memorial plaque in St Anne's Church, Kew.

Campbell Island, a mere day's sailing to the south east, is forty square miles of rugged terrain, steep and rocky, and in the path of prevailing westerly gales. It had been discovered in 1810 by Captain Frederick Hasselburgh, an employee of a firm in Sydney. A mile from the shore Hooker could see the vivid yellow of *Bulbinella rossii* on hillsides. The flora was similar to that of Lord Auckland Islands, more abundant perhaps but not so large. Both groups of islands had large tussocks, one or two feet across, of the grass *Chionochloa bromoides*, ideal nesting sites for albatrosses. Some sailors carelessly started a fire amongst this grass, and being absolutely dry, it quickly spread through the brushwood and woodland and only a timely storm prevented it from engulfing the encampment.

Fourteen of the sixty-eight flowering plants Hooker collected were new to him. In his notebook he jotted down random thoughts on the influence of latitude on plant populations. He wondered why these southern latitudes should have so many big plants when 'small and densely tufted plants' would be more appropriate in such a harsh climate.

After just two days on Campbell Island the ships headed for Antarctica on 17 December. They had left England fifteen months earlier and, at last, their principal mission – the precise location of the South Magnetic Pole – was under way. On Boxing Day they saw an iceberg, an immense block with perpendicular sides and a tabular top. By New Year's Day, when they crossed the Antarctic Circle, many monumental bergs were drifting by the ships. A

Hand-coloured lithograph of *Bulbinella rossii* by Fitch. (Hooker. *Flora Antarctica,* vol. 1, 1844–45, plates xliv–xlv). 'Perhaps no group of islands on the surface of the globe, of the same limited extent and so perfectly isolated, can boast … such beautiful plants … It is very natural that the great size and luxuriance of this and several other plants of the high southern latitudes should excite surprise'.

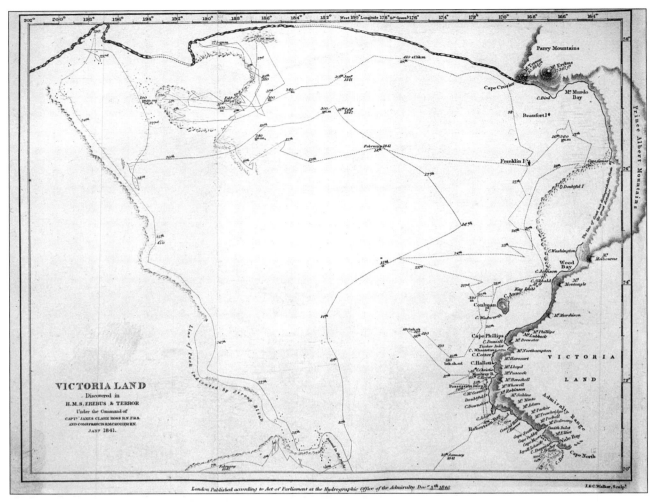

Map of Victoria Land. J.C. Ross. *A Voyage of Discovery and Research,* vol. 1, 1847. The ice barrier, charted by Ross for many miles, starts from Mount Erebus. Franklin Island where Hooker narrowly escaped drowning lies off it.

mud-coated lump of rock, retrieved from one of them, turned out to be of volcanic origin. For three or four days persistent gales prevented their entering the pack ice which encircled the Antarctic continent, varying in height and thickness, and drifting at the whims of winds and currents. For a while they were confined to a small pool of water in the enclosing pack, and when heavy seas broke it up they were threatened by cascading blocks of ice. Both ships suffered damage in the ensuing storm but in the calm that followed, the ice parted allowing them to reach the safety of open water.

Ross who continued his course to the south-west was rewarded by the sight of land early in the afternoon of 11 January 1841. Hooker hastily sketched 'a mass of immense mountains, all peaked or newly so, formed into cones and pyramids of an immense height, covered with snow except in a very few places where some brown streaks showed that the land was too steep for the snow to lie on'.[19] The ships had reached latitude 70°14′, and having passed the furthest point south reached by Cook in 1774, the crew were given extra rations of grog. On 12 January this land, believed by some of the crew to be

19. *Antarctic Journal* (typescript), f. 142.

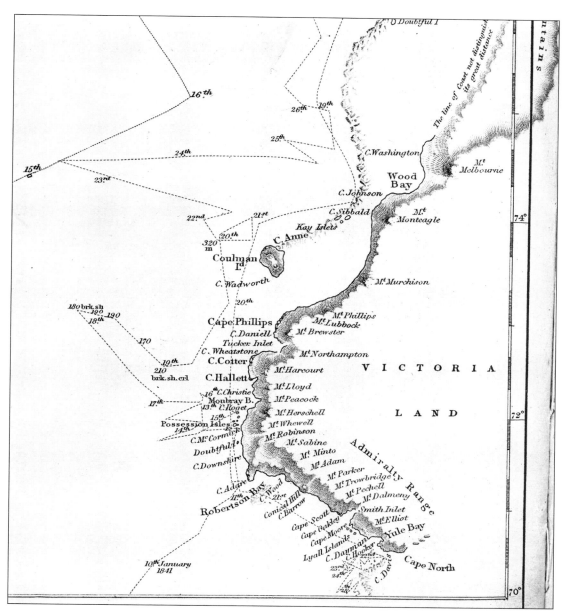

Detail of Ross's map showing topographical features named after politicians, civil servants, scientists and members of Ross's expedition. Cape Hooker appears at the bottom of the coastline.

the 'southern continent', was taken possession of in the name of Queen Victoria (later known as Victoria Land). As it was impossible to land there, the ceremony was held on an offshore island, appropriately dubbed Possession Island. 'I did not observe the faintest trace of vegetation, not so much as a lichen on the bare volcanic rocks, not even a seaweed in the shoal', reported McCormick who had joined the landing party, 'but our stay was so brief – only some twenty-five minutes – in consequence of the threatening aspect of the weather'.[20] The penguins there defied their intruders with raucous cries, and thick guano with the elasticity of a dried-up peat bog was evidence of their long occupation of the island.

20. R. McCormick. *Voyages of Discovery in the Arctic and Antarctic Seas and round the World: being Personal Narratives of Attempts to reach the North and South Poles*, vol. 1, 1884, p. 154.

Plate XXXIX–XL

Veronica Benthami Hook fil

Hand-coloured lithograph of *Hebe benthamii* by Fitch. (Hooker. *Flora Antarctica*, vol. 1, 1844-45, plates xxxix-xl). 'Found in rocky places on Lord Auckland and Campbell Islands ... of a most beautiful blue colour'.

Plate VIII.

Fitch del et lith.

pre^d lith. Vincent & comp.

Anisotome latifolia Hook. fil.

Hand-coloured lithograph of *Anisotome latifolia* by Fitch. (Hooker. *Flora Antarctica,* vol. 1, 1844–45, plate viii). 'This is certainly one of the noblest plants of the natural order to which it belongs, often attaining a height of six feet, and bearing several umbels of rose-coloured or purplish flowers, each compound umbel as large as a human head. The foliage is of a deep shining green, and the whole plant emits, when bruised, an aromatic smell'.

In a lane of water between the ice and the shore Ross followed the coast seeking an anchorage and a place to land in order to proceed with magnet-ometric observations on 20 January, one of the days internationally agreed for simultaneous observations. Rounding a cape on 15 January an impressive panorama of sky and mountains confronted them. Hooker, sketch pad in hand, tried inadequately to record it.

> Just above the water's edge the snowy precipices were seen covered with an immense bank of broken clouds, each tinged of a golden colour by the never-setting sun; above these rose the immensely high peaks of land, towering up against a beautifully clear blue sky, above which, was another canopy of dark, lowering clouds, their lower edges of a bright golden red colour. It was one of the most gorgeous sights I ever witnessed, and called to my mind the descriptions of the Himalayas and Andes.[21]

Ross baptised this chain of peaks, over 10,000 feet high, with the names of fellows of the Royal Society and the British Association for the Advancement of Science. One particularly fine peak was reserved for the Prime Minister, Lord Melbourne.

The pack ice, now extending some forty or fifty miles from the shore, frustrated any close examination of the land still clearly visible on the horizon. On 27 January a boat from each ship rowed to an island with high cliffs of black volcanic rock. Hooker, who had not been able to land on Possession Island, found himself a member of this landing party. Getting ashore proved extremely tricky. One way was to wait until the boat reached the crest of a breaker and then jump on to ice-covered rocks. Hooker slipped, fell into the sea, and was momentarily in danger of being crushed between the boat and the rocks. He was fortunate to suffer no more than the numbing cold of the water. He never saw Franklin Island, named in honour of the Governor-General of Tasmania. He had to rely on Ross's report that not 'the smallest trace of vegetation, not even a lichen or piece of sea-weed [was] growing on the rocks'. Ross now had no doubt 'from the total absence of it at both the places we have landed, that the vegetable kingdom has no representative in antarctic lands'.[22]

The next day puffs of smoke could be seen rising from what appeared to be a hill in the distance. As they got closer the hill resolved itself into an active volcano 'emitting immense clouds of black smoke, rising perhaps 300 feet above it, its margins tinged white by the sun, with a distinct red tinge from the fire below'[23] The volcano reaching over 12,000 feet, went down on the chart as Mount Erebus and its extinct companion as Mount Terror.

The coastline beyond them was replaced by a perpendicular wall of ice, extending to the east as far as the eye could see. It rose well above the mast-heads of the ships. No break could be seen anywhere in it: 'we might with equal chance of success try to sail through the Cliffs of Dover, as penetrate such a mass', wrote Ross. After following it for 100 miles it still stretched

21. *Antarctic Journal* (typescript), f. 143.
22. J.C. Ross. *A Voyage of Discovery*, vol. 1, 1847, p. 215.
23. *Antarctic Journal* (typescript), f. 149.

relentlessly ahead of them, sometimes reaching a height of 300 feet. We now know this formidable ice barrier which Ross called Victoria Barrier as the Ross Ice Shelf which fills a huge bay of more than 300,000 square miles, that is approximately the size of France.

By 12 February they had hugged this barrier of ice for 300 miles but with deteriorating weather and thickening pack ice Ross abandoned his easterly course. He turned back for one more attempt to reach the Magnetic Pole and to find a winter harbour. Three days later they passed Franklin Island and a berg four miles long. Mount Erebus with a scarf of cloud across it still erupted. They were only about 160 miles from the Pole. Ross and his second-in-command conferred. Had it been possible to find a safe harbour for the winter, a party might have reached the Pole across the snows the following spring.

As they passed mountains, capes, bays and inlets on the coast of Victoria Land they identified them with the names of the crew – the masters, mates, pursers and surgeons. In due course Cape McCormick and Cape Hooker appeared on the map. Their last glimpse of Victoria Land coincided with the first display they saw of the Aurora Australis.

On 6 March when the two ships were afloat in the centre of the mountainous terrain depicted on Lieutenant Wilkes's chart as the Antarctic continent, Ross smugly noted that the American commander had obviously misidentified 'dense, well-defined clouds as land'.

A heavy swell drove them towards a cluster of more than eighty huge bergs which threatened to crush them. 'For eight hours', wrote Ross, 'we had been gradually drifting towards what to human eyes appeared inevitable destruction'. They were saved by a wind which, filling their sails, took them away from disaster.

After nearly five months' absence, the two ships returned to their base at Hobart. It had been 'a most glorious and successful cruise to the southward', Hooker told his parents.[24] Aware of their anxieties, he concealed the hazards of the voyage: 'we have been in no dangerous predicaments and have suffered no hardships whatever'. Naturally he said nothing about nearly drowning off Franklin Island.

During the three months' stay in Tasmania the ships were repaired, refitted and loaded with provisions for the next three years. The officers responded to the generous hospitality they had enjoyed with a grand ball. Both ships were lashed together, covered by a canvas awning, and the decks draped with festoons of native flowers. Ross's cabin served as a ladies' room with mirrors, brushes and combs for their use. Over 300 dined on board and dancing continued until daybreak. One wonders whether Hooker enjoyed or grimly endured this and other farewell parties. There is no mention of them in his journal.

24. *J.D. Hooker. Letters and Journal, 1839-43*, f. 181.

Raising of the British flag on Possession Island off the coast of Victoria Land, 11 January 1841. Watercolour by John Edward Davis, second master on H.M.S. *Terror*. Members of the crew are killing penguins for food. (*Scott Polar Research Institute.*)

Franklin Island, another addition to British possessions, was named after the distinguished Arctic explorer, at that time Governor of Van Diemen's Land (Tasmania). Watercolour by J.E. Davis. (*Scott Polar Research Institute.*)

Watercolour by Hooker of Mount Erebus and Mount Terror. (Hooker. *Antarctic Journal,* f. 130). On 28 January 1841 an active and a dormant volcano were observed. 'This was a sight so surpassing everything that can be imagined and so heightened by the consciousness that we have penetrated into regions far beyond what was ever dreamed practicable, that it really caused a feeling of awe to steal over us, at the consideration of our comparative insignificance and helplessness'.

The ice barrier. Watercolour by J.E. Davis. 2 February 1841. (*National Maritime Museum, London.*)

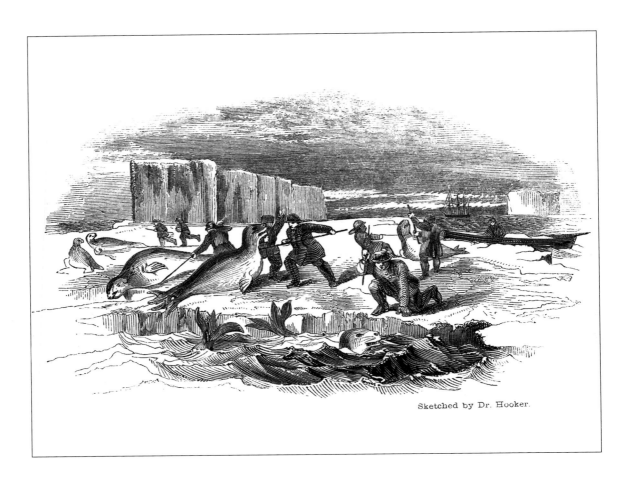

Sketched by Dr. Hooker.

Sketched by Dr. Hooker.

Catching penguins and slaughtering seals. Based on sketches by Hooker. (J.C. Ross *A Voyage of Discovery and Research,* vol. 2, 1847, pp. 33, 90.)

Pencil sketch by Hooker
of *Erebus* leaving Port
Jackson, Australia on 5
August 1841. (*Family of
the late R.A. Hooker.*)

Ross arrived at Sydney on 14 July to carry out scientific observations similar
to those he had just completed at Hobart. Their short stay permitted only
casual botanising on walks Hooker made in the hills about the harbour.
Alexander Macleay, a former Colonial Secretary and another of Sir William
Hooker's many correspondents, invited him to his home overlooking
Elizabeth Bay, set in spacious grounds filled with ornamental plants from
Australia and abroad. This elegantly furnished house made Hooker acutely
conscious of the primitive conditions endured by the ordinary settler. He
overheard some women, newly arrived from Britain, speculating on the
domestic comforts that awaited them. 'One talked of having a nice house,
with a verandah, on a hill near the water, with a garden, etc.; and really her
husband must provide her such a one. Little did she think that she will perhaps
have to spend two years in a mud hovel, with a marsh before the door and the
bush for a verandah'.[25] The poverty of the aborigines equally depressed him.
'The most degraded-looking savages, both men and women, with nothing but
a blanket thrown diagonally across their person, abominably foetid, dirty and
squalid, tall, gaunt and wiry, with no calves to their legs, nearly black, with
bushy black hair, broad faces, large mouths and high cheek bones'.[26] He did
not seem to have any regrets about leaving the colony.

The *Erebus* and *Terror*, heavily laden with supplies, sailed slowly to New
Zealand for another of their scheduled series of scientific experiments. On 17
August they anchored in the bay speckled with islands where the *Endeavour*
had sheltered in 1769. Captain Cook gave it the name by which it is still
known, The Bay of Islands, at the tip of the North Island. Some sixty years
later the *Beagle* called on its small British settlement. It had become a
convenient anchorage for passing ships; d'Urville had made use of it and an
American corvette was just leaving when Ross arrived. He set up his
observatory about a quarter of a mile from the spot where the body of the

25. *Antarctic Journal* (typescript),
ff. 177–78.
26. Ibid., f. 180.

Watercolour by J.E. Davis of *Erebus* and *Terror* skirting the ice barrier. (*Family of the late R.A. Hooker.*)

French navigator, Marion du Fresne, who discovered the Marion and Crozet Islands, had been cooked and eaten by Maori warriors in 1772. A Maori chief who had objected to Ross's men felling tall trunks of *Metrosideros* for replacement spars for the ships, was placated with a present of two rifles (he had demanded double-barrelled guns), perhaps an unwise choice in view of resentment still shown by the natives towards the settlers.

Long periods at sea with only marine life and coastal scenery to sketch were no substitutes for botany and drawing flowers. The prospect of returning to the desolation of Antarctica disheartened Hooker. 'Could I with honor leave the expedition here, I would at once and send home my plants for sale as I collected them; but now my hope and earnest wish is to be able on my return home to devote my time solely to botany, and to that end the sooner we get back the better for me'.[27] If it were not possible to live at home with his parents, he resolved to earn his living by collecting plants like a former pupil of his father, George Gardner who collected in Brazil for subscribers.

His confidence and sense of purpose were restored when he met William Colenso, another useful contact his father had advised him to seek out. Colenso, a Cornishman, had been sent as a printer to Paihia in The Bay of Islands in 1834 by the British and Foreign Bible Society. He was still plying that trade when Hooker was introduced to him, 'a brisk and active man'. A man with a lively curiosity, Hooker could have added. He filled his leisure studying history, folklore and languages to which natural history was added after meeting Darwin in 1835. Hooker admired his collections of shells, minerals and insects and the local flora which he cultivated in his small garden, but some flowering double violets from England pleased him most.

With Colenso often as his guide, he explored the neighbouring fern-covered hills and valleys. He judged Tasmania's tree-ferns superior to those of

27. Hooker to his father. 24 August 1841. L. Huxley. *Life and Letters ...* , vol. 1, 1918, pp. 115-16

Watercolour by J.E. Davis of Cape Hooker. (*Family of the late R.A. Hooker.*)

Kororarika, Bay of Islands, New Zealand in 1836. Engraved frontispiece to J.S. Polack. *New Zealand,* 1838. 'The country is hilly, with a smooth outline, and is deeply intersected by numerous arms of the sea extending from the bay. The surface appears from a distance as if clothed with coarse pasture, but this in truth is nothing but fern'. (Darwin on H.M.S. *Beagle.*)

Drawing by R. McCormick of the Falls of Keri Keri in his *Voyages of Discovery in the Arctic and Antarctic,* 1884. 'The river in the shape of a rapid stream, runs through open fern-lands, and suddenly precipitates itself over a mass of trap (basaltic columns) 76 ft. high in one clear fall, an immense wooded basin receives the flood, and a beautiful rainbow spans the dark ravine'. (Hooker. *Journal.*)

New Zealand, dismissing *Cyathea dealbata* as 'miserably herring-gutted lanky things with black stems, a few inches in diameter, and naked tuft [of] horizontal dark green fronds, with silvery undersides, the latter their only beauty'.[28] But another species in full fruit, he liked unreservedly. 'It is by far the most handsome of the tree-ferns. The trunks are jet black and stout, 12–14 feet high, the tufts of fronds are not horizontal but at an angle of 45°, gracefully curved outwards, the stipites stout deep black, ten feet long'.[29]

Like Joseph Banks before him, he carefully noted in his journal the uses Maoris made of *Phormium* fibres in making clothing, mats and cordage.

Colenso took him to the spectacular Falls of Keri-Keri, flanked by dark green *Coprosma*, the lighter glaucous *Laurus*, intermingled with the waving fronds, looking like 'magnificent plumes of feathers', of the ubiquitous tree-fern. The floor of the dark ravine at the base of the seventy-six feet high falls was densely covered with ferns and mosses.

He also had to see a forest of tall Kauri trees (*Agathis australis*). On a similar pilgrimage Darwin had found a specimen thirty-one feet in circumference. Hooker measured one twenty-seven feet in girth. These trees soared in 'a perfectly straight taper' to sixty and sometimes 100 feet with never a branch until near the top. Copious trickles of resin exuded from their trunks to coagulate in lumps on the ground, often the only evidence that these trees had stood there before natives had destroyed them by fire.

Webber, a shipmate, joined him on some of his exploratory walks. During one of them they got separated in a wood. While Hooker was trying to find his way with a compass, he was hailed by a Maori on the lake. He leapt ashore from his canoe . . .

28. *Antarctic Journal* (typescript), f. 191.
29. Ibid., f. 238.

Hand-coloured lithograph of New Zealand tree-fern, *Cyathea medullaris*, by Fitch. (W.J. Hooker. *Garden Ferns*, 1862, plate 25.)

Kauri trees. 'The forest was here almost composed of the Kauri; and the largest trees, from the parallelism of their sides, stood up like gigantic columns of wood. The timber of the Kauri is the most valuable production of the island'. (Darwin on H.M.S. *Beagle*.)

. . . shouting and singing. On seeing me, he became impetuous in his noise, the more so on seeing me walk into the wood. For my part I had no idea what he wanted with me, and as there had latterly been a battle in the neighbourhood, I did not like the idea of this tattooed customer with sharks teeth in his ears. Seeing, however, that he was determined to have me for good or evil, and as he gave chase to me in the wood, I thought it better to give in with a good grace, much fearing I had been trespassing on tabooed ground, and this fellow wanted to avenge his father's angry shades. After a great deal of persuasion, I entered his canoe, not knowing what better to do; and at the same time determined to resist any attempts he might make to roast me for ki ki (eating). I lay down in the canoe, but he was very sulky, talking angrily to me in lingo, to which I made answer of kapai, kapai (good, good) on all occasions. Finding me incorrigible, he left off, and landing with his frail bark, signed me to follow to some smoke in the wood.[30]

To his relief he was led to Webber, who had sent the native to look for him, busy cooking potatoes in the home of a Maori family. Both men were hospitably received. One proudly showed Hooker his copy of a native version of the New Testament; a little girl shyly brought her pet pig to be admired. In turn they inspected Hooker's plants and 'finding that I had gathered one out of flower, one of them immediately started off for the wood and returned with flowering specimens . . . an old knife and a few sixpences delighted them all, and we rubbed noses on parting, although I believe it . . . should be on meeting'.

On 23 November, his last day in New Zealand, Hooker wrote to his father[31] that a box of almost 250 herbarium specimens from Tasmania and New Zealand, plus duplicates, and most of his cryptogams, notes and sketches had been despatched. Insects and shells had been submitted to Ross to extract any items he might want for the official collection. He also had about forty bird skins for him. He reckoned he had gathered sufficient data on New Zealand plants to compile a flora. He had one dismal piece of news. Ross had heard from Lady Franklin that Hooker's collection sent from Tasmania had been lost at sea.[32]

30. *Antarctic Journal* (typescript) ff. 222-23.
31. *J.D. Hooker. Letters and Journal, 1839-43*, f. 253.
32. Fortunately this turned out not to be the case.

66

Chapter 4

THE SEARCH FOR THE SOUTHERN CONTINENT

On his second tour of Antarctica, Ross decided to plot a more easterly course to reach the place on the Victoria Barrier where he had been forced to turn back. But first he planned to stop at Chatham Island for routine scientific tests and to investigate its suitability for colonisation or as a base for whalers. Thick fog, strong winds and uncharted reefs deterred him from landing, a disappointment for Hooker who had hoped to study its little-known flora.

The ships sailed south through dense fog, keeping in touch with each other by firing muskets, sounding the gong and ringing the bell. It thinned just in time to reveal three looming icebergs. By 19 December they had penetrated the pack-ice for nearly a hundred miles. Christmas passed manoeuvring the ships trapped in a diminishing pool of open water. As a diversion McCormick, Hooker and the junior mate pursued and caught a penguin on an ice floe. The year ended with both ships moored to a low, flat iceberg to prevent a collision. On New Year's Eve they crossed the Antarctic Circle, and on New Year's Day 1842 every member of the crew received a box-cloth jacket and trousers, a red guernsey shirt, two comforters, a worsted cap known as a 'Welsh wig', a pair of boot stockings, and needles and thread. A reclining Venus de Medici about eight feet long, was sculpted in hard snow by Hooker and John Davis, second master on the *Terror*. Snow was also shaped into sofas in readiness for a ball that evening. The Royal Standard, the Union Jack and any other colourful flags decorated the floe. Captain Crozier and his consort 'Miss Ross', opened the ball with a quadrille. The ice was now so tightly packed that a couple of days later McCormick went for a long walk across it. On 6 January some cracks in it enabled the ships to move cautiously. They left behind their snow Venus, still intact.

Whenever there was no wind the ships' boats towed the *Erebus* and *Terror* through gaps and prevented them colliding with large pieces of ice. Trapped yet again in a small stretch of clear water, unable to use their sails, they moored with hawsers to a floe. A dispersal of the ice-pack on 18 January promised escape at last but a violent gale hurled huge fragments of loose ice against them. The *Erebus* lost the use of its rudder and that of the *Terror* was completely destroyed. The thud of ice against the ships and the creaking and grinding of towering bergs filled everyone with foreboding. The ships came

Sepia watercolour by J.E. Davis of the *Erebus* and *Terror* about to collide. (*Family of the late R.A. Hooker.*)

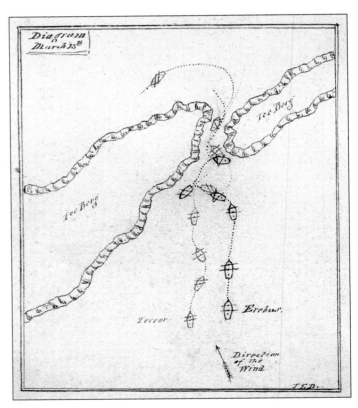

J.E. Davis's diagram of the collision. Captain Ross described how the two ships 'hanging together, entangled by their rigging, and dashing against each other with fearful violence, were falling down on the weather face of the lofty berg under our lee ... Sometimes she [*Terror*] rose high above us, almost exposing her keel to view, and again descended as we in turn rose to the top of the wave, threatening to bury her beneath us whilst the crashing of the breaking upperworks and boats increased the horror of the scene' (J.C. Ross. *A Voyage of Discovery and Research*, 1847.) (*Family of the late R.A. Hooker.*)

perilously close. 'Indeed, there seemed to be but little probability of our ships holding together much longer, so frequent and violent were the shocks they sustained'.[1] Eventually the heavy swell subsided, the wind moderated, and the crippled vessels were attached to a floe for examination and repair. It was a tribute to the shipwrights at Chatham Dockyard who had strengthened the vessels that even after this pounding by ice and waves, they remained absolutely watertight. In a motionless sea the *Erebus's* rudder was refitted and that of the *Terror* replaced with the spare it carried.

1. J.C. Ross. *A Voyage of Discovery*, vol. 2, 1847, p. 168.

Watercolour by J.E. Davis of a gale in the pack ice which threatened to destroy both ships, 20 January 1842. (*Family of the late R.A. Hooker.*)

Lithograph of J.E. Davis's drawing of *Erebus* passing through the narrow gap between two icebergs on 13 March 1842. (J.C. Ross. *A Voyage of Discovery and Research,* 1847.)

J.E. Davis's watercolour of this event was reinterpreted as an oil painting by Richard Brydes Beechey. Beechey, who had served in the Royal Navy, pursued another career as a marine painter. With his predilection for the drama of ships in distress and disasters at sea, the plight of *Erebus* was an irresistible subject. (*National Maritime Museum, London.*)

All the time the pack ice was drifting northwards returning them almost to their position of three weeks earlier. A providential wind came up on 23 January, once more taking them in the right direction. The pack obligingly opened, the wind freshened to a gale from the north, and the ships expeditiously ploughed their way through the thinner ice. It soon consolidated again, however, threatening to trap them, so whenever cracks appeared they unhesitatingly warped and heaved through spaces, sometimes hitting bergs, ignoring the dangers of navigating in the dark, until they at last reached the open sea after forty-six days in the pack.

The great ice barrier came into view on 23 February. Prudently keeping a few miles away, they followed it eastwards. The hope of seeing land was raised when stones and soil were spotted on some of the low bergs. They followed the barrier behind which appeared to be the undulating profile of mountains until pack ice once more impeded them. With the sea fast freezing over, a decision was taken to seek a winter sanctuary in the Falkland Islands. A long line of bergs, 'the heaviest masses of ice' Ross could remember, dictated a course to the north east. A few shreds of drifting *Macrocystis* encouraged them to continue in that direction.

On 12 March when they thought they had left the icebergs behind them, a large one unexpectedly loomed out of the darkness. The *Erebus* tried to avoid it, but the *Terror* unable to clear both the berg and her companion, collided with the *Erebus*. Briefly their rigging tangled them together but miraculously they parted again. The *Erebus*, now disabled, drifted dangerously close to the berg. Only consummate seamanship saved it; in the gale the crew climbed the rigging to loosen the main-sail, all the while the lower yard-arms repeatedly hit the towering cliffs of ice. The *Erebus* cleared the berg only to be faced by another one coming up from behind. Its only means of escape lay between the two bergs, a space barely three times the width of the ship. Yet somehow it got through into quieter waters beyond. The *Terror* had come off relatively lightly but the *Erebus* had suffered severe damage. Temporary repairs enabled the ship to proceed to the Falkland Islands, still several thousand miles away. One of the few casualties during the entire expedition occurred when the quartermaster fell from the mainyard and was drowned. After 138 days at sea, much of the time encircled by ice, they sailed into Berkeley Sound in the Falkland Islands on 6 April.

John Davis, an English navigator, had discovered these islands in 1592; William Dampier named them a century later. Comte de Bougainville brought French settlers there in 1764 and 1766. His chaplain, A.J. Pernety, as an amateur naturalist, examined their vegetation. In 1816 Admiral Louis de Freycinet persuaded the French Government to back a scientific voyage with a botanist and a zoologist on the complement of the two ships, one of which was wrecked in the Falklands in 1820. The botanist (Gaudichaud) salvaged part of his collection of dried plants and, on his return to France, published the first flora of the islands. Dumont d'Urville, then second in command on a French corvette which anchored there in 1822, concentrated on the abundant algae around its shores. Sir William Hooker's curiosity about the islands was aroused after receiving a set of its plants from W.E. Wright in 1841. He wrote to his son: 'How much I wished I could have reached you with letters at the Falkland Islands. I would like you to investigate the botany & ecology of those islands to the utmost of your power'.[2] The densely tufted cushion plants, compared by Wright to 'small haystacks', intrigued Sir William. The tussock grass 'must be very remarkable if Wright's drawing & description are accurate'.

With so much already collected, one assumes that Joseph Hooker never anticipated finding anything new. Certainly his first impressions did not encourage expectations. 'Kerguelen's Land is a paradise to it', he wrote.[3] He endorsed Darwin's perception of land 'with a desolate and wretched aspect'. The little Ross says about the islands in his published narrative of the voyage is largely confined to two contributions by Hooker, one a lengthy and spirited account of a wild cattle hunt, and the other his resumé of its vegetation.

Though hindered by bad weather or marshy terrain, Hooker persevered in exploring the low hills behind the settlement and their broad, flat-bottomed valleys, swarming with rabbits originally introduced by the French. At low water he searched the beaches. His excursions took him up Mounts Châtellux, Vernet and Lowe and over the sandhills between Ports William and Jackson. He noticed that the vegetation became less varied, largely confined to a few grass species, the farther he penetrated inland.

With the onset of winter flowering plants were scarce, Nevertheless he gathered a yellow violet (*Viola maculata*), a white primrose (*Primula magellanica*), *Calceolaria fothergillii*, *Olsynium filifolium* whose 'nodding white blossoms recall the snowflakes', the island's largest shrub, *Hebe elliptica*, and a red crowberry, *Empetrum rubrum*. Grasses had adapted exceptionally well to the peaty soil, the most common, *Poa flabellata*, grew in communities of large tufts, a favourite food of the wild cattle. Just as prominent was the balsam-bog (*Bolax gummifera*), hemispherical hummocks four feet high, pale or yellowish green in colour, exuding a fragrant, resinous smell. Since they grew on barren soil, the settlers called them 'misery balls'. When Sir William Hooker saw a sketch of a field full of them, he said they reminded him of 'gigantic pincushions or Norfolk dumplings'. Joseph Hooker attributed the total absence of trees to the configuration of low hills and broad valleys which provided no shelter.

Two of the few ferns he collected – *Blechnum penna-marina* and *B. magellanica* – he was to encounter again in Tierra del Fuego. He had seen several large fungi but left it too late in the season to collect them. He had some difficulty in sorting out the smaller cryptogams compacted in the thick turf but lurid

2. 20 March 1842.
J.D. Hooker. Correspondence received, 1839-45, f. 120.
3. Hooker to his father, 8 April 1842.

(Right) Hand-coloured lithograph of *Calceolaria fothergillii* by Fitch. (Hooker. *Flora Antarctica,* vol. 2, 1847, plate cxvii). Hooker judged this common flower to be 'among the prettiest of the wild flowers of the Falkland Islands'.

(Below) Hand-coloured lithograph of *Olsynium filifolium,* based on a drawing by Matilda Smith. *Curtis's Botanical Magazine,* 1885, plate 6829. 'One of the most abundant and elegant plants in the Falkland Islands, where the grassy plains are, in the spring month of November, almost whitened by the profusion of its pendulous snowy bells'. (Hooker.)

Plate CXVII

Fitch del et lith.　　　　　　　　　　Reeve imp:

Calceolaria Fothergilli: Ait:　　　　C. Darwinii: Benth:

6829

M.S. del J.N.Fitch lith.　　Vincent Brooks Day & Son Imp.

lichens on rocks and cliffs were delightfully easy to spot; he identified about thirty species.

The islands' seaweeds were not easy to gather. The loose strands of *Macrocystis pyrifera* and *Durvillea antarctica* intertwined into thick cables, several hundred feet long. *Lessonia* grew to 'the thickness of a man's thigh . . . In many places the plant is so copious that it forms a submerged forest'.[4]

He now revised his original unfavourable impressions of the Falklands. 'Every day adds something new to my collection, especially among the lower tribes . . . Altogether this place is better for botany than I had expected, and but for lichens, etc. it beats Kerguelen's Land, [though] collecting here is no sinecure, for the days are very short and the nights long'.[5] Towards the end of August he boasted that he had found all but three or four of the plants enumerated by Gaudichaud.

4. J.C. Ross. *A Voyage of Discovery,* vol. 2, 1847, p. 267.
5. Hooker to his father. 3 May 1842. *L. Huxley. Life and Letters ... ,* vol. 1, 1918, p. 132.

Watercolour by Fitch of the balsam-bog, *Bolax gummifera*. Early travellers usually commented on these enormous balls which were a distinctive feature in the landscape. (*Family of the late R.A. Hooker.*)

The British settlement at Port Louis in Berkeley Sound on East Falkland Island. Watercolour, probably by Davis. On 15 January 1842 Lieutenant R.C. Moody was formally installed as its first Lieutenant-Governor. The British flag flies over his official residence. A few years later the settlement moved to a better anchorage at Port William (now Stanley). (*Family of the late R.A. Hooker.*)

Wood engraving of tussock grass, *Poa flabellata*, (W.J. Hooker. *Notes on the Botany of the Antarctic Voyage*, 1843, p. 55). Copied from a drawing by W.E. Wright, who had been to the Falklands, and published in *Gardeners' Chronicle*, 1843, p. 131.

Governor Anson asked him to list the colony's useful plants.[6] Hooker who considered the grasses to be of prime importance, had already discussed the economic potential of tussock grass with the previous Governor. *Poa flabellata* provided excellent fodder. 'No bog, however rank, seems too bad for this plant to luxuriate in'. The area of cultivation of *Poa annua*, a British introduction, now well established, should be extended. The reputed efficacy of *Bolax gummifera* in the treatment of gonorrhoea deserved further investigation. He recommended the wild celery (*Apium prostratum*) as an effective antiscorbutic. The little cress (*Cardamine glacialis*) and wood sorrel (*Oxalis enneaphylla*) might also be used in treating scurvy.

In great excitement Sir William Hooker informed his son that he had been recognised as 'the most fortunate discoverer of the most wonderful grass in the Falkland Islands' (*Poa flabellata*).[7] But paternal pride had distorted the facts. Bougainville's botanist, Pernety, had described it as 'tall bullrushes or cornflags' in 1766. Gaudichaud had drawn attention to the 'nourishing food' yielded by the 'great grass *Festuca flabellata*'. Joseph Hooker could claim the credit of being the first to describe it botanically. This he did at the behest of the Governor of the Falklands, R.C. Moody, then engaged in writing an official report on the colony. Tussock grasses are a notable feature in the landscape of the southern hemisphere. Hooker found them in New Zealand, on some of the oceanic islands, and on Tierra del Fuego, but none competed in luxuriance with those on the Falklands. They reminded Hooker of groves of diminutive palm trees covering vast tracts of land, especially where the soil was sandy. Their roots develop into huge balls, up to five or six feet above the ground, and measuring as much across. From them project gracefully curving leaves, six or seven feet long. Growing close together, the spaces between them are, what Hooker called, a 'labyrinth'. It appeared to flourish on pure sand, on the edge of peat bogs, and on the exposed coast. According to

6. *J.D. Hooker. Indian, Moroccan and Syrian Journals*, ff. 767–69.
7. 5 January 1843. *J.D. Hooker. Correspondence received, 1839–45*, f. 121c.

Wood engraving of a sketch by Hooker of the tussock grass. (J.C. Ross. *A Voyage of Discovery and Research,* vol. 2, 1847, p. 212). Although this drawing is credited to Hooker, he was obviously influenced by Wright's composition.

Governor Moody, who carried out trial experiments with it in his garden, its roots had provided a subsistence diet for two unfortunate Americans stranded on West Falkland for fourteen months. Some settlers boiled its roots as a tasty vegetable.

When the Colonial Office printed Moody's report in 1842, Sir William Hooker lauded the virtues of this tussock grass in a letter to the Royal Geographical Society.[8] He promptly despatched some Wardian cases to the Falklands to bring specimens to Britain for trial cultivation. Kew Gardens was inundated with requests for the grass from owners of useless bogs in Ireland and Scotland. A report in the *Gardeners' Chronicle* [9] confirmed its hardiness on non-productive land, and the Royal Agricultural Society presented Moody with a gold medal. Joseph Hooker never expected it to grow so tall in Britain's drier climate, although he shared public optimism about its agricultural merits, but he, his father, estate managers and farmers were to be disappointed. Seeds often failed to germinate and when, at last, it was established in Orkney and the Hebrides, its growth rate was too slow to make it a viable crop.

Before the *Erebus* and *Terror* left the islands for a short visit to Tierra del Fuego, Hooker packed three boxes and a cask of plants and seeds for despatch: New Zealand tree-ferns, a sampling of the flora of the Campbell and Falkland Islands, shells and the skins of birds. Identification is always a challenge for any collector. Hooker felt reasonably confident dealing with flowering plants and mosses but often wished he had some reference books on unfamiliar lichens and algae.

After the battering the two ships had endured, they were beached, caulked below the water-line, and made fit to sail again. The scientific equipment which had been erected near the ruins of Bougainville's fortifications was reloaded for similar experiments in the vicinity of Cape Horn. Gales persisted all the way to that notorious headland which a disappointed Hooker found fell short of its reputation. The archipelago of islands off the southern extremity of

8. *Journal of Royal Geographical Society,* vol. 12, 1842, pp. 267-68.
9. 4 March 1843, p. 131.

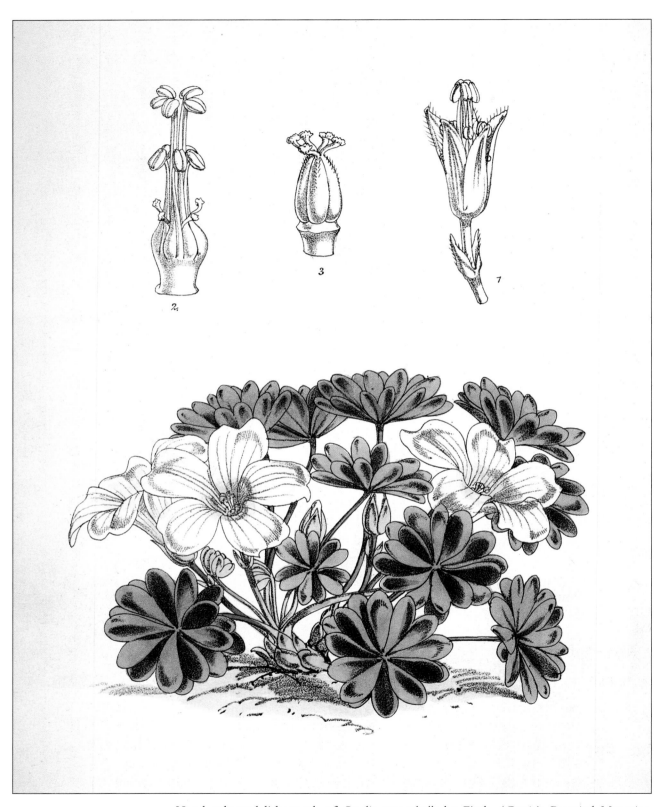

Hand-coloured lithograph of *Oxalis enneaphylla* by Fitch. (*Curtis's Botanical Magazine,* 1876, plate 6256). An 'excellent antiscorbutic' and an 'agreeable pot herb', Hooker saw it growing 'in such profusion at Berkeley Sound, on banks overhanging the sea, as to cover them with a mantle of snowy white in the spring month of November'.

(Above left) Hand-coloured lithograph of *Berberis ilicifolia* by Fitch. (*Curtis's Botanical Magazine*, 1847, plate 4308). Of one consignment of Tierra del Fuego plants despatched by Hooker, only the *Berberis* survived. In March 1847 it flowered at Kew, 'its deep orange-coloured blossoms, which, taken in conjunction with its bright, glossy, holly-leaved foliage, induced Dr. Hooker to consider it, and justly so, the handsomest known species of the genus'. (Sir W.J. Hooker.)

(Above right) Hand-coloured engraving of *Fuchsia magellanica* by James Sowerby. (*Curtis's Botanical Magazine,* 1789, plate 97). First introduced into Kew Gardens in 1788 when it was placed in a hothouse where it flowered throughout the summer. Later discovered to be extremely hardy, it is used for hedging in Ireland.

Christmas Sound, Tierra del Fuego. Engraving of a drawing by W. Hodges, the official artist on Captain Cook's second voyage. (J. Cook. *A Voyage towards the South Pole and around the World,* vol. 2, 1777). Cook reported that it was not so barren as he had expected: 'we could see trees distinctly through our glasses and observe several smokes made probably by the natives as a signal to us'.

South America had been named Tierra del Fuego, 'Land of Fire', by Magellan, a reference, presumably, to the Indian camp fires he saw at night. Captain Cook passed through the islands in 1769 and again in 1774. On his first voyage Joseph Banks and his companion, Daniel Solander, collected about a hundred plants, most of them new species. The local scurvy grass and wild celery provided vegetables for the crew's soup. When Darwin stepped ashore from the *Beagle* in 1832, the 'still solitudes' of dense forests oppressed him. 'Death, instead of life, seems the predominant spirit'.

The crews of the *Erebus* and *Terror* may also have been similarly intimidated but they welcomed the first trees they had seen since leaving New Zealand a year earlier. The ships hove to in St Martin's Cove on Hermite Island, one of the southernmost in the group. An amphitheatre of snow-capped hills rose to heights of between 1,200 to 1,700 feet. A deep green belt of evergreen beeches ascended to about 1,000 feet, topped by a band of the contrasting green of deciduous beeches. The trees were tightly enmeshed, an impenetrable barrier except by paths hacked out by the Indians.

The beeches of the northern hemisphere are all deciduous whereas the southern beeches have only a few deciduous species amongst its predominantly evergreen ones. *Nothofagus betuloides*, the principal evergreen escorted *Nothofagus antarctica*, a smaller deciduous species. Together with another prominent tree – Winter's bark (*Drimys winteri*) – they occupy, according to Hooker, the same status in Tierra del Fuego as the birch, oak and mountain ash in Scotland.

Determined to reach the summit of Kater Peak, Hooker forced his way through the beech forest, his boots frequently impaled by spiny twigs. He wanted to see the small, hardy alpines above the tree line but found mainly mosses and lichens, among them 'the handsomest of all lichens', the black or sulphur-coated *Usnea melaxantha*.

He judged few of the plants to be really spectacular but *Hebe elliptica*, in his opinion, deserved to be introduced to British gardens. The holly-leaved barberry (*Berberis ilicifolia*), then covered with bright orange-yellow-flowers, and *Fuchsia magellanica* met with his approval.

To the forty or so species of flowering plants he collected, he added mosses and lichens. 'Fuegia is richer in mosses than any other Antarctic island; perhaps no part of the globe of equal extent yields more or finer species than Hermite Island'.[10] A 'miniature forest' of *Dendroligotrichum dendroides*, 'the noblest of mosses', carpeted the ground. He collected sixty species of mosses, suspecting that had he more time he would have found others.

He boasted in his *Flora Antarctica* that he had found many of the plants described by the botanists on Cook's first two voyages, and by Archibald Menzies on Vancouver's voyage in a region he called 'the greatest botanical centre of the Antarctic Ocean'.[11] The two ships were loaded not only with his cargo of plants but also with about 800 deciduous and evergreen beeches for

10. J.C. Ross. *A Voyage of Discovery*, vol. 2, 1847, p. 300.
11. Ibid., p. 295.

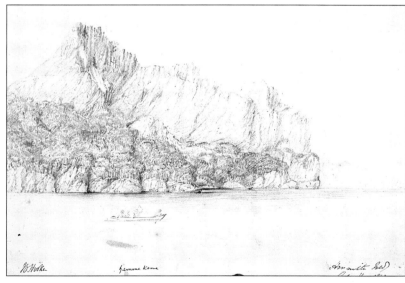

Pencil drawing by Hooker of Hermite Island. 'The mountains rise abruptly out of the water in a succession of steep precipitous banks and cliffs ... clothed with the densest matting of flat-topped, stag-headed beech trees of a lovely green colour; with here and there masses of the purple-leaved deciduous beech, forming a lurid contrast to the other. (Hooker. *Journal*). (*Family of the late R.A. Hooker.*)

(Right) Hand-coloured lithograph of *Durvillea antarctica* by Fitch. (Hooker. *Flora Antarctica*, vol. 2, 1847, plates clxv–vi). Hooker saw this seaweed in the Falklands and encountered it again on Hermite Island. He also found a species of the giant kelp *Macrocystis* and a huge *Laminaria* from which the native Fuegians made cups.

(Below) Watercolour and pencil drawing of *Lecanora miniata*. (Hooker. *Antarctic Botany: Notes and Drawings*, f. 193). Hooker collected this and five other lichens on Cockburn Island. (See p.152 for the specimen Hooker collected in the Himalayas.)

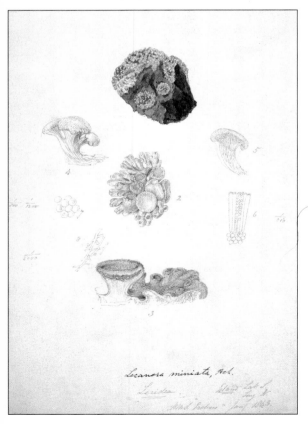

Lecanora miniata, Ach.

planting in the treeless Falklands, and many tree trunks for roofing the houses there.

Just as memorable as the vegetation were the island's inhabitants. Cook had castigated them as 'miserable a set of people as are this day on Earth', without the desire or initiative to make themselves more comfortable. Darwin could not believe 'how wide was the difference between savage and civilised man'. They daubed their bodies with bands of red, white or black pigment. Their clothing, if they wore any, consisted of a single seal or otter skin, or a guanaco cloak slung across the shoulders. Hive-like huts, constructed of bent branches covered with twigs, gave them shelter. They appeared to live on shellfish – often raw – wild

A native of Tierra del Fuego. (R. Fitzroy. *Narrative of the Voyage of H.M.S. Adventure and Beagle, 1826–36*, vol. 2, 1839). 'The men are broad-shouldered with long, spare muscular arms and legs, the latter almost without calves, like the natives of Australia. Their chests are flat as are their faces, with high square cheek bones, flat, thick lips and nostrils, large mouths, and eyes small. The hair is long and dishevelled, cut only over the eyes on the forehead often powdered with wet or dry chalk or wood ashes, as are their bodies sometimes'. (Hooker. *Journal.*)

celery and the yellow fungus (*Cyttaria hookeri*), parasitic on *Nothofagus antarctica*. On an earlier voyage, Captain FitzRoy had taken four of them to England, and had eventually brought them back, 'civilised' and soberly dressed in European clothes, accompanied by a missionary. The well-intentioned experiment was a disaster. When the *Beagle* returned some weeks later, two had absconded to the interior and FitzRoy was confronted by an emaciated third, dishevelled with only a blanket around his waist. The missionary, having been threatened by the tribe, thankfully rejoined the ship. When Ross saw them, he, too, dismissed them as 'the most abject and miserable race of human beings'. Hooker concurred. But he felt sorry for the women who appeared to do most of the work. 'One I saw, wading for many hours up to her middle, in water at 38° with snow falling, quite naked, of course, procuring limpets for her husband who sat in his wigwam, roasting or rather warming them'.[12] Darwin charitably came to the conclusion that 'we must suppose that they enjoy a sufficient share of happiness, of whatever kind it may be, to render life worth having'.

12. Hooker to The Revd James Hamilton. 28 November 1842. *J.D. Hooker. Letters and Journal, 1839-43*, f. 395.

On 14 November the ships began discharging their cargo of trees and timber in the Falklands. Hooker later learned that not a single plant from Tierra del Fuego had withstood the neglect of the settlers and the voracious appetite of goats. He had better luck with the Fuegian plants he sent to his father. He included germinating seeds of Kerguelen's Land cabbage, a moss (*Leptostomum macrocarpum*) that he had kept alive in a bottle since leaving New Zealand, and a representative collection of Falklands seaweed. This, he admitted to his father, was 'sad smuggling' since everything he collected should go to the Admiralty for disposal, 'but I cannot bear staying so long out of England, & not sending home, for anyone's benefit, the products of our labor . . . I have one or two beautiful skinned penguins for the hall at home; but they are not dry enough to forward'.[13] Casualties were a regular occurrence in the shipment of plants by sea, and a good number of Hooker's despatches were dead on arrival in England. These included most of the mosses from Tierra del Fuego and the tussock grass Sir William Hooker so desperately wanted. However the deciduous and evergreen beeches had survived – the first to be introduced alive, claimed Sir William – and the Winter's bark joined another healthy specimen at Kew, then the only one in the country.

The ships were overhauled for the third sortie to the south polar regions. Some calves, pigs and sheep with tussock grass for fodder ensured a supply of fresh meat on the voyage. They departed on 17 December to survey part of Louis Philippe Land, discovered by d'Urville. Should that prove impossible, Ross proposed to retrace Weddell's route to latitude 74° 15´S. to find the open sea Weddell claimed he had seen.

The first icebergs drifted past on Christmas Eve, the vanguard of the pack ice which appeared on Boxing Day. Lyall, the *Terror*'s assistant surgeon and botanist, gave some strands of an unusual seaweed to Hooker who identified it as a new species of *Sargassum*. He traced the southernmost limits of seaweed during this trip.

The ships cautiously skirted Joinville Island. Large tabular bergs, some up to three miles long, now blocked the horizon. The first day of 1843 was the warmest Hooker could recall in Antarctica. The sea was calm and visibility good. The First Lord of the Admiralty, Lord Haddington, was commemorated in the discovery of a mountain about 7,500 feet high, which stood on what is now James Ross Island.

Another senior sea lord gave his name to a conical island nearby, Cockburn Island. Hooker never expected to find any vegetation on its bare volcanic rocks. In the three hours he had ashore he collected thirteen species: algae in the sea, minute mosses in the fissures of rocks, and several lichens including one he had collected on other Antarctic islands, *Lecanora miniata*. He was to see it again high up in the Himalayas. There were no flowering plants but it was, as he told his father, 'a great consolation to me after such a long and

13. *J.D. Hooker. Letters and Journal, 1839-43*, f. 382.

82

dreary cruize to gather any plants in a situation much nearer to the South Pole than vegetation hitherto had been supposed to reach'.[14] He found seaweed in ice-bound waters another surprise. He often noted birds in his Antarctic journal. His ornithological skill in succinctly tabulating their essential features is evident in this description of shags on Cockburn Island.

> . . . the back beautifully bronzed with blue iridescence and a white band between the wings, the cere much carunculated and golden yellow, crest none, ring of the eyes prominent and bright blue, iris yellow brown, pupil black, bill dirty red, sides of neck and whole throat and belly white, legs flesh colored.[15]

As they probed thick fog, both ships fired guns and banged gongs to keep in touch at a safe distance. After days of being either moored to a floe or tacking in pools of water, sometimes tantalizingly in sight of land, aware that the end of the navigating season was close, Ross admitted defeat. On 1 February he made a last attempt to find Weddell's open water to the south. He searched the perimeter of about 160 miles of the pack without finding any access. He concluded that Weddell's open sea had been an aberration of the winds moving the pack ice. As they crossed the Antarctic Circle on 1 March the weather improved. A cloudless sky, a bright sun, a light wind, and a moderately calm sea raised spirits but it was a short-lived reprieve. Violent squalls, heavy snow, spray freezing as it fell on the rigging and decks, and always the presence of pack ice, eventually forced a retreat. The squat little ships pitched and rolled, their hatches battened down. The gales, the fogs and the blizzards had never been so severe on their previous attempts. In his old age Hooker still retained a clear

14. Hooker to his father. 7 March 1843. *J.D. Hooker, Letters and Journals, 1839-43,* f. 432.
15. *Antarctic Journal* (typescript), f. 347.

The expedition reached Cockburn Island on 6 January 1843. '... its appearance is that of a truncated cone, low, round, and the slope at an angle of nearly 45 degrees formed of loose stones, here and there tinged with yellow red, but otherwise of a uniform pale brown'. (Hooker. *Journal*.)

recollection of the mood of the entire ship's company: tense and apprehensive, anxiously alert to every movement and sound in the vessel.

> Officers and men slept with their ears open, listening for the look-out man's cry of "Berg ahead!" followed by "All hands on deck!" The officers of the *Terror* told me that their commander never slept a night in his cot throughout that season in the ice, and that he passed it either on deck or in a chair in his cabin. They were nights of grog and hot coffee, for the orders to splice the main brace were many and imperative, if the crew were to be kept up to the strain on their nerves and muscles.[16]

The officers had concealed their reluctance to undertake this last cruise in the ice. When they had volunteered for this epic voyage they had expected 'all those agreeable recreations which the North Polar expeditions have afforded'.[17] Ross, forced to abandon his mission, set a course northwards for the Cape of Good Hope.

> 'And I cannot tell you how rejoiced we are to be leaving it for good, & all. Captain says he would not conduct another expedition to the South Pole for any money & a pension to boot. Nor would any individual of us join if he did; I am sure I would not for a baronetcy'.[18]

The Antarctic Circle was crossed for the last time on 11 March. An attempt *en route* to find the elusive Bouvet Island failed and Ross, like Cook before him, concluded that the Frenchman had mistaken a large iceberg for land. On the journey north Hooker drafted a paper on the 'Geographical Distribution of the Antarctic Plants … their relation to those of the Arctic regions, & the affinities between the Antarctic, Polynesian & American floras'.[19]

Being too late in the season to collect seeds when he landed at Cape Town in April, he relaxed and met congenial residents like Baron Ludwig who promised to exchange plants with Kew Gardens. A local nurseryman, Joseph Upjohn, who had already despatched bulbs to Kew, filled a Wardian case with a sampling of the Table Mountain's flowers for the Gardens.

The ships called at St Helena where Hooker collected twenty-two species of ferns. On Ascension Island he gathered another eight ferns of which only two had been found on St Helena. About a dozen flowering plants, all introductions, made up Ascension's flora. When Darwin was there he had not seen a single tree but Hooker found that one had survived an acute shortage of water. At the request of the Admiralty he proposed remedial action with a generous planting of vegetation similar to that on St Helena. Kew Gardens subsequently supervised a programme of planting trees and shrubs capable of withstanding persistent sea breezes. By 1865 Ascension Island had about a hundred naturalised plants, fresh vegetables for its military garrison, and an improved water supply. Nevertheless, Hooker had misgivings about the successful outcome of the project. 'The consequences to the native vegetation

16. *Geographical Journal*, vol. 3, 1894, pp. 28-29.
17. Hooker to his father. 7 March 1843. *J.D. Hooker. Letters and Journal, 1839-43*, f. 439.
18. Ibid.
19. Ibid., f. 448.

of the Peak [on Ascension Island] will, I fear, be fatal, and especially to the rich carpet of ferns that clothed the top of the mountain when I visited it'.[20]

At midnight on 4 September 1843 the *Erebus* and *Terror* anchored off Folkestone, then proceeded to Woolwich where the crews who had been at sea for four years were paid off.

Ross had fulfilled the principal objective of the voyage, the investigation of terrestrial magnetism, conscientiously and methodically. At all times he maintained meticulous weather records. He devised a technique for taking deep sea soundings. With Hooker's assistance he collected microscopic marine life but never wrote up his discoveries. However he always encouraged the researches of his surgeon naturalists.

His voyage is probably best remembered today as the first reconnaissance of the Antarctic which confirmed the existence of a continent much of whose coastline he charted. He discovered Victoria Land, the Ross Sea, the Ross Ice Shelf, McMurdo Sound and numerous small islands. With hindsight Hooker qualified these achievements by declaring that they were 'due rather to accidental circumstances than to foreknowledge, forethought, or foresight'.[21]

Ross spent four laborious years writing his account of the expedition: *A Voyage of Discovery and Research in the Southern and Antarctic Regions, during the years 1839–43*. He acknowledged the scientific research of McCormick and Hooker and incorporated some of their geological and botanical observations. A few of Hooker's landscape sketches were reproduced. Darwin who found the book disappointing except for Hooker's 'botanical summaries', wondered if the only thing he had really enjoyed, a racy narrative of a wild cattle hunt in the Falklands, had been written by Hooker. Hooker himself was peeved that Ross had not mentioned that he had been 'the sole worker of the tow-net, bringing the captures daily to Ross, and helping him with their preservation, as well as drawing a great number of them for him'.[22]

The expedition had tested Ross's undoubted qualities of courage, tenacity and organisation but it also revealed his arrogance and professional jealousy. McCormick deplored his 'prejudices' which made him 'so difficult to reason with'. Hooker, while gratefully conscious of the consideration Ross had always shown him, confessed to his father that 'love him I never can or could'. Ross had resented the presence of d'Urville and Wilkes in the Antarctic, but they were never serious rivals since their ships had not been strengthened to venture far into the pack ice. Ross and the crews of the *Erebus* and *Terror*, the last sailing ships to explore so far south, won the admiration of a later polar explorer, Roald Amundsen.

> Few people of the present day are capable of rightly appreciating this heroic deed, this brilliant proof of human courage and energy. With two ponderous craft – regular 'tubs' according to our ideas – these men sailed right into the heart of the pack, which all previous explorers had regarded as certain death'.[23]

20. *J.D. Hooker. Indian, Moroccan and Syrian Journals*, f. 665.
21. *Geographical Journal*, vol. 3, 1894, pp. 27-29.
22. *L. Huxley. Life and Letters...*, vol. 1, 1918, p. 47.
23. R. Amundsen. *The South Pole*, vol. 1, 1912, p. 12.

Chapter 5

An Interlude

When Hooker left England in 1839 his father was teaching botany at Glasgow University; on his return he was managing a small botanic garden at Kew. Within a few years of taking up his Glasgow appointment in 1820, Sir William regretted being so far from the country's scientific activities centred on London, and resolved to return south as soon as possible. Rumours about the imminent retirement of W.T. Aiton, the Director of the royal gardens at Kew, not far from London, focused his hopes on being his successor. To improve his chances of getting this congenial post when it became vacant, he solicited the help of the sixth Duke of Bedford whom he knew through mutual horticultural interests. As the years passed and the aged Aiton showed no desire to retire, Sir William despaired of ever achieving his ambition. He abandoned all hope of it when it seemed likely that the royal gardens might be disbanded as part of a Treasury cost-cutting exercise. In 1838 a working party composed of an eminent botanist and two gardeners had recommended the transformation of part of the royal estate into a national botanic garden, funded by the State, but the Government predictably showed no enthusiasm for the proposal. Sir William gloomily wrote to his son on H.M.S. *Erebus*, 'it seems that nothing will be done with Kew & that there really is nothing I can ask for'.[1]

In November 1840, however, Aiton at last intimated his intention to relinquish charge of the botanic garden which passed to the control of the Commissioners of Woods and Forests. Sir William was appointed its first Director. Writing from the Athenaeum on 10 March 1841 he told his son that although he was sorry to be leaving Scotland, 'England & especially the vicinity of London have many powerful attractions'. Kew Palace, Queen's Cottage and the Royal Kitchen Garden remained with the Crown, and the King of Hanover (formerly the Duke of Cumberland) exercised game rights over several hundred acres of the rest of the estate. Eleven acres were all that Sir William controlled but he planned to expand the grounds and its stock of plants. His son was one of many people he began importuning. 'I long for a plant in Kew Gardens of the Kerguelen's Land cabbage. Remember to get me seeds or live plants whenever you can by purchase or otherwise. I am as keen for dried plants as ever & a 1000 times more so for living ones'.[2]

1. W.J. Hooker to his son. 13 April 1840. *J.D. Hooker. Correspondence received, 1839-45*, f. 100.
2. W.J. Hooker to his son. 16 July 1841. Ibid., f. 116.

When Sir William Hooker left Glasgow to become Director at Kew Gardens, he acquired West Park less than a mile away as his residence. He described his new home in a letter he wrote to his son on 16 July 1841. 'The house commodious, the rooms however rather small but plenty of them & the whole air of the place thoroughly gentlemanly & paddock of 7 acres, excellent kitchen garden, a greenhouse, stables and a coach house'. Joseph Hooker joined his parents there on his return from Antarctica.

Joseph Hooker learned of his father's appointment through an announcement in the *Athenaeum* newspaper when he reached Sydney. Macleay volunteered to send Australian plants to Kew, and Gunn in Tasmania was asked to send hardy species. Sir William continued to bombard his son with requests. 'While at the Cape you will do all you can to provide seeds & bulbs for Kew Gardens, of all kinds of seeds of Proteaceae, even the commonest kinds will be acceptable'.[3] Another letter thanked his son for seeds of the Falkland Islands' tussock grass. 'They have been carefully sown in the Royal Gardens & heartily do I hope they may flourish. But I fear they may refuse to vegetate like the still more valued seeds of the Kerguelen's Land cabbage'.[4] Such failures also depressed Joseph Hooker. 'I hope the beeches, especially, may have reached England alive! They were in such order when despatched'. He longed to see a new fern house at Kew. 'The noble tree-

3. W.J. Hooker to his son. 20 March 1842. *J.D. Hooker. Correspondence received, 1839-45,* f.120.
4. W.J. Hooker to his son. 19 March 1843. Ibid., f. 123.

ferns, huge *Acrosticha* and *Stegassiae* with the *Hymenophylla* creeping on the ground, would be a splendid novelty'.[5] In his first annual report Sir William proudly drew attention to 'those rare and singularly beautiful trees, the most southern in the world, the evergreen and deciduous beech trees of Tierra del Fuego, which promise to be alike useful and ornamental on our soil, and which we have been happily able to distribute pretty extensively'. The same report announced that tussock grass, received from Governor Moody in the Falkland Islands, was also being grown at Kew.

Joseph Hooker's more informative letters to his family were diligently copied several times for circulation among relatives and friends. Darwin who had read one addressed to Lyall, congratulated Sir William on his son's 'agreeable' style. When Sir William was invited to Buckingham Palace in March 1842 to show the Prince Consort copies of Joseph Hooker's sketches of Mount Erebus and 'a curious iceberg with a hole in it', he seized the opportunity to read extracts of his son's letters to his royal audience. This publicity given to his letters and drawings alarmed Joseph Hooker, fearful of Captain Ross's disapproval. He knew perfectly well that he had transgressed an Admiralty prohibition when he summarised his official journal in his letters. He sharply rebuked his father for his thoughtlessness. 'Do remember that I do extremely dislike having my letters shown to those I do not know, and that with regards to the drawings it is not fair to me to make them known far and wide, inasmuch as I have defrauded the Expedition of them'.[6] Thoroughly chastised, Sir William made sure that he obtained the Admiralty's permission before he published a précis of his son's letters in his *London Journal of Botany* in 1843.[7] He reprinted them as a separate pamphlet dedicated to Prince Albert. His actions all along had been well-intentioned, that is, simply to promote his son's reputation at the beginning of his chosen career.

Joseph Hooker had never contemplated the Royal Navy as a career when he joined in order to be a naturalist on the Antarctic expedition. Friends in Tasmania had tried to persuade him to get a discharge on medical grounds and to stay there as a botanist. As the end of the voyage drew near he considered his preferences. Employment in his father's private herbarium might be feasible for a while. Foreign travel still appealed to him, especially in the South Seas. The Himalayas were another option but they were already being explored by officials of the East Indian Company. If Ross were to command an excursion of about eight months to the North Pole he would like to join it as a naturalist, 'but I could not afford to spend 3 years in any such climates'.[8] Ross urged him to remain in the Navy given an assurance that he would be employed only on scientific expeditions, and as an inducement, offered to recommend him for promotion. Hooker was non-commital: if no suitable appointment turned up on shore, he would remain in the Navy for the time being. Ross advised him to stay on its pay-roll (perhaps on half-pay) in order

5. *Hooker's London Journal of Botany*, vol. 2, 1843, p. 327.
6. Hooker to his father. 5 December 1843. *J.D. Hooker. Letters and Journal, 1839-43*, f. 407.
7. 'Notes on the Botany of the Antarctic Voyage'. *Hooker's London Journal of Botany*, vol. 2, 1843, pp. 247-329.
8. Hooker to D. Turner. 17 April 1843. *J.D. Hooker. Letters and Journal, 1839-43*, f. 475.

to write up the botanical results of the voyage. Sir William approved of his son's caution and welcomed his offer of assistance in his private herbarium. Joseph Hooker was absolutely certain that botany was his vocation. A gentle admonition from the American botanist, Asa Gray, may have helped to resolve his dilemma. 'You now stand in a perfectly unrivalled position as a botanist as to advantages, etc. with the finest collections and libraries of the world within your reach; and if you do not accomplish something worth the while, you ought not to bear the name of Hooker'.[9]

It had been assumed by the family that the botanical results of the Antarctic voyage would be published. With that thought in mind Dawson Turner had offered to help sort and edit Joseph Hooker's papers on his return. In their correspondence father and son tried to plan the hypothetical book. Only a few months into the voyage Joseph Hooker was already defining its limits.[10] By May 1842 Sir William had extended the flora to cover New Zealand and Tasmania as well as Antarctica,[11] which would also incorporate collections from the British Museum and the *Beagle* voyage. He proposed that a government subsidy towards its publication might be sought and that he would be happy to make a personal contribution. He tried to convince Ross of the merits of publishing the scientific results of his voyage, and reminded him that specimens collected on Cook's voyages were languishing in the British Museum, still awaiting an editor. If Sir William had his way, the projected flora would include all the islands Ross had visited. Excited by the challenge but daunted by its magnitude, Joseph Hooker had reservations about the inclusion of New Zealand and Tasmania. 'I fear you overrate my botanical powers, for I am very ignorant of plants that I have not actually seen'.[12] He agreed, however, to incorporate the Auckland and Campbell Islands, Kerguelen's Land, and the Falklands. From this exchange of ideas the dimensions of a conceivable published flora gradually emerged.

The next step was to obtain the support of the Admiralty and the Treasury. The Admiralty rejected a request for a grant of £1,000. In strictest confidence Sir William appealed to Ross. Joseph Hooker's collections deserved a work with 500 plates, some of them coloured, he argued. 'Surely our country would not like to see d'Urville's Botany superior to ours: yet it will & must be so unless the above sum is granted'.[13] This astute reference to the publication of a rival voyage made Ross an ally. Robert Brown at the British Museum gave his support to a petition sent to the Prime Minister, Sir Robert Peel. In March 1844 the Treasury sanctioned £1,000 for the production of 500 plates. Moreover, while he was engaged on the flora Joseph Hooker would receive £200 a year, an enhancement of his assistant surgeon's pay. A sinecure appointment on one of the Queen's yachts ensured he would not be distracted by official duties.

It was anticipated that five royal quarto volumes would be required to

9. Gray to Hooker. 1 March 1844. *Letters of Asa Gray*, vol. 1, 1893, p. 317.
10. Hooker to his father. 1 and 17 March 1840. *J.D. Hooker. Letters and Journal, 1839-43*, f. 103.
11. W.J. Hooker to his son. May 1842. *J.D. Hooker. Correspondence received, 1839-45*, f.121.
12. Hooker to his father. 25 November 1842. *J.D. Hooker. Letters and Journal, 1839-43*, f. 385.
13. W.J. Hooker to Ross. 3 November 1843. *Antarctic Voyage. Letters from W.J. Hooker*, f. 17.

describe and illustrate the floras of Antarctica, New Zealand and Tasmania. Relevant collections at the British Museum (the plants of the Cook and Menzies voyages) and in private hands would be incorporated. Leading London publishers like Bailliere, Longmans and Murray calculated that the lithographic work could not be done at the stipulated price of a pound a plate, and the initial financial outlay deterred Smith and Elder who showed some interest. At this point a young man, anxious to get established as a publisher, impetuously offered to undertake the project. Lovell Reeve with a shop in the Strand in London selling natural history specimens and conchological books also had a lithographic press. He agreed to produce the text and the plates provided any fees for the drawings were waived and that no copies of the work would be presented to potential purchasers. The first of twenty-five numbers of *Flora Antarctica* appeared on 1 June 1844 with eight plates. In its review of the work the *Athenaeum* commended the drawings by Fitch: 'we know of no productions from his pencil, or, in fact, any botanical illustrations at all, that are superior in faithful representation and botanical correctness'.

Walter Hood Fitch, a Glaswegian, had served a brief apprenticeship as a lithographer before finding employment drawing patterns for Henry Monteith, a calico printer. In his spare time he mounted dried plant specimens for Sir William Hooker who, impressed by his industry and talent, taught him how to draw plants with the scientific accuracy demanded by botanists. His first published drawing when he was only seventeen, appeared in *Curtis's Botanical Magazine*, edited by Hooker. When Sir William came to Kew he brought Fitch with him, paying his wages out of his own pocket. Fitch was to become one of the most prolific of all Victorian botanical artists with a style instantly recognisable: fluent competent lines and bold colouring, encapsulating the character of plants in exuberant portraits. Joseph Hooker showed his appreciation of his ability by naming in 1845 a new genus, *Fitchia*, found on an island in the South Pacific.

The first volume of *Flora Antarctica* comprising ten issues, described material mostly collected by Hooker. The second volume (fifteen issues) included plants already in published literature which Hooker made use of with due acknowledgement. He enlisted the help of specialists for the determination of cryptogams: T. Taylor for lichens and liverworts, W. Wilson for mosses and W.H. Harvey for algae.

The two volumes were completed by October 1847, the first dedicated to Queen Victoria, the second to Lord Minto, First Lord of the Admiralty. The author wrote at considerable length about some of his spectacular finds: Kerguelen's Land cabbage, Falkland Islands' tussock grass, and the giant kelp. Fitch's interpretation of his dried specimens and floral sketches pleased him, especially his rendering of *Bulbinella rossii*, 'the most beautiful botanical drawing we have ever seen published', he told Ross. He postulated floristic

Walter Hood Fitch (1817–1892). The botanical artist who illustrated most of Hooker's publications.

relationships between the Lord Auckland and Campbell Islands and New Zealand, and between Tierra del Fuego and oceanic islands some 5,000 miles to the east. He saw such islands as a key to the understanding of the geographical distribution of the world's vegetation. *Flora Antarctica* made Hooker's reputation as a systematist and plant geographer, and he was still a young man. He felt relief as well as pride that it was finished. 'The *Flora Antarctica* nearly broke my back; and except the Flora of New Zealand and Van Diemen's Land, I do not contemplate any other such great work'.[14]

Charles Darwin heavily marked some of Hooker's statements on plant geography in his copy of *Flora Antarctica*. Early in 1843 he had congratulated Sir William Hooker that his son was embarking on a flora of his voyage. 'I have long felt much curiosity for some discussion on the general character of the flora of Tierra del Fuego'.[15] His collection of plants from that archipelago were at his son's disposal, he added. In mid-November 1843 he introduced himself to Joseph Hooker, expressing pleasure that Hooker had accepted his small collection of Tierra del Fuego's alpine flowers. 'Do make comparative remarks on the species allied to the European species for the advantage of botanical ignoramuses like myself'[16] Hooker had been delighted to have them since few of the alpines he had collected had been in flower.[17] He also shared Darwin's interest in a comparative study of the floras of the North and South Poles. Thus began a long and productive correspondence between the two

14. L. Huxley. *Life and Letters...*, vol. 1, 1918, p. 255.
15. Darwin to W.J. Hooker. 12 March 1843. *Correspondence of Charles Darwin*, vol. 2, 1986, pp. 350-1.
16. Darwin to Hooker. 13 or 20 November 1843. Ibid., pp. 408-9.
17. 28 November 1843. Ibid, pp.410-13

scientists, letters soliciting information and exchanging opinions. 'Is not the similarity of plants of Kerguelen's Land & S. America very curious', mused Darwin.[18] Hooker agreed. 'I do not think that there is in the north any instance of the floras of two such remote spots as Kerg. Land & Cape Horn being identical'. As they used each other as a sympathetic listener, so their mutual regard grew. Hooker was the first to hear of Darwin's hypothesis that species, far from being immutable, were adaptable. At that time Hooker subscribed, albeit with reservations, to the conventional view on the permanence of species. Darwin entrusted the elucidation of his Galapagos Islands plants to Hooker, hoping he might discover whether, like the birds, there were significant island variations in species. The endemics that Hooker identified were largely confined to one island, a piece of research duly digested by Darwin.[19]

Hooker became a frequent visitor to Darwin's home at Down House in Kent. He dealt with all the botanical queries that his host had accumulated for him, raised pertinent points on his researches on barnacles, showed him how to use microscopes, and generally became his confidant. 'I congratulate myself in a most unfair advantage of you' wrote Darwin, 'viz in having extracted more facts & views from you than from any other person'.[20] In July 1844, Darwin, always paranoiac about his health, instructed his wife that, in the event of his death, his draft essay on species should be edited by one of his dependable supporters. Shortly afterwards he specifically mentioned Hooker as a suitable editor. The prospect of Hooker's departure to Edinburgh in the spring of 1845 dismayed Darwin who consoled himself with the thought that 'I know I shall live to see you the first authority in Europe on that grand subject, that almost key-stone of the laws of creation, Geographical Distribution'.[21]

The necessity to secure employment had precipitated Hooker's move north. Dependence on his father's hospitality embarrassed him. Sir William hoped that his transformation and enlargement of Kew Gardens would in due course provide an opening for his son. Joseph Hooker could have had the vacant post of Curator of the Sydney Botanic Garden in November 1844, but neither of them viewed that option with much enthusiasm. Much closer at hand, and certainly more attractive, was the chance of an appointment at Edinburgh University. The Professor of Botany there, Robert Graham, through poor health desired an unpaid assistant to give a series of lectures beginning in the late spring of 1845. As this temporary assignment could be a stepping-stone to the chair at Edinburgh, Joseph Hooker accepted an invitation to be the lecturer, but somewhat reluctantly since shyness and a nervous disposition always made him ill at ease in front of an audience. He discovered that Graham's method of lecturing was chaotic – no syllabus and, worst of all, no notes that he could use. At first he floundered but confidence came with practice, his tension relaxed, and, we are told, students appreciated his

18. Darwin to Hooker. 12 December 1843. *Correspondence of Charles Darwin*, vol.2, 1986, pp. 419-20.
19. J.D. Hooker. 'Plants of the Galapagos Archipelago'. *Transactions of Linnean Society*, vol. 10, 1845-46, pp. 163-233, 235-62.
20. Darwin to Hooker, 10 February 1846. *Correspondence of Charles Darwin*, vol. 3, 1987, p. 287.
21. Darwin to Hooker, 10 February 1845. Ibid., pp. 139-40.

informality. When Graham died in August, Hooker marshalled an impressive band of eminent people to confirm his suitability for the post. The name of Baron von Humboldt dominated his foreign supporters. Captain Ross and the Arctic explorers, Edward Parry and John Richardson, reminded the University of Hooker's distinguished service in Antarctica. Some of Britain's foremost botanists – Brown, Bentham and Lindley, for instance – vouched for his botanical expertise. Darwin supplied a laudatory testimonial. In the event, the appointment went to a former Edinburgh man, John Balfour, nine years Hooker's senior. Balfour's previous post of professor at Glasgow University was offered to Hooker who declined it.

When Sir Henry de la Beche, Director of the Geological Survey of Great Britain, wanted a botanist to investigate the connections between plants and geological formations, he consulted Sir William Hooker who immediately thought of his son. The salary was only £150 a year but the duties were not onerous. He would be required to visit a couple of sites a year (travelling expenses paid); the rest of the time he would be free to work on the *Flora Antarctica*. There was a subsidiary reason for considering the post. The Geological Survey reported to the Office of Woods and Forests, which was also Kew's parent department, a fact not lost on Sir William who thought it might facilitate his son's transfer to Kew at a later date. On 1 April 1846 Joseph Hooker entered the employ of the Geological Survey in London.

Palaeobotany, then in its infancy, could yield clues on the migration of plants through many millennia. In his first published paper for the Geological Survey Hooker wrote:

> As a field for botanical research there is none so novel as the coal formation, the few yards of shaft being more than equivalent to the longest voyage, in respect of the amount and kind of difference between the vegetation the naturalist is acquainted with and that he seeks to understand.[22]

During the Antarctic voyage he had published a short paper on a fossil tree embedded in Tertiary basalt in Tasmania. His researches on fossil plants of the Carboniferous and Eocene periods appeared in a couple of papers in the *Memoirs of the Geological Survey*.[23] Others were published in the *Journal of the Geological Society* in 1855. He was to demonstrate his understanding of geological structures and rock types during his Indian tour when he also supplied Lyall and Darwin with data on glaciers in the Himalayas. Fossils, however, never had the same appeal as living plants although in his old age he returned to a problem of his youth in a paper on the Silurian fossil, *Pachytheca*.[24]

Congenial employment with the Geological Survey, satisfactory progress on the *Flora Antarctica*, his engagement to Miss Frances Henslow, and his election to the Royal Society could not assuage his longing to travel again to get firsthand experience in the field. In absolute confidence, he told his

22. *Memoirs of the Geological Survey*, vol. 2, 1848, p. 394.
23. Ibid., pp. 387–430, 431–39.
24. *Annals of Botany*, vol. 3, 1889, pp. 135–40.

grandfather that 'I shall be ready to make any sacrifice to get to the tropics for a year, so convinced am I that it will give me the lift I want, in acquiring a knowledge of exotic botany'.[25] He rejected the Andes in favour of India where Hugh Falconer, Superintendent of the Calcutta Botanic Garden, promised assistance. Once there, a botanical tour in the neighbourhood and perhaps an excursion to the Himalayas might be arranged. Another friend, Thomas Thomson, whom he had known from student days, had been detailed to join a commission to regulate the border between Kashmir and Chinese Tibet. Hooker wondered how he might exploit this connection. Sir Henry de la Beche encouraged these aspirations, seeing an opportunity to get Indian fossils for the Geological Survey. But India did not meet with the approval of the Admiralty, still his paymaster, which suggested he might join an official expedition to the Malay islands in 1848.

Joseph Hooker put his case to the First Lord of the Admiralty, Lord Auckland, a former Governor-General of India, who sanctioned two years in India on half-pay for Hooker with a third year in Borneo where he would join the official expedition. When Lord Auckland died in 1849, the Borneo excursion was cancelled and an additional year in India substituted. His father had spotted an opportunity of increasing his son's pay, by submitting a case to send a man to India to collect plants for Kew Gardens. Not surprisingly, he nominated his son as his collector. The Commissioners of Woods and Forests approved the application and granted Joseph Hooker an allowance of £400 a year.[26] Sir William himself made good the shortfall in his son's expenses. Nothing had been finally settled about where he should go in India but the Himalayas beckoned.

Through trade and conquest, some of India's trees and flowers had reached the classical world. Herodotus singled out cinnamon, Theophrastus cited plants collected by Alexander's troops, and Pliny the Elder extolled its spices. A doctor practising in Portuguese Goa, Garcia da Orta, grew native medicinal plants. A soldier and administrator in the Dutch possessions in the south of the sub-continent produced the first regional flora.[27] One of Linneaeus's students, Johann Koenig, introduced his teacher's system of classifying and naming plants to the few European botanists then in India. Most of them served in the medical branch of the East India Company, surgeons who had been taught basic botany as students, and the Company encouraged them to identify plants with any commercial application. It therefore supported a scheme to create a botanic garden in Calcutta in 1787 for the collection, cultivation and distribution of plants of economic value. Sir Joseph Banks, adviser to George III on the management of his gardens at Kew, maintained a personal interest in the development of this embryonic garden. He recommended that foreign crops should be naturalised in India and that useful Indian plants might be grown in British colonies. He obtained ornamental Indian shrubs and flowers for the

25. Hooker to D. Turner. 7 July 1847. *Letters from J.D. Hooker*, vol. 13, f. 317.
26. 20 November 1847. *Kew Collectors*, vol. 11, f. 11.
27. H.A. van Reede tot Drakenstein. *Hortus Indicus Malabaricus*, 1678–93. 12 vols.

Hooker's work with the Geological Survey involved searching for fossil plants in the Welsh coal-beds. He was persuaded by the Royal Institution of South Wales to give a public lecture on his recent voyage at Swansea.

grounds and greenhouses at Kew. It was his initiative that led to the publication of the sumptuous folio, *Plants of the Coast of Coromandel* (1795–1820), a selection of flower drawings by Indian artists. So when Hooker arrived in India he found that a great deal had been done towards identifying and classifying its exotic flora.

Chapter 6

ONCE MORE ON HIS TRAVELS

Hooker's attempts to get to India were followed by Charles Darwin with some disquiet. 'I shall feel quite lost without you to discuss many points with, & to point out (ill luck to you) difficulties & objections to my species hypotheses'.[1] However, he could not resist the chance of using his friend on a fact-finding mission while he was out there. Such data, culled from many sources, often relayed to him by friends, enabled him to formulate plausible theories. At that moment Darwin needed specific information on breeds of domesticated animals, native and imported, in India. Hooker's first letter to him from India obediently attempted to answer his queries on the subject.

Alexander von Humboldt was also quick to take advantage of Hooker's tour, especially as some thirty years earlier he had been thwarted in his ambition to explore Ceylon, India, Tibet and the East Indies. He asked Hooker to take temperature readings at different heights, to discover the altitudinal limits of individual plant families, to examine geological formations, and much else. He modestly concluded 'Je cesse pour ne pas vous ennuyer de choses que vous savez mieux que moi'.[2]

Hooker got a free passage on the frigate, H.M.S. *Sidon*, taking Lord Dalhousie, the new Governor-General, to Alexandria, the first stage of his journey to India. The ship left Portsmouth on 11 November 1847 and Hooker botanised whenever he could. At Lisbon he joined an excursion to Cintra, unimpressed by the trees and flowers of the countryside. He brightened up when he saw lichens carpeting rocks but then dismissed them as being inferior to those in Antarctica. He found fault with much of Lisbon whose inhabitants were 'naturally dirty, indolent and immoral'.

At Gibraltar where *Sidon* refuelled, the Palmetto or dwarf fan-palm reminded him of species he had seen in New Zealand. He recalled that *Phytolacca dioica*, a South American plant introduced by the Portuguese and the Spanish, grew well on Ascension Island. Frequently throughout this new expedition he would be reminded of his Antarctic voyage, sometimes seeing the same species.

He condemned Alexandria as 'a ruinous city of dirty white houses, straggling round a broad bay with nothing but its antiquities and associations to interest a stranger'. Here the *Sidon's* passengers transferred to a boat which

1. Darwin to Hooker.
7 April 1847. *Correspondence of Charles Darwin*, vol. 4, 1988, pp. 29-30.
2. Von Humboldt to Hooker. 30 September 1847. *Hooker's London Journal of Botany*, vol. 6, 1847, pp. 604-7.

took them to the Nile where a small steamer brought them to Cairo. After an extremely uncomfortable night on this steamer, Hooker and some of the passengers went to a Turkish bath, a novel experience for most of them. Dressed only in 'airy garments', they were led into 'a dark, dirty, domed chamber, with a bath of muddy water at 94° in one corner, the stone-work of which abounded in cockroaches'. Having been 'flayed with small hair-brushes', scrubbed with black soap, shaved without soap or lather, Hooker submitted apprehensively to a vigorous massage. He left with 'a crick in his neck' to attend an official reception at the Pasha's palace. Guns fired a salute as guests arrived and a band played the National Anthem and a selection of sprightly polkas. 'The gateway was crowded with tame-looking, fiercely-armed Egyptians, equipped with gorgeous sashes, diamond-hilted scymetars [sic] and the like'. They were conducted to the private audience chamber hung with mirrors on pale satin walls embroidered with crimson and gold flowers, a motif which was repeated on cushions scattered around the room. After formal introductions, each member of the party, including Lady Dalhousie, was handed a hookah, 'its amber mouth-piece as thick as my wrist, and eight inches long, studded with brilliants'. Coffee followed in 'little egg-cups, set in gold filagree holders, blazing with diamonds'.

Like all good tourists, Hooker marvelled at the Sphinx and crawled through the passageway of one of the Pyramids. He even climbed to the top of one of them assisted by two urchins, 'scrambling like cats', and pulling him up 'from ledge to ledge'. Near the summit he was rewarded by colonies of lichens which he naturally sampled. A trip into the desert to see the 'Fossil Forest', some eight to ten miles out of Cairo, probably excited him much more. Small fragments of fossil wood littered the sand, here and there large trunks protruded and occasionally whole trees, seventy or more feet in length. 'Their colour is generally dark reddish-brown: they are all chalcedony and agate of a coarse description, with the rings of the wood well preserved . . . Contrasted with the surrounding sterility, this record of a once luxuriant vegetation is a very impressive object, for it is not confined to a few miles only of desert, but (I am given to understand) extends forty or fifty in one direction'. He gathered as many fragments as his mules could carry, adding some plants he had collected on the way.

He tried unsuccessfully to interest Lord Dalhousie in his finds. He had expected the former President of the Board of Trade to show at least a passing curiosity in a piece of Gum Arabic (*Acacia senegal*) but 'he chucked it out of the carriage window; and the Rose of Jericho, with an interest about it of a totally different character, met with no better fate'.[3] The Governor-General was more concerned about the state of India's tea industry which he invited Hooker to investigate.

His lordship's indifference to botany in no way affected their good relations.

3. Hooker to his father. 24 December 1847. *Letters from J.D. Hooker*, vol. 8, f. 126.

Indeed he included him in his suite on the overland journey from Cairo to Suez. A convoy of carriages and vans, flanked by a couple of outriders, got to the Red Sea in nineteen hours, Hooker braced in his swaying vehicle, his two precious barometers slung round his neck to prevent their getting broken.

Aden's black, volcanic rock struck him as being 'one of the most remarkable places' he had ever seen. In some respects it reminded him of St Helena, and its barrenness of Ascension Island. The commonest plants seemed to be a bushy green *Capparis* and a mignonette (*Reseda*). The valleys protected species belonging to Asclepiadaceae and Euphorbiaceae. He failed to find any algae or maritime plants along the shoreline but collected lichens at 1,500 feet.

While the ship anchored at Point de Galle off the coast of Ceylon, Hooker spent several days with George Gardner, a former pupil of his father, and now Director of the Botanic Garden at Peradeniya. Hooker could not have wished for a better guide on his first introduction to Asia's exotic flora.

Two miles off Madras passengers waited for massalah boats to take them through the dangerous surf that pounded the beaches. These flat-bottomed boats were specially constructed to ride the successive lines of waves, and although their crews were dextrous oarsmen, disembarking was always an alarming experience.

> The steersmen watched minutely every cresting wave, putting the boat round when any too big to be kept ahead of us approached, and urging the paddlers, who screamed and yelled all the more discordantly as each surf tumbled beside the boat and carried her on the top of its foaming crest, letting her down bodily on the hard sand every time, with a crack that would break any ordinary vessel to pieces.[4]

The Governor-General was met by the Governor of Madras in dress uniform, his aides-de-camp at his side, the cavalry and native infantry lined up, and the regimental bands playing. Civilians on horseback and crowds of Indians followed the entourage to Government House. Hooker, reclining in one of the carriages, thought it was 'a gorgeous and stunning sight'. 'This India is a wonderful place', he told his mother, '& quite equal to all my expectations'.

The captain, mindful that he had the Governer-General on board, cautiously navigated his ship up the treacherous River Hooghly to dock at Calcutta on 12 January 1848. From a small settlement in 1690 the city had become the seat of government in British India. Its classical Georgian mansions, stuccoed and whitewashed, set among smooth lawns and shade-giving trees, substantiated its claim to be a 'city of palaces'. It had theatres, many societies, a race-course, and a botanic garden.

The Calcutta Botanic Garden had evolved from a modest proposal made in 1786 by Colonel Robert Kyd, the Military Secretary to the Government in India. He believed that the Sago palm and the Persian date palm could provide

4. Hooker to his father. 10 January 1848. *Letters from J.D. Hooker*, vol. 7, f. 41.

alternative sources of nutritious food for the native population in times of severe famine. A nursery could propagate them on a large scale and the saplings distributed throughout British India. The favourable response to this plan encouraged him to extend the range of crops to those of commercial benefit to India and Britain. He had in mind spices, cotton, tea, coffee, tobacco and teak. The East India Company, assured it would not be an expensive operation, agreed. Some derelict land on the banks of the River Hooghly was requisitioned and gradually stocked with useful crops.

When Kyd died in 1793, William Roxburgh, a surgeon who had managed some experimental horticultural plots in South India, succeeded him, bringing to the appointment professional skills that Kyd had lacked. Plants of purely botanical interest were also grown and he trained Indian artists to make pictorial records of them. His *Flora Indica* was posthumously published. His policy of combining botanical, commercial and recreational activities was continued under Nathaniel Wallich, the next Superintendent of the Botanic Garden. During an absence on a long period of sick leave, his temporary replacement, William Griffith, with youthful impetuosity, destroyed much of Wallich's layout. Plants grown for decoration and display were dug up, venerable trees were felled, and the garden redesigned to present botanical themes. The devastation – for that was how Wallich perceived it on his return to India – was more than he could bear. Within a few years he resigned, an embittered man, but the transformation of the garden continued under another locum, John McClelland. He was still officiating as acting Superintendent when Hooker arrived in India. Some of his alterations met with Hooker's approval – the clearance of undergrowth, additional drainage, more paths, a new arboretum – but he deplored 'the indiscriminate destruction of the useful and ornamental which had attended the well-meant but ill-judged attempt to render a garden a botanical class-book'.[5] When Hugh Falconer eventually took charge, Hooker expected a change in policy, and a restoration of a traditional botanic garden but, as he pointed out to his father, 'Falconer has, after all, a much easier job than you had at Kew'.

Both Falconer and Lord Auckland had independently recommended reclusive Sikkim in the Himalayas to Hooker as a country deserving botanical exploration. The Himalayas which the twentieth-century plant collector, Frank Kingdon Ward, described as an 'immense reservoir of hardy plants', extends from the Karakoram range in the west to the Brahmaputra river in the east. A mission in 1796 to the ruler of Garhwal at Srinagar gave Thomas Hardwicke an opportunity to collect plants in the north-western Himalayas. William Moorcroft on his way to central Asia in 1819 borrowed two Indians from Wallich to collect plants in Kashmir. Its legendary scenery and floral treasures soon attracted other European collectors – the three Gerard brothers, Godfrey Vigne, the Austrian Baron von Huegel, and the Frenchman Victor

5. J.D. Hooker. *Himalayan Journals*, 1891, p. 2.

Old Tamarind trees Feb 10 1848

Pencil drawing by Hooker of the trunks of tamarind trees in Bengal. Note the figure at the base of one of them.

Jacquemont. Farther east Francis Buchanan, a surgeon at the British Residency in Khatmandu, employed native collectors in Nepal where Wallich also botanised in 1820. When George Bogle passed through Bhutan in 1774 on a mission to Lhasa, Warren Hastings asked him to note its fauna and flora. A surgeon on another diplomatic mission in 1783 wrote the first account of the geology and botany of Bhutan and Tibet. William Griffith spent four and a half months collecting in Bhutan in 1838. His native collectors also worked for him in neighbouring Sikkim in 1843, but Joseph Hooker was to be the first European to collect there.

Since it was not the right season to explore the Himalayas, Hooker joined the geologist David Williams, who was just about to survey a coalfield near the Soane river. When he was an employee of the Geological Survey of Great Britain, Hooker had studied some of Williams's Indian fossil plants. He hired a servant of Portuguese descent, an Indian plant collector, four bearers to carry his luggage and stacks of drying paper, and a torch bearer. For nearly three days he endured a jolting ride in a palanquin, sweltering if he kept its doors closed, covered in dust if he left them open. This near relative of a sedan chair was borne on the shoulders of four men. Richard Burton who had travelled many miles in India in one wrote that 'after a day or two you will hesitate which to hate most, your bearers' monotonous, melancholy, grunting, groaning chaunt [sic], when fresh, or their jolting, jerky, shambling, staggering gait, when tired'. When he reached Williams's camp, Hooker thankfully transferred to an elephant for the next stage of the journey. He boasted to his aunt that he had become quite adept in reaching the creature's back by means of ropes or, more agilely, 'by stepping on a tusk, and gripping at a broader ear. If I drop anything, hat or book, he picks it up with his trunk and adroitly tosses it over his head into my lap'.[6]

They overtook crowds of pilgrims, mostly on foot, a few in carts with gleaming brasswork. Their route took them through arid country – stunted

6. Hooker to Mrs Ellen Jacobsen. 8 April 1848. *Letters from J.D. Hooker*, vol. 10, f. 1.

rossing the Soane. Feb. 20. 1848

Crossing the Soane river at Tura with the Kymore Hills beyond, 20 February 1848. Here the river was nearly three miles wide and so shallow that elephants and carts could easily cross. This pencil drawing by Hooker was adapted by Fitch for publication in *Himalayan Journals*.

trees, no plants in flower and few in fruit _ then into valleys with a richer vegetation than he had expected: leafless *Oroxylum indicum* with large pendant sword-shaped pods, and shade-giving *Neonauclea purpurea*. The party ascended Parasnath, a conical mountain sacred to Jains, through a forest of Sal (*Shorea robusta*) and other trees draped with climbing *Bauhinia*. At about 3,000 feet Hooker collected five species of ferns and some rather dry mosses. Higher up he found more. Jain temples near the summit stood among plantain and banyan trees. He noticed few altitudinal changes in the vegetation apart from a limited tropical zone near the top. He gathered sixteen species of flowering plants close to the edge of nearby hot springs whose waters he bottled for future analysis. The landscape featured some splendid specimens of mango, banyan, fan-palms and peepul trees (*Ficus religiosa*) and a small wood of Indian olibanum (*Boswellia serrata*) with fragrant, transparent gum trickling down their trunks. He heard and saw his first wild peacocks. This journey across plains, over hills, through a picturesque pass, well wooded with *Bombax*, *Cassia* and *Acacia*, eventually brought him to the banks of the Soane river. All the time he had been recording the temperature of the air and of the soil at various depths, and sent details of his meteorological observations to Professor Wheatstone. 'My objects are purely botanical; but I hope, by the careful use of good instruments, to obtain data for calculating the effects of climate on the vegetation of large areas'.[7]

They crossed the Soane river, the elephants pushing the heavy waggons of mining equipment. The land on the other side of the river was intensively cultivated with cereals, cotton, sugar cane, indigo and poppies. In the damp coolness of some palace ruins he found healthy specimens of species barely surviving on the exposed plains. The fallen masonry at the hill fort at Rohtas accommodated both wild and naturalised garden plants. Particularly invasive was the little yellow-flowered *Kickxia ramosissima*, the Indian equivalent of the British ivy-leaved toadflax.

7. 15 February 1848. *J.D. Hooker. Indian Letters, 1847-51*, f. 47.

Butea frondosa. Lac tree

Watercolour and pencil sketch of *Butea frondosa* (i.e. *B. monosperma*) by Hooker. Its clusters of bright orange flowers suggested the name, 'Flame of the Forest'. The leaves follow the flower. It is common throughout India.

Cochlospermum.

Watercolour sketch of *Cochlospermum religiosum* with hill fort in background by Hooker. Also known as the yellow silk-cotton tree. 'The bark abounds in a transparent gum, of which the white ants seem fond, for they have killed many trees. Of the leaves the curious rude leaf-bellows are made, with which the natives of these hills smelt iron'. (Hooker. *Himalayan Journals.*)

At night Indian farmers lit fires to scare tigers and bears from prowling around the places where they cut wood and bamboo. Villagers living close to the river had also to watch out for crocodiles. Hooker saw one which had just been killed after swallowing a small child. 'The brute was hardly dead, much distended by the prey, and the mother was standing beside it'. He watched an unsuccessful tiger hunt from the safety of a high tree. The beaters, drumming and shouting, scoured the hills but no living thing, much less than a tiger, was flushed out. More to his taste was the spectacle of *Butea monosperma*, rampantly in flower. 'In mass the inflorescence resembles sheets of flame, and individually the flowers are eminently beautiful, the bright orange-red petals contrasting brilliantly against the jet-black velvety calyx'.[8] On undulating hills of limestone he found *Cochlospermum religiosum* with clusters of golden-yellow flowers 'as large as the palm of the hand'. Near the river a dominant specimen of *Hardwickia,* about 120 feet tall, caught his eye.

Hooker parted company with Williams on 3 March on 'a small, fast and woefully high-trotting elephant', bound for Shahgung and a bungalow's

8. *Himalayan Journals*, 1891, pp. 35-36.

comfort. The elevated table-land he crossed paraded gum-arabic trees (*Acacia arabica*), and the lurid blossoms of mangoes strongly scented the air. He stopped at villages to buy suitable items for the Kew Gardens museum — resins, drugs, cultivated grains, and artefacts made from plants like, for example, a pair of bellows fashioned out of leaves with a bamboo spout. His host's bungalow stood on a small hill surrounded by an orderly display of roses, sweet peas and mignonettes. He must have observed during this tour that British residents compulsively gardened wherever they lived, resolutely accepting the challenge of poor soil, the extremes of climate, and the dubious skills of native gardeners. As a guest in their houses he was flattered to discover that many had already heard of him through Captain Ross's account of his Antarctic voyage or from reviews of the book. At Mirzapur, a major centre of carpet manufacture, he again enjoyed the hospitality of the European community. An army officer enthralled him with stories about his work in suppressing thuggee, the criminal practice of strangling unsuspecting travellers. He learned, too, about dacoits, robbers who stopped short of murder,and a caste of poisoners who drugged their victims with *Datura* seeds before stealing their possessions.

At Mirzapur he abandoned his elephant for a boat, forty feet long, fifteen feet wide, and not 'unlike a floating haystack, or thatched cottage'. In a rudimentary cabin with a palanquin as a bed, he spread out his papers and plants, hung up his telescope, barometer and thermometer, and finally finished off a letter he had started some three weeks earlier to Charles Darwin. 'Though our correspondence has not ebbed so low for full four years, you have been so constantly in my mind that it appears far from strange to be writing to you'.[9]

His researches on his friend's behalf had started as soon as he set foot in Madras where impeccable authorities answered Darwin's queries about the cheetah. They assured Hooker that they never bred in confinement; only fully grown creatures were selected for hunting; and that the youngest were poor hunters. Like the cheetah, the two species of bird used in falconry never hunted for more than a year. Hooker reported some of the habits of elephants of which he had personal experience. Any titbit about the unusual appearance or behaviour of animals he automatically relayed to Darwin, adding that he had no idea whether this information had any significance. He had been told that imported dogs would freely interbreed with domesticated Indian dogs but not with those in the wild. He thought it worth mentioning that common squirrels on the west side of the mountainous Ghats were black-headed while those on the east side sported 'a rufus tinge'. As in other parts of the world, Indian animals dwelling in the plains could ascend up to about 6,000 feet whereas those inhabiting higher altitudes never came down to lower levels. Millions of spiders occupied deserted sand martins' nests in the banks of the

9. Hooker to Darwin.
20 February-16 March 1848.
Correspondence of Charles Darwin,
vol. 4, 1988, pp. 114-20.

Pencil sketch by Hooker of a sundial at Benares (the diameter of the face of the dial was two feet two inches). Erected by the Rajput Maharajah, Jai Singh II, an 18th century patron of astronomy. Altogether he established five observatories in India, the biggest and best known being at Jaipur.

Equinoctial dial.

Soane river but never once did he see any birds eating them. He even fed Darwin's relentless curiosity with hearsay like the belief that swallows in the Nilgiri Hills in the south never nested. He felt on more secure ground with a botanical fact: the sighting of a barberry (*Berberis* species) at 5,000 feet similar to English and Cape Horn species. Confidentially, he revealed to Darwin his anxiety about palpitation and pain down his left side. This long, informative letter ended with an invitation to Darwin to 'put every question about this quarter of the globe you can think of'.

The boat's crew of 'six all but naked Hindoes' brought him to Benares (Varanasi), the 'Athens of India', one of the country's seven cities sacred to Hindus. One suspects that Hooker responded much more instinctively, more spontaneously to natural than to man-made beauty. Some of the most lyrical passages in his journals were evoked by a panoramic view, a florid sunset, a patchwork of lichens. He liked the octagonal minarets of the mosque built by the Moghul Emperor Aurangzeb but little else in Benares. The bank of the Ganges crowded with temples and shrines and flights of steps in the 'burning ghats' were 'far from picturesque'. The chaotic jumble of roofs and squalor reminded him of the view of the Thames from the Blackwall railway: 'the eye wanders in vain for some attractive feature or evidence of the wealth throughout the East for all these atttributes'.[10] He drew some of the large stone astronomical instruments in Maharajah Jai Singh's observatory, 'the most interesting object in Benares', but like so much else in the city suffering from neglect and decay.

His hosts at Ghazepore (Ghazipur) on the north bank of the Ganges took him to Lord Cornwallis's mausoleum designed by Flaxman. Acres of roses around the town were grown and harvested for the perfume distilled from their petals.

The slow progress of the boat gave him time to sort his plants, to write his journals, to sketch, and to scrutinise the high river banks. Seeing few trees and no ferns, mosses or lichens, the birds attracted his attention: the adjutant-bird 'with his head sank on his body and one leg tucked up', gorgeous orange-brown Brahminy ducks, and flocks of grey pelicans splashing the water with

10. *Himalayan Journals*, 1891, p. 49.

their broad wings to drive fish into the shallows. Along the sandy shore marked with the prints of birds and crocodiles, some English plants – dock, nasturtium, fumitory and common vervain – grew among the withered grass. When occasionally the boat stuck fast to a bank in the middle of the river it provided a welcome diversion from hours of passive observation.

He escaped from the restrictions of the boat at Patna to inspect official opium warehouses. Some of the drug was sold in India, hospitals received an allocation, but most of it was destined for China. Doctors also used another local plant, mudar (*Calotropis gigantea*). Hooker already knew the smaller purple-flowered variety but dysentery was treated with the larger white-flowered plant. One doctor claimed to have cured leprosy with it.

Monghyr, rated by Hooker to be the prettiest town he had so far encountered on this river trip, looked rather European with white villas climbing wooded hills. A couple of days at Bhaugulpore (Bhagalpur) gave him an opportunity to take a good look around its Horticultural Gardens spread over fifteen acres that four years earlier had grown indigo. Fifty gardeners and labourers tended fruit trees, many of them imported, grapes on a long covered walk, varieties of sugar, cotton, coffee and English vegetables. It survived by selling its produce and seeds, a model, Hooker thought, for similar establishments elsewhere in the subcontinent. In a letter to his father on the day he left the town, he took stock of what he had achieved so far during the two months he had spent on this trip.[11] He blamed the paucity of his collection – only about 700 species – on the dry season and the barrenness of the region, but he anticipated a richer flora on the Rajmahal Hills. 'I cannot describe how glad I shall be to reach Darjeeling & to see a luxuriant vegetation once more'.

He headed north east in the direction of the Himalayas less than 200 miles away. A higher level of humidity was confirmed by changes in the vegetation: ferns and mosses were more common while *Butea, Boswellia, Grislea, Carissa* and other trees and shrubs of drier regions were seldom or never seen. A different species of bamboo formed groves of straight stems up to twenty feet high. He stopped at Silligoree (Siliguri) on the edge of the terai, a belt of low-lying swamp and Sal scrub, which marked a transition to the flora of the Himalayas. From now on he proposed an intensive ecological investigation of the vegetation taking into account the impact of soil, climate and altitude. The stunted trees of the terai gave way to a forest of *Duabanga, Terminalia, Cedrela* and *Gordonia* among a density of smaller trees and shrubs. Some trees were hosts to *Dendrobium* and other epiphytic orchids; ferns flourished under the forest canopy. Torrents crashed down steep hills rising to over 5,000 feet. With his scanty stock of paper already full of plants, he collected very little. That night he rested in a dak bungalow, his sleep disturbed by a discordant chorus of cicadas.

11. Hooker to his father. 7 April 1848. *J.D. Hooker. Indian Letters, 1847-51*, f. 59.

Wood engraving of a sketch by Hooker, reproduced in his *Himalayan Journals*. It shows the dak bungalow at Punkabaree in the foothills of the Himalayas. 'All around the hills rise steeply five or six thousand feet, clothed in a dense deep-green dripping forest. Torrents rush down the slopes ... From the road ... the view is really superb'. (*Himalayan Journals.*)

Next morning he mounted a pony sent to him from Darjeeling and followed a road made by the army through an even greater mass of vegetation as he ascended the side of the valley. Tall timber trees were linked by cables of climbing *Bauhinia* and *Robinia*. Bamboos, 'as thick as a man's thigh at the base', soared to 100 feet and more. At about 4,000 feet, still twenty-five miles from Darjeeling, the vegetation changed again: a scattering of oaks (*Quercus lamellosa*), 'a very English-looking bramble', and banks colonised by mosses and lichens. Hooker assumed that he had now left the winter of the tropics and entered the spring of the temperate zone. On a ridge he saw his first tree-fern, *Cyathea gigantea*, and thought it inferior to those he had seen in Tasmania. Above a bungalow at Kursiong (Kurseong) where he rested briefly, a sinuous path pointed the way through a forest of chestnut, oak, walnut and laurel.

> It is difficult to conceive a grander mass of vegetation – the straight shafts of the timber-trees shooting aloft, some naked and clean, with grey, pale or brown bark; others literally clothed for yards with a continuous garment of epiphytes, one mass of blossoms, especially the white orchids (*Coelogynes*), which bloom in a profuse manner, whitening their trunks like snow. More bulky trunks bore masses of interlacing climber, Araliaceae, Leguminosae, vines and Menispermeae, Hydrangea and Peppers, enclosing a hollow, once filled by the now strangled supporting tree, which had long ago decayed away. From the sides and summit of these, supple branches hung forth, either leafy or naked, the latter resembling cables flung from one tree to another, swinging in the breeze, their rocking motion increased by the weight of great bunches of ferns or orchids, which were perched aloft in the loops. Perpetual moisture nourished this dripping forest, and pendulous mosses and lichens are met with in profusion.[12]

At over 7,000 feet, he saw 'English-looking' plants, but it was too early in the season to identify them with any certainty. The lemon-scented blossoms of a white rhododendron compensated for the rarity of epiphytes. The absence of any species of Leguminosae and Cruciferae surprised him and he had expected to find more native grasses. This elevation was too high for tropical plants, too moist for temperate ones, and too low for alpines. Ahead of him he could see Darjeeling on a narrow ridge at a little over 7,000 feet.

12. *Himalayan Journals*, 1891, p. 75.

Chapter 7

Arrival at Darjeeling

The British had acquired Darjeeling and some of its surrounding hills in 1835. Sikkim, a small, thinly populated and impoverished state, had reason to fear its neighbours – Tibet to the north, Nepal and Bhutan on either side, and British India to the south. Nepal which had already grabbed some of its territory annexed the southern perimeter known as the terai in 1814. The British forced Nepal to withdraw but when the Nepalese raided Sikkim again in 1834, a permanent British presence was deemed necessary and Darjeeling was ceded. Its population was a mixture of migrants: Lepchas, thought to be of Indo-Chinese stock, who, centuries earlier, came from Nagaland; Bhutias who probably infiltrated from Tibet; and Limbus who crossed from Nepal.

Darjeeling had already become a summer retreat from the heat of the plains, a place to convalesce, and a resort for retired officers and their families when Hooker arrived on 16 April 1848. He found lodgings in a guest-house and hired several Lepcha boys whom he trained to collect and dry plants while he drew, dissected and labelled them. He liked these short, well-built men with broad, flat faces, and plaited tails of hair, and respected their agility and resourcefulness on trek. Skilled woodsmen, they could construct a waterproof hut of bamboo and banana leaves in an hour. They cleared the jungle for their crops by the universal method of slash and burn, and at night their fires were visible from Darjeeling, the noise of exploding bamboo clumps sounding like artillery salvoes. As plant collectors, the Lepchas with their knowledge of jungle life and folklore of plants were unsurpassed.

After a couple of months in the guest-house, Brian Hodgson invited Hooker to share his bungalow on a wooded ridge some distance from the settlement. Being 500 feet higher it commanded one of the best views of the Snowy Mountains dominated by the twin peaks of Kangchenjunga, forty-five miles to the north. 'It is a wonderful panorama, startling in its effect when first revealed by the rising mists on a cloudless morning. The eye spans the intervening gulf of interlacing ranges, divided by rushing streams and clothed with tropical forests, until it is arrested by the dazzling amphitheatre of silvery crests'.[1]

Hodgson combined the intellectual curiosity of a Renaissance scholar, the single-mindedness of a dedicated collector, and the skills of a competent artist.

1. J.D. Hooker's reminiscences in W.W. Hunter. *Life of Brian Houghton Hodgson*, 1896, p. 250.

As British Resident in Khatmandu, he had studied Nepalese life and culture, became an authority on Buddhism, and collected Sanskrit manuscripts. Zoology, however, was his first love, and ornithology his passion. Tribesmen collected specimens for him, and he taught three native artists to draw them with scientific precision, adding to their paintings his meticulous observations on size, colour, habitat and behaviour. Lord Ellenborough who had succeeded Lord Auckland as Governor-General of India, insisted that all British Residents should be neutral and impartial in their dealings with rulers and their court officials. Hodgson refused to withdraw from his close involvement in Nepalese affairs and consequently resigned. This 'most unclubbable of men' could not endure retirement in Britain and returned to India. Barred from Nepal, Darjeeling was the nearest he could get to the eastern Himalayas.

Mutual regard and affection evolved between this reclusive and aloof man and Hooker who at that time still felt ill at ease in society. He believed Calcutta to be 'a detestible place, & its society equally so'.[2] Hodgson advised his young friend on his preparations for exploring the mountains, and gave him the freedom of his books on the Himalayas and runs of Indian scientific journals. They discussed the geology and glaciers of the region, Hodgson from his experience of Nepal, and Hooker from the perspective of his travels in Antarctica. 'We are working together every evening at Himalayan and Thibetan geography and Nat. Hist., and though I say it myself, it is true that I ought in a month or two to have a better knowledge of these aspects of India than any man, having every advantage that an excellent library and tutor can afford'.[3] 'Dear Hodgson' which had formerly prefaced Hooker's letters had become 'Dear old Brian' by December 1849.

The only other local resident, privileged to enjoy Hodgson's hospitality, was his former assistant at Khatmandu, Archibald Campbell, now British Political Agent to Sikkim. He supplied Hooker with facts on Sikkim, its ruler and people, the vegetation, and useful titbits gleaned from Tibetan traders. Welcomed to the Campbell household, Hooker played with their children, and became godfather to Josephine who was born while he and Campbell were captives in Sikkim. He instructed his father that a new rhododendron he had collected was to be named after Mrs Campbell.

As Political Agent Campbell undertook negotiations for Hooker's admission to Sikkim. He assured the Secretary to the Government of India that he was 'satisfied that Dr Hooker's temper and disposition towards the natives are worthy of entire confidence, and that nothing untoward need be apprehended on that score from his anticipated travels'.[4] Lord Dalhousie, who had formed a good opinion of Hooker's abilities, agreed. Campbell was required to inform the Rajah that the Government of India expected adequate protection and every reasonable facility to be rendered to Hooker. With no response from Sikkim, Hooker decided that his plan to reach the Tibetan passes in the north

2. Hooker to his father. 7 April 1848. *J.D. Hooker. Indian Letters, 1847-51,* f. 61.
3. Hooker to his mother. 23 June 1848. *L. Huxley. Life and Letters ... ,* vol. 1, 1918, p. 248.
4. *J.D. Hooker. Indian Letters, 1847-51,* f. 1.

Brian Houghton Hodgson (1800-1894.) '... a great naturalist who is ill & nervous to such a degree that he fancies the Darjeeling doctors want to kill him, & he will have no other medical attendant than myself '. (Hooker to Frances Henslow, 26 May 1848.)

of the country was doomed to failure. Although the Rajah never wished to provoke the British, he feared even more exacerbating relations with China which governed Tibet. Hooker privately blamed Campbell for not challenging Sikkim's prevarications, and insisting on a positive, unambiguous response. Only the personal intervention of the Governor-General persuaded the Rajah to sanction Hooker's tour which had to be postponed until 1849.

During these protracted negotiations Hooker botanised in the neighbourhood. The spur on which Darjeeling stood and neighbouring Sinchal (Senchal) offered the curious botanist various ferns, lichens, mosses, orchids, and arums, the large-leafed *Rhododendron argenteum*, a purple

Pencil sketch by Hooker of the path to the Great Rungeet river.

magnolia, and colonies of fungi in its damp woods. The diameter of the caps of some of the agarics was eight to ten inches; one reached fourteen inches, the largest Hooker had ever seen.

He and Charles Barnes, a local resident, explored a different flora on a trip to the Great Rungeet (Rangit) river some eleven miles to the north. The descent to the lower valley passed through successive vegetational zones: at the top oak, chestnut and magnolia were the dominant genera; below 6,500 feet *Cyathea gigantea* appeared, common throughout Nepal to Malaya, also species of the palms *Calamus* and *Plectocomia* and various plantains; *Gordonia* and *Cedrela* had their own territory at 3,000 feet. Here the oaks and chestnuts were different from those higher up, and bamboos replaced tree-ferns.

They camped at 2,000 feet above the river. Within twenty minutes their Lepchas had constructed a table and two bedsteads out of forked sticks and flat split pieces of bamboo bound together with strips of rattan palm stems; layers of bamboo leaves served as mattresses. The descent next morning down steep banks to the river gorge was almost as difficult as Hooker's attempt to cross a cane bridge, typical of many spanning Sikkim's rivers. A large fig tree served as

A typical suspension bridge spanning a river. (*Royal Geographical Society, London.*)

one of its piers; canes from a species of *Calamus* provided the basic structure of hand rails and looped ribs. Anyone crossing it grasped the hand rails firmly, feet placed precariously on the bamboos which were arranged loosely in the loops of cane. All the time the bridge would sway alarmingly. 'With shoes it is not easy to walk; and even with bare feet it is often difficult, there being frequently but one bamboo, which, if the fastening is loose, tilts up, leaving the pedestrian suspended over the torrent by slender canes'.[5] On this occasion Hooker was thankful to be able to cross on a bamboo raft.

He was now beyond British jurisdiction, aware that any native caught guiding Europeans was likely to be severely punished. Large tropical butterflies hovered above the banks of the river which he and his companion followed towards the east; whip-snakes lazed in the sun. He slept that night on a ridge away from the heat of the sun, trying to ignore black ants which invaded everything, especially their food. Their walk ended where the dark green and very clear waters of the Great Rungeet merged with the sea-green and muddy waters of the Teesta (Tista) river. They returned to Darjeeling by the same route. The trek had not been particularly difficult and he had been rewarded

5. *Himalayan Journals*, 1891, p. 103.

with three rhododendrons, 'one, the most lovely thing you can imagine', he told his father, 'a parasite on gigantic trees, three yards high, with whorls of branches, and 3–6 immense white, deliciously sweet-scented flowers at the apex of each branch' (i.e. *Rhododendron dalhousiae*).[6] Falconer in Calcutta confirmed that three of his magnolias were also new to science. His Lepchas had performed well but the three Bengali collectors loaned by the Calcutta Botanic Garden had been uncooperative; 'one actually objected to carrying the vasculum 6 miles' while the Lepcha porters uncomplainingly bore loads of 80–100 pounds.

Another excursion in May, this time a circuitous thirty miles, brought him to Tonglo (Tanglu), a mountain in the Singaleleh (Singalila) range on the Nepalese border, visible from Darjeeling on a clear day. The arduous journey which took three days to push through dense vegetation, constantly climbing and descending valleys, following vestigial tracks, and in appalling weather, gave Hooker a foretaste of what to expect on his major tour.

Again with Barnes as his companion, he set out with a party of Lepchas, Ghurkas and Bengalis carrying a small tent, blankets, provisions, instruments, and plant drying paper. The Lepchas placed their loads in large conical baskets supported on shoulder straps. Their familiarity with plants impressed Hooker. They could recognise about a dozen kinds of bamboo, distinguishing those that could be eaten and the one whose seeds made a fermented drink. The tallest made water buckets, others were shaped into bows, arrows, quivers, and walking sticks. They made cloth and cordage out of nettles, and cooked the tops of two of them. Edible figs, walnuts and brambles were valued in a country where the produce of orchards was usually poor in quality.

Cultivated crops and groves of peaches were left behind at 4,000 to 5,000 feet, and a little-used track above the monastery of Simonsbong (Selimbong?) ran along ridges and cut through forests of oaks and magnolias on its ascent of Tonglo. The fallen scarlet blossoms of *Agapetes serpens* and the white ones of *Rhododendron dalhousiae* covered the ground. When torrential rain called a halt in mid-afternoon, the porters quickly constructed a shelter of bamboo and leaves of wild plantain, improvised a table and chairs, and laid a carpet of leaves. Hooker saw some spectacular climbing plants, one of which he sketched and later identified as a species of *Wightia*. The rain never ceased. The Lepchas sat around their fire until late, chatting and playing their only musical instrument, a flute made, inevitably, from bamboo. 'Except for the occasional hooting of an owl, the night was profoundly still during several hours after dark – the cicadas at this season not ascending so high on the mountain. A dense mist shrouded everything, and the rain pattered on the leaves of our hut. At midnight a tree-frog broke the silence with his curious metallic clack, and others quickly joined the chorus, keeping up their strange music till morning'.[7]

6. L. Huxley, *Life and Letters ...*, vol. 1, 1918, p. 256.
7. *Himalayan Journals*, 1891, p. 114.

They continued their climb next day up a slippery, muddy path. At 8,000 feet they met the first of the large rhododendrons, *R. arboreum. R. argenteum* ('in the point of foliage the most superb of all the Himalayan species') and *R. barbatum* soon followed – Hooker noted that liverworts and lichens never adhered to their smooth paper bark. Near the summit at 9,000 feet *Magnolia campbellii*, *Skimmia*, *Symplocos*, the white-flowered *Rosa sericea* were common, the purple orchid *Pleione praecox* graced many trees and irises bordered pools. Hooker recorded the absence or scarcity of ten families on this mountain – Umbelliferae, Geranieae, Fumariae, Ranunculaceae among them – but C.B. Clarke who followed in his footsteps a quarter of a century later found

Fitch's rendition of the climber *Wightia*, from a sketch by Hooker. Wood engraving in *Himalayan Journals*. 'Trunk-like root of *Wightia gigantea*, ascending a tree, which its stout rootlets clasp'. (Hooker.)

View of Kangchenjunga from Brian Hodgson's House. Watercolour, probably by Fitch. 'The view from his windows is one quite unparalleled for the scenery it embraces, commanding confessedly the greatest known landscape of snowy mountains in the Himalaya and hence in the world'. (Hooker. *Himalayan Journals*.)

Watercolour of a Lepcha girl and a Buddhist monk by Miss Colvile. '... the girls are often very engaging to look upon, though without one good feature: they are all smiles and good nature; and the children are frank, lively, laughing urchins'. (Hooker. *Himalayan Journals*.)

many of them to be reasonably represented.[8] Hooker was also struck by the rarity of pines not only at Tonglo but also on the outer ranges of Sikkim between 2,500 and 10,000 feet, an observation confirmed by Clarke.

Sikkim, lying in the direct path of the monsoon, lived up to its reputation for being one of the wettest regions in the Himalayas. The tent in which they slept collapsed under the weight of rainwater. 'By propping the slopes with sticks, and laying the wax cloth of my plant papers over our shoulders, we got through the night'.[9] Miserably wet and cold, some of the Lepchas went down with a fever. With little hope of the mist lifting and of enjoying the celebrated view, they left the summit and did not emerge from the clouds until they got down to 6,000 feet where the little monastery at Simonbong gave the entire party shelter for the night.

Buddhism like so much else in Sikkim had been imported from Tibet. The larger and richer monasteries or gompas usually conformed to an architectural style of tapering white-washed walls and projecting roofs of thatched bamboo. The one that offered Hooker refuge was one of the poorest and was constructed entirely of wood. It had only one large room with sliding shutter windows and a shingled roof. Its focal point was a black, red and white chequered altar displaying seven brass cups full of water, a human thigh-bone, sprigs of flowers in some ordinary black bottles, a large conch shell with the sacred lotus carved on it, and a spray of peacock feathers in an elegant Chinese brass jug. A prayer wheel, a low seat, and a table with devotional objects on it faced the altar. Close by were some planks of wood, the austere beds of two young monks. These were surrendered to Hooker and Barnes who slept well after two uncomfortable nights under canvas. They were woken by the two boys whose beds they were occupying, banging gongs with great gusto, and blowing the thigh-bone trumpet and conch shell. When they had subsided, a scarlet-robed abbot entered, performed ritual prayers, punctuated by vigorous ringing of a bell. As he glimpsed Hooker sketching, 'his excitement knew no bounds, he fairly

8. *Journal of Linnean Society. Botany*, vol. 15, 1876, p. 118.
9. *Hooker's Journal of Botany*, vol. 2, 1850, p. 149.

Watercolour drawings of *Boletellus emodensis* by Hooker who collected it at Darjeeling. It has been described as 'one of the most splendid of the Himalayan fungi and the pride of its genus'. Hooker found fungi 'very brittle and difficult to preserve'. The Revd M.J. Berkeley identified and described them for him.

turned round on the settee, and, continuing his prayers and bell-accompaniment, appeared to be exorcising me, or some spirit within me'.

Back at Darjeeling, Hooker dealt with a backlog of mail. He complained to his fiancée about the behaviour of his Bengali collectors on the Tonglo venture – 'utterly useless either at gathering plants or anything else'.[10] He criticised the performance of two he had sent 'beyond the snow for plants'. Their specimens were in such a deplorable condition that they could not be identified. 'Then came two more men with plants, vowing they also are from across the snow, but all [the plants] are the same as I gathered a few days back at Tonglo, and I recognise these dirty fellows as having traversed the mountain while I was there, so that story won't do'. A letter to his father contained a succinct observation on Himalayan botany. 'In travelling N. you come upon genus replacing genus, Natural Order replacing Natural Order. In travelling E. or W. (i.e. N.W. or S.E. along the ridges) you find species replacing species, and this whether of animals or plants. Don't forget to send this to Darwin'.[11]

Darwin had not forgotten Hooker. On its way was another interrogative communication.[12] He had been much impressed by Hooker's long, informative letter of 20 February – 16 March 1848. 'Such a letter would have cost me half a day's work'. He advised him to save these fascinating facts on animals for the Indian journal he hoped he would one day publish. Could Hooker investigate silkworms and domestic bees? He queried the accuracy of Hooker's account of the mating of the wild Bhil (cattle) with domestic breeds to produce sterile offspring – 'surely they must be different species? . . . I have been much struck about what you say of lowland plants ascending mountains, but the alpine not descending . . . what a grand subject alpine floras of the world would be'. He wondered whether Hooker might find time to consider insular floras and to make a comparison of Arctic and Antarctic vegetation.

Five months passed before Hooker replied to Darwin. Confined to Hodgson's bungalow by the rainy season, he employed eighteen native collectors to scour the hills and the terai. Their finds were placed on a circle of chairs in front of the fire. Two rooms were requisitioned to dry paper for pressing them; when the supply ran out he substituted sheets of newspaper. Many of his consignments of living plants destined for Kew died before they reached Calcutta docks. Hooker's life was regulated by the daily routine of regular readings of the barometer and thermometer, examining every new delivery of plants, noting their native names and local uses, and selecting a few to draw. Using a pocket sextant and compass lent by the Deputy Surveyor-General, he calculated the height of neighbouring mountains. 'I worked out in two hours the height of Kinchin [Kangchenjunga] from this place and made it 28,000 ft [it is 28,169 feet]. Sinchul I have worked barometrically with no trouble at all, and made it 8,653 feet. Tonglo, Mr Müller [an amateur scientist convalescing at Darjeeling] and I have just worked out from the observations I took in May, and

10. Hooker to Frances Henslow. 26 May 1848. *Letters from J.D. Hooker*, vol. 6, f. 172.
11. Hooker to his father, 18 May 1848. L. Huxley. *Life and Letters ...* , vol. 1, 1918, p. 258.
12. Darwin to Hooker. 10 May 1848. *Correspondence of Charles Darwin*, vol. 4, 1988, pp. 138-42.

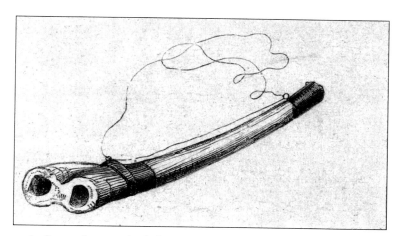

Trumpet made from a human thigh-bone. (Wood engraving in *Himalayan Journals*.) This instrument was often accompanied by 'a double-headed rattle, or small drum, formed of two crowns of human skulls, cemented back to back' and filled with 'some pebbles'.

it is 10,009 feet'.[13] When eventually he did write to Darwin, his excuse for the delay was that 'the very rich flora of this place has kept me busy & Hodgson is so complete a Himalayan naturalist that I have paid little other attention to Zoology, than bottling beetles & applying to my host for information on all other branches'.[14] He now made amends with a recitation of scientific data obtained either from Hodgson or from scientific journals published in India. He diffidently offered his own interpretation of the geology of the region: clay slate in tropical valleys, hornblende schists and gneiss at high altitudes; he suspected that Kangchenjunga was granite. He answered more of Darwin's queries. According to Hodgson, the yak bred freely with the domestic buffalo, producing zobo, a hybrid with desirable attributes. The domestic mountain fowl interbred with the domestic Chittagong fowl. 'Hodgson has repeatedly had the eggs of the wild jungle fowl brought him, & hatched the chick, but they never live – in short we cannot *reoriginate* the domestic breed'. The domesticated silk moth fed on *Ricinus* leaves whereas the wild species chose Sal, *Terminalia* and other sources of food. The progeny of the Junma goat, introduced into the temperate regions of the Himalayas, was either prematurely born or died of congenital goitre.

Hooker's main item of news for Darwin was that he had been given permission to enter Nepal where a military escort would conduct him to the Tibetan passes: '5 or 6 marches take me to the snows of Kinchinjunga where the guard is to meet me at the N.W. corner of Sikkim; but the Sikkim Rajah hesitates allowing me to pass through his territories'. Up to that time he had not seen any vegetation above 10,000 feet. He hoped to make a reconnoitring trip to the Snowy Mountains, lasting about a month. He and Hodgson had planned to make a joint excursion and, if the opportunity arose, to sneak through one of the Tibetan passes to measure the height of the plateau and to record its animal and plant life. All rested on the consent of the Rajah who was still evasive, now making religion an excuse for barring Hooker. 'The Gods and Divinities of my country are numerous and very watchful . . . I have consulted the lamas as to whether it is good and proper that the British gentleman should examine the trees and plants of my country. The result is that it will not be proper'.[15] He

13. Hooker to his father.
1 October 1848. L. Huxley.
Life and Letters ..., vol. 1, 1918,
p. 263.
14. Hooker to Darwin.
13 October 1848.
Correspondence of Charles Darwin,
vol. 4, 1988, pp. 171-78.
15. Rajah of Sikkim to
Campbell. 7 October 1848.
*J.D. Hooker. Indian Letters,
1847-51*, f. 238.

Hand-coloured lithograph of *Rhododendron dalhousiae* by Fitch, based on a sketch by Hooker. (Hooker. *The Rhododendrons of Sikkim-Himalaya*, 1849–51). Hooker collected it in 1848. It first flowered in Britain in a hothouse on the Earl of Rosslyn's estate in 1853.

RHODODENDRON DALHOUSIÆ, Hook. fil.
(*in its native locality*)

Tab. I

Rhododendron arboreum. Hooker found it common in East Nepal and Sikkim at about 5,000 to 6,000 feet, especially 'on dry slopes of mica-slate rocks'. (*Roy Lancaster.*)

would require Tibet's authority before any foreigner could visit Kangchenjunga, a holy mountain. Nevertheless, he would be willing to send Hooker any particular plants he desired. Campbell's brusque reply reminded the Rajah that dire consequences from vengeful deities had been prophesised when the British occupied Darjeeling but nothing had happened. He now issued an ultimatum that should the Rajah fail to co-operate his annual remittance from the Government of India would cease. Permission was reluctantly granted but limited to one visit only, a condition immediately rejected. Hooker gave his father perceptive portraits of the two emissaries who brought the Rajah's reply. His vakeel or official representative was 'stern, grave

Interior of Simonbong temple.

Sepia drawing by Fitch of Hooker's sketch of the interior of the Buddhist monastery at Simonbong. (Wood engraving in *Himalayan Journals*.)

and stolid, thoroughly obstinate and impracticable; thin lips, a good chin, thin arched nose and narrow nostrils, high cheek bones and forehead, cold grey eyes and handsome brows; no beard or moustache, and a nut brown, but not bronzed complexion. His years must be above sixty and his hair was scant and grizzled'. His companion was 'a little old staid withered Thibetan, leaning on his long bamboo bow, simply clothed in a woollen robe, his grey hair floating in the wind, bowed with age, of mild expression, and stone blind'.[16] With no satisfactory conclusion to these prolonged negotiations in sight, Campbell obtained permission for Hooker to visit the Tibetan passes west of Kangchenjunga through Nepal but it was due to Hodgson's friendship with the ruler of Nepal, Jang Bahadur, that this concession was won.[17]

16. Hooker to his father. 20 October 1848. *J.D. Hooker. Indian Letters, 1847-51,* ff. 115-17.
17. W.W. Hunter. *Life of Brian Houghton Hodgson,* 1896, p. 254.

Boodhist monuments.

Sepia interpretation by Fitch of Hooker's sketch of *Pinus roxburghii* in the valley of the Great Rungeet river. Prayer flags wave on Buddhist chortens or shrines. (Wood engraving in *Himalayan Journals*.)

Chapter 8

A Tour in East Nepal

Since the monsoon was late in 1848, it was not until 27 October that Hooker and his party of fifty-five men departed for eastern Nepal, the first European to attempt to reach the Tibetan passes by this particular route. Ill-health denied him the company of Hodgson who lent the services of his bird and animal hunter, a collector and a taxidermist. Hooker had Adok, a Bhutia, as his interpreter, and a half-caste Portuguese as a personal servant. He took three of his best Lepchas to climb trees and to change plant papers. A team of porters carried his equipment, his tent and bedding, and provisions including rice, ghee, salt and flour for the porters. There were also placatory presents of snuff, tobacco, beads, boxes and hand mirrors for villagers whose help he might need.

Hooker recruited more porters than he actually required, anticipating that he might have to discharge a few who proved unsatisfactory. Friends at Darjeeling contributed useful items. Hodgson gave a tent and a stock of tea, sugar, brandy and preserved meat. Hooker accepted mittens, comforters and a veil to shield his eyes from snow glare from Mrs Campbell but resisted her offer of jars of preserve and cases of salmon. Tin boxes came from the Müller brothers who also calibrated his instruments and offered on his return to consolidate his readings of longitude, latitude and elevation. The Assistant Surgeon-General added a chronometer to his scientific equipment (compass, telescope, thermometers, barometers, sextant and artificial horizon). He had an escort of five Nepalese sepoys commanded by a havildar (sergeant) dressed like 'a sea free-booter' in a silk-braided purple jacket over a white cotton garment, pulled in at the waist by a check sash. As well as protecting Hooker, he took charge of his money to buy food *en route* to supplement their stores. His men, who wore scarlet jackets and skull caps perched on their long black hair, were armed with kukris and swords. Assembling this party cost Hooker £100. His principal concern was that the unpredictable behaviour of his porters might threaten the success of the expedition.

His route lay five marches north to Jongri (Zongri), then west over the spurs of Kangchenjunga, and north west to Nepal's passes into Tibet. 'I cannot tell you how comfortable I feel at the prospect of realising the fondest dream I ever harboured as a traveller and botanist', he told his father.[1] Campbell believed that Hooker's 'journey is the most interesting that has ever been undertaken in this part of the Himalaya, and as the passes in this direction have

1. Hooker to his father. 20 October 1848. *J.D. Hooker. Indian Letters, 1847-51*, ff. 15-17.

120

never been penetrated by a European, his attempt is fully as interesting and important as any that has ever been made in any direction, either in the Himalaya or in other unknown lands'.[2] Hodgson confided to Sir William Hooker that his son hoped to slip unobserved into Tibet to establish 'the barometric elevations of that wondrous plateau'.[3]

Hooker's foreboding about his Bhutia porters was realised on the very first day when they failed to turn up at his camp site compelling him to spend the night without food or a bed. They arrived late next day complaining about their excessive loads, and through their tardiness only four miles were covered the following day. He would have dismissed them had it been possible to replace them without delaying their progress. The party crossed the border and descended into the beautiful Myong valley guarded by a Ghurka hill fort. In order to avoid the Myong river's many tributaries they left the valley along a spur of Tonglo, and camped near the summit of Nangki. From that vantage point in the clarity of early morning he could see Kangchenjunga, 'a dazzling mass of snowy peaks, intersected by blue glaciers, which gleamed in the slanting rays of the rising sun'. The undisciplined Bhutia porters who had been raiding his stores found the cold too much for them and deserted, though a few did return, leaving Hooker with no choice but to make a detour to ensure finding villages where he might hire porters on a daily basis. Unfortunately the region was sparsely populated and he had to send all but essential baggage back to Darjeeling. Now less burdened, the party climbed a ridge through a forest populated by the Great Indian Hornbill, easily recognised by its huge yellow bill and broad black and white wings. A common tree at 7,000 feet was the broad evergreen oak (*Quercus semecarpifolia*). A lack of water on the ridge made it imperative to camp at a spring at 8,500 feet. Hooker scrambled to the top of an outcrop of gneiss and looked westwards to the plains of India.

> The firmament appeared of a pale steel blue, and a broad low arch spanned the horizon, bounded by a line of little fleecy clouds (moutons); below this the sky was of a golden yellow, while in successively deeper strata, many belts or ribbons of vapour appeared to press upon the plains, the lowest of which was of a dark leaden hue, the upper more purple, and vanishing into the pale yellow above. Though well defined, there was no abrupt division between the belts, and the lowest mingled imperceptibly with the hazy horizon. Gradually the golden lines grew dim, and the blues and purples gained depth of colour; till the sun set behind the dark-blue peaked mountains in a flood of crimson and purple, sending broad beams of grey shade and purple light up to the zenith, and all around. As evening advanced, a sudden chill succeeded, and mists rapidly formed immediately below me in little isolated clouds, which coalesced and spread out like a heaving and rolling sea, leaving nothing above its surface but the ridges and spurs of the adjacent mountains. These rose like capes, promontories, and islands, of the darkest leaden hue, bristling with pines, and advancing boldly into the snowy white ocean, or starting from its bed in the strongest relief. As darkness came on, and the stars arose, a light fog gathered round me, and I quitted with reluctance one of the most impressive and magic scenes I ever beheld.[4]

2. Campbell to W.J. Hooker. 2 November 1848. *J.D. Hooker. Indian Letters, 1847-51*, ff. 15-17.
3. Hodgson to W.J. Hooker. 8 December 1848. Ibid., f. 119.
4. *Himalayan Journals*, 1891, p. 131.

When he returned to the camp illuminated by fires for cooking and warmth, his 'tent' had been erected – a blanket thrown over a branch of a tree and supported with a frame. His box of clothes had been stowed beneath an improvised bed, his books and papers stacked under a table on which a solitary candle burned, and a white napkin bore a knife and fork. His barometer lay in one corner of the tent, other instruments were at hand, and his thermometers hung under a canopy of plaited bamboo and leaves near the tent. After a supper of stewed meat with rice and tea and biscuits, he wrote up his journal, plotted his maps, and labelled his specimens. As soon as he went to bed at ten, a sepoy guard rested on a blanket in the tent. Before they moved on at ten next morning, the Lepchas changed the plant papers, Hooker explored the immediate vicinity, made his weather checks, and breakfasted. This became a regular routine, an ordered pattern to the day, which he observed as far as possible throughout the tour.

Spectacular views were now commonplace. From a knoll at over 9,000 feet he again surveyed the wide sweep of plains south of Nepal; from the main ridge of Sakkiazung a succession of wooded hills led the eye to the western snows of Nepal and the peaks of Kangchenjunga. An abrupt descent brought them to Pemmi at 2,000 feet, a dreary landscape of boulders, thorny bushes, brambles and nettles relieved by an occasional large tree like a *Toona ciliata* with a girth of thirty feet at five feet above the ground. On 13 November they reached the east bank of the turbulent Tambur (Tamur?) river at its junction with the Khawa river. They followed its course for three days and whenever they crossed it in boats the Bhutias draped bushes with votive scraps of rags and the Lepchas made a token offering of water to the river god.

At the village of Mywa Guola Hooker heard from Campbell that the Rajah had capitulated; he was now free to return through any part of Sikkim. The Lepcha messenger who brought the letter, looking smart in a scarlet jacket over a blue-striped dress, became a co-operative and knowledgeable addition to Hooker's retinue.

After six marches they arrived at Wallanchoon where the Mewa river was crossed by a sturdy suspension bridge with firm planks of Sal rather than insecure bamboo to walk on. A single plank substituted for the next bridge which had been washed away. The Tambur below, raced through a narrow gorge, a torrent of waves and foam. Tropical vegetation clothed its banks below 5,000 feet; above that altitude *Rhododendron arboreum* took over.

As the natural features of the country changed so did its inhabitants. Tibetans with hairless faces and high cheek-bones replaced Limbus and tribal people. Men wore leather-belted blanket robes, women short sleeveless cloaks over long flannel petticoats. Both sexes displayed rings and amulets or reliquaries. What especially caught Hooker's fancy was a bull-headed Tibetan mastiff, 'his glorious bushy tail thrown over his back in a majestic sweep, and a

Syamjung Khola above Thudam. Photographed by Roy Lancaster during his tour in East Nepal in 1971. This steep river valley is typical of the terrain encountered by Hooker. (*Roy Lancaster.*)

thick collar of scarlet wool round his heck and shoulders, setting off his long, silky coat, to the best advantage'.[5] The inhabitants of Lelyp, who had never seen a European before, found Hooker not only strange but singularly amusing; his spectacles sent one woman into fits of laughter.

He had searched vainly for the moss *Lyellia crispa* at Darjeeling. Now at last he was able to write to his father's friend, Charles Lyell, after whom the genus had been named, that he had found it near the Tambur river at about 4,000 feet.[6] As they left the river with its lichens and pendulous mosses behind and entered the temperate zone, Hooker examined his first conifer, the Himalayan hemlock (*Tsuga dumosa*), a pyramidal tree with spreading branches, gracefully drooping. One specimen measured twenty feet in girth. Alpine rhododendrons grew near the village of Wallanchoon at over 10,000 feet.

The village was set in a bleak landscape where few trees had survived felling for building and fuel. The long threads of 'tree moss', the lichen *Usnea* which festooned the remnants of the former forest, were dyed yellow with the leaves of *Symplocos* and worn as a hair ornament. Wooden houses, rising from twenty to forty feet, sprawled in the direction of a red and grey-painted monastery, several storeys high. Yaks, the villagers' most prized possession, grazed in large herds. A dependable pack animal at high altitudes in this inhospitable land, its hair made ropes, it yielded milk and meat, and its dung and bones fuelled their fires. Hooker saw few of the smaller hybrid (zobo or zho) which had interested Darwin. The tent in which Hooker lodged, made of yak's hair and dyed in blue and white stripes, offered little protection against the cold wind. It was in this tent that he formally received the herdsman who presented him with a kid, fowl, eggs, some rice, and spikenard roots, a favourite perfume. Despite this friendly overture he questioned whether Hooker's passport allowed him to visit the border passes. In this he was supported by the havildar who insisted he had received no orders to visit them. Hooker countered the herdsman's assertion that snow had blocked the passes with the observation that a caravan of traders with their yaks had just come through them from Tibet. He demanded a guide, provisions and snow boots for the small party which would join him on his climb to the passes.

On 25 November Hooker led his men out of the village, up through a belt of fir and juniper and into an alpine flora of dwarf trees and rhododendron bushes. None was in flower but he gathered the seed of a good number of species. Much to his surprise, he discovered two British plants, shepherd's purse and the grass *Poa annua*.

Such incidents as these give rise to trains of reflection in the mind of the naturalist traveller; and the farther he may be from home and friends, the more wild and desolate the country he is exploring, the greater the difficulties and dangers under which he encounters these subjects of his earliest studies in science; so much keener is the delight with which he recognises them, and the

5. *Himalayan Journals,* 1891, p. 142.
6. Hooker to C. Lyell. 20 November 1848. *Letters from J.D. Hooker,* vol. 10, f. 278.

more lasting is the impression which they leave. At this moment these common weeds more vividly recall to me that wild scene than does all my journal, and remind me how I went on my way, taxing my memory for all it ever knew of the geographical distribution of the shepherd's purse, and musing on the probability of the plant having found its way hither over all Central Asia, and the ages that may have been occupied in its march.[7]

At 13,000 feet, suffering from altitude sickness, he took shelter from the keen wind in a stone hut soon heated by a fire of juniper wood. The steep climb to the pass was resumed next morning. Just before he reached the perpetual snows a carved head of a demon with protruding eyes and blood-stained cheeks, placed in a rocky cavity, glowered at him. They followed a stream (which had cut a path through deep snow) in order to get to the summit at over 15,000 feet (Tipta-La pass). A prayer flag on a cairn marked the boundary which the havildar refused to cross, fearful he would be reprimanded if he took Hooker into Tibet. Hooker, however, was too exhausted to argue. He wrote to Hodgson that he 'could see nothing of Thibet but had no strength to crawl farther'. He 'never felt more ill' in his life, yet in his *Himalayan Journals* he stated that apart from 'an excrutiating headache' he had felt no ill effects from the climb.[8]

Ill or not, he still managed to gather *Arenaria*, some grasses and composites, and *Saussurea gossypiphora* which formed 'great clubs of the softest white wool, six inches to a foot high, its flowers and leaves seeming uniformly clothed with the warmest fur that nature can devise'.[9] Oncoming darkness during the descent forced them to spend the night under the shelter of enormous boulders at 13,500 feet. When he got back to the village next morning the headman refused food for further expeditions and only when Hooker threatened to report him did he grudgingly sell some inferior rice at an exorbitant price. Hooker resolved this crisis in supplies by retaining only nineteen men, the rest he sent back to Darjeeling with his collections of plants and minerals.

His party had enough food for seven days. The march through the narrow gorge of the Yangma valley was a testing one over a rocky road, up ladders 'and along planks lashed to the faces of precipices' above the rapid river which they crossed several times by plank bridges. As the valley widened so the river subsided into a tranquil flow. An impressive moraine 700 feet above the valley floor stretched for about three quarters of a mile and they descended the slopes of enclosing mountains. Hooker attributed its formation to a time 'when a glacial ocean stood high on the Himalaya, made fiords of the valleys, which the wind and currents would deposit along certain lines'.[10] Before the valley contracted again, they passed a forlorn monastery, a huddle of mortuary shrines (chortens or chaits), devotional paths, and mani walls with mantras carved on their stones. At about 13,500 feet they camped at the village of Yangma where Hooker proposed to stay for as long as his provisions,

7. *Himalayan Journals,* 1891, p. 153.
8. Ibid., p. 157.
9. Ibid., p. 156.
10. Ibid., p. 162.

Coloured lithograph in *Himalayan Journals* based on Hooker/Fitch drawings. The Tambur river and valley, looking north from Chingtam.

originally intended for only three days, lasted; the rest had been left in the valley near the first moraine. The tents the villagers lent them were little more than rags, and the additional food, meagre rations of yak milk and small potatoes. Hooker ate what remained of Hodgson's preserved meats; his companions made do with their customary diet of rice, ghee and chillis. He explored the neighbouring Kanglachen valley which was also blocked by a gigantic moraine. He recorded such features in his notebook and took his bearings with an azimuth compass and pocket sextant.

Wallanchoon village. Sepia drawing by Fitch after a sketch by Hooker. (Wood engraving in *Himalayan Journals*.)

Pen and ink sketch of a yak by Hooker. 'The yak is a very tame, domestic animal, often handsome ... Their ears are generally pierced, and ornamented with a tuft of scarlet worsted; they have large and beautiful eyes, spreading horns, long silky black hair, and grand bushy tails; black is their prevailing colour, but red, dun, parti-coloured and white are common'. (Hooker. *Himalayan Journals*.)

Drawing by Hooker of *Larix griffithiana* (Wood engraving. *Gardeners' Chronicle,* 5 June 1886). Hooker sent seeds of this Himalayan larch from Nepal in 1848. Kew Gardens germinated them and distributed the seedlings widely but few withstood viral infection.

11. *Himalayan Journals*, 1891, p. 186.
12. Douglas Freshfield who followed the same route half a century later stated that there was no pass there. Hooker had probably misidentified a plateau north of Kangla-Nangma.

He discovered a new rhododendron on his ascent to the Kambachen or Nangpo Pass (also known as Hunza or Khunza). Bright green leaves sixteen inches long, undersides brown, were a distinctive characteristic. The ground beneath it (he named it *Rhododendron hodgsonii*) had been showered with thin flakes of its flesh-coloured bark. At 14,000 feet Hooker's numbed fingers clung to rocks on a path alarmingly close to the edge of precipices. Another 1,000 feet got him on a crest of a ridge, snow emphasising the contours of glacial valleys on Nangpo still above him. More valleys had to be traversed before he reached the Sikkimese frontier. In the absolute stillness he could hear every word of his porters some 400 yards away. He left them far behind during a descent in the dark. At about 13,000 feet he camped, sleeping on a layer of rhododendron and juniper twigs beneath a blanket draped across a boulder. Next day he breakfasted on an indigestible pheasant. The East Himalayan larch, *Larix griffithiana*, had been discovered by William Griffith in Bhutan, and Hooker rediscovered it, the only Indian species of the genus, on an old moraine at the bottom of Kambachen valley. He was to meet it again on grassy and bushy slopes but always in association with rocks and good drainage.

It surprised him that anyone could live in this valley, 'by far the wildest, grandest, and most gloomy' he had seen, isolated every winter by deep snows. Yet several families survived here on a few acres of grass, growing barley, celery and radishes. They gave him some of their winter stock of potatoes, no bigger than walnuts, a leg of a musk deer, and the services of a guide to take him through Choonjerma pass. His party skirted ancient moraines as they climbed out of the valley, diverted by snow drifts, ascending above the mist which looked like 'a calm, unruffled ocean'. A spectacular sunset fleshed the snow and tinted the peaks with fleeting colour. 'I have never before or since seen anything which for sublimity, beauty, and marvellous effects, could compare with what I gazed on that evening from Choonjerma pass'.[11] Although it was a moonlit night, he waited anxiously for his porters to appear at his camp in the Yalloong valley. When eventually they arrived, grunting and staggering under their baggage, he was so relieved that he shared his precious bottle of brandy with them.

Some travellers with their flock of salt-laden sheep informed him that the villagers of Yalloong had left for winter quarters at Yankutang two marches distant. Much more disturbing was the news that his chosen route through the Kanglanamo pass had been made impassable by heavy snow.[12] Forced to abandon that way into Sikkim, he decided to go south along the west flank of the Singalelah range, hoping to cross one of its many passes. At about 10,000 feet his path took him among tall *Rhododendron falconeri* with the largest leaves of all the species he had so far seen – some measured nineteen inches. His descent took him through thickets of *Rhododendron arboreum* and *R. barbatum* and past

Pen and ink sketch of Hooker and his dog in a letter to Archibald Campbell, 9 June 1849 (Hooker. *Indian Letters,* 1847–51, f. 173). 'He had grown a most beautiful dog, with glossy black hair, pendant triangular ears, a high forehead and jet black eyes, bold & erect, with such a tail, straight legs & arched back.' (Ibid., f. 198.)

some magnificent specimens of *Quercus lamellosa*. He made his way south, occasionally seeing Kangchenjunga, some twenty miles away, rising above the broad mass of the Singalelah range, all the time seeking a valley that looked a likely exit to Sikkim. Although he was travelling through a populous region with prosperous villages, he had difficulty in buying provisions nor did he receive any of the presents usually given to strangers. He eventually discovered that his havildar, whom he had trusted, had kept all the presents and even some of the food purchased with Hooker's money. 'In the mountains he bought a whole deer (& never paid for it I am assured) & 3 days afterwards offered me a most microscopic portion. This was greedy & unfair, but I found no fault till the total want of food was accompanied by an equal want of respect on the part of the villagers & latterly of himself'.[13]

They now struck east through a valley, taking two days to hack a way through the humid forest up to 10,000 feet. Ticks penetrated his clothing and got into his hair, making sleep at night impossible. He ate the last of his store of meat with some rice and chilli vinegar before crossing the Islumbo pass[14] at 11,000 feet into Sikkim. A few stones indicated the frontier. In the mist he could just make out dwarf bamboo, roses and berberis, all coated in ice. He put some mosses in a box before beginning the descent through snow and sleet to the Kulhait river.

At Lingcham (Linchyum) villagers welcomed him with a salute of muskets and a feast. Next day the headman brought a calf, a goat and chicken, eggs, rice, vegetables, fruit, rancid butter, milk and fermenting millet seeds to brew the local beer. Most appreciated were the supplies that had just arrived from Hodgson in Darjeeling. Self-indulgently, Hooker ate a whole loaf for breakfast. Squatting beneath a shelter of branches and leaves he drank a bamboo jug of beer while presents piled up on the ground in front of him. On the third day of

13. Hooker to Hodgson. 22 December 1848. Zoological Society of London.
14. Freshfield who queried Hooker's name for this pass, called it Tumbok; another person identified it as Chiabhanjan pass.

Ancient moraine (800 ft high) crossing Yangma valley

Coloured lithograph in *Himalayan Journals* based on Hooker/Fitch drawings. Ancient moraine in the Yangma valley at 11,000 feet.

Kanglachem 16 500 ft

Watercolour by Fitch of Hooker's sketch of Kanglachen pass at over 16,000 feet. (Wood engraving in *Himalayan Journals*). 'A gulf of moraines and enormous ridges of debris, lay at our feet, girdled by an amphitheatre of towering, snow-clad peaks, rising to 17,000 and 18,000 feet all around'.

Sea of mist from 16000 ft elev.
from Choonjerma. Pass.

W. Fitch

Watercolour by Fitch of Hooker's impressions of the view from Choonjerma pass. 'I saw a sea of mist floating 3,000 feet beneath me, just below the upper level of the black pines; the magnificent spurs of the snowy range which I had crossed rising out of it in rugged grandeur as promontories and peninsulas'. (Hooker. *Himalayan Journals*.)

this fulsome hospitality he received a letter from Archibald Campbell requesting his presence at Bhomsong where the Rajah was holding court. Hooker left immediately accompanied by the headman and a boy carrying a supply of Murwa beer which was replenished at every village they passed through. Fortunately for Hooker it was a fairly mild drink tasting like rather sour sherry. He paused at Pemiongchi (Pemayangtse) monastery where the lama, 'a most jolly fat monk', added to his accumulation of presents. A well-known mendong or wall several hundred yards long, ten feet high and more than six feet broad lay close to the junction of the Kalhait and Great Rungeet rivers. Shortly after he had crossed the latter river, he bought a black puppy, a cross between a Tibetan mastiff and a Sikkimese hunting dog. His pet, which he called Kinchin, became a constant companion for many months.

The headman from Lingcham introduced him to some of the culinary uses of native plants. Succulent nettles made excellent soups; a sauce was concocted from the stalks of a yellow-flowered *Begonia*; a particular tree-fern was edible, and the large fern, *Botrychium virginianum*, which was, as with the Maoris in New Zealand, served as a vegetable. A servant from the Rajah's Dewan or chief minister, sent Hooker a pony for the last stage of the march. He climbed on to the high-peaked, silver-ornamented saddle with stirrups attached to shortened straps and promptly fell off. He chose to walk until close to Bhomsong when, out of courtesy to the Dewan, he remounted, a man supporting him on either side, and rode into Campbell's camp pitched in an orange grove.

Presents from the Rajah awaited Hooker: a brick of Tibetan tea, yak butter packed in yak-hair cloth, rice, bread, chicken, fruit, salt and the inevitable Murwa beer. The Dewan, a well-built, clean-shaven Tibetan, related to one of

Hooker/Fitch drawing of chaits or chortens and the weeping cypress, *Cupressus corneyana*. (Wood engraving in *Himalayan Journals*.)

the Rajah's wives, welcomed them that evening. His courtesy and politeness initially impressed Hooker who was soon to perceive his deviousness in opposing Campbell's overtures of friendship, and in ignoring his warning of the dangers of violating the recent treaty. He persisted in trying to persuade Campbell who had already waited a week to see the Rajah to return to Darjeeling. One reason followed another: the Rajah was sick, he had gone to Tibet, he was participating in a religious festival.

With Campbell impervious to these excuses, an audience with the Rajah was at last granted. Campbell was sartorially prepared for this reception; Hooker had to make do with a shooting jacket borrowed from his companion, a travelling cap and a plaid. They were led into a bamboo shed hung with faded Chinese silk. A platform, six feet high, stood at one end, covered with purple silk embroidered with white and gold dragons. Beneath a canopy of tattered blue silk over this platform a little man of about seventy squatted. The Rajah, Cho-phoe Namgye, was dressed in yellow silk and wore a pink, broad-brimmed hat with silk side pieces. The Dewan, a striking figure in an embroidered purple silk robe, presented Campbell and Hooker before an assembly of the Rajah's relatives, his counsellors, and a congregation of monks, one of whom rhythmically swung an incense holder of burning juniper. The ruler never acknowledged the emissaries' salutation nor responded to Campbell's request that he should send a responsible representative to Darjeeling. At this impasse presents were brought in and white scarves draped around their necks, a sign that the audience was over. Before they withdrew Campbell informed the Rajah that Hooker would be returning in the spring to explore the east side of Kangchenjunga. This ceremonial display and the reverential regard shown by his subjects did not conceal his poverty nor his dependence on his Dewan. Campbell and Hooker paid a farewell visit to the Dewan in his trophy-hung hut

Pencil sketch by Hooker of one of the three temples in the monastery at Tassiding; 'painted red, and encircled with a row of black heads, with goggle eyes and numerous teeth, on a white ground'. (Hooker. *Himalayan Journals*.)

where he received them in a fawn-coloured silk gown lined with soft wool, and entertained them with some melodies on a Tibetan stringed instrument.

Having a few free days before returning to Darjeeling, Campbell joined Hooker on Christmas Day on a trip to climb Mount Mainom, 11,000 feet high, and to visit some of the principal monasteries. At the start of the ascent Hooker showed his companion the English common duckweed (*Lemna minor*) and pondweed (*Potamogeton natans*) on a small lake. They found *Primula petiolaris*, 'stemless flowers spread like broad purple stars on the deep green foliage', at 8,000 feet, and camped that night in a wood of bamboo, magnolia and rhododendron. When they reached the summit the following day their view was restricted by a density of silver firs. The Himalayas appeared to rise out of a black mass of pine forests, surmounted by the russet-brown of rhododendron shrubs. Hooker reflected on the manner of their creation: the upward thrust of granite from great depths and the convulsions of stratified rocks. The day ended with a sublime sunset. On their descent next day they pitched their tents at 7,000 feet near a partially-built temple at Neongong. The local people were celebrating a festival with offerings for the temple, six monks solemnly prayed, and acolytes blew long copper horns and conch shells or banged cymbals. Out of a number of larger monasteries close at hand they decided to visit Tassiding (Tashiding), said to be among the oldest in the country.

It was perched on a conical hill above the confluence of the Rungeet and Ratong (Rathang) rivers. Most temples planted the weeping cypress, imported from Tibet, in order to burn its fragrant red wood as incense. At Tassiding their branches shaded a group of chortens enclosed within a wall of stones on each of which was carved a Buddhist mantra. Its three temples were oblong in shape, with sloping walls and projecting roofs of split bamboo. The murals in their dark interiors depicted events in the life of the Buddha whose statue dominated the room, and the subdued light softened the garish colours of the wooden beams and pillars. 'The countenances of the images are all calm, and their expression solemn', wrote Hooker. 'Whichever way you turn, the eye is met by some beautiful specimen of colouring or carving, or some object of veneration'.[15]

15. *Himalayan Journals*, 1891, p. 229.

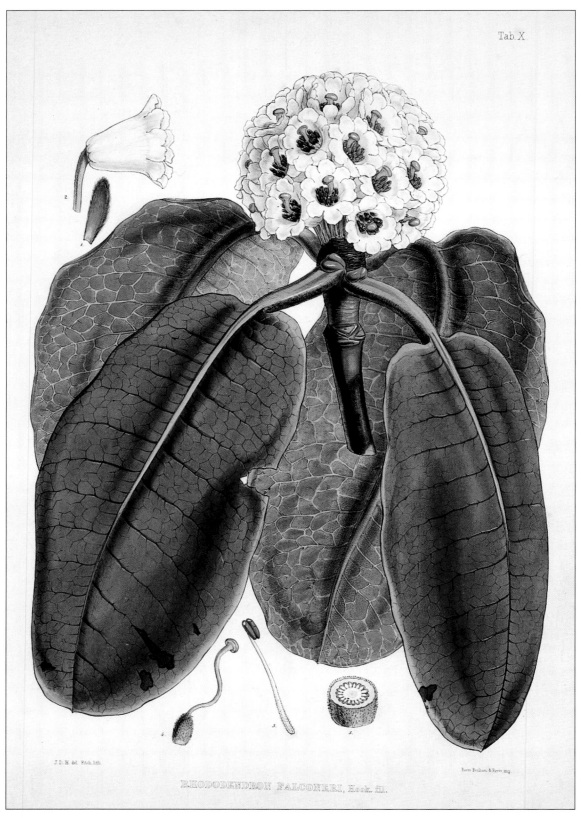

Tab. X

RHODODENDRON FALCONERI, Hook. fil.

Fitch's lithograph of *Rhododendron falconeri*, based on Hooker's sketch (opposite). *Rhododendrons of the Sikkim − Himalaya*, 1849-51. One of the hardiest of the genus introduced by Hooker.

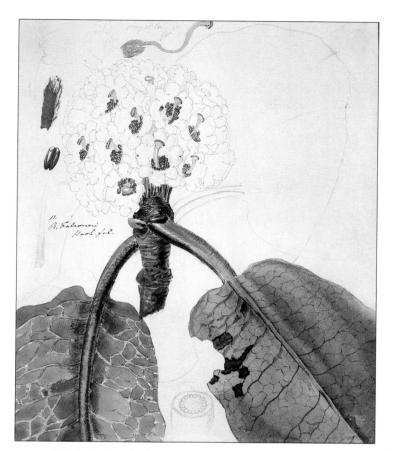

Hooker's sketch of *Rhododendron falconeri.*

(Above right) Watercolour and pencil drawing of *Quercus lamellosa* by one of the Indian artists employed by J.F. Cathcart. Hooker rated it in *Illustrations of Himalayan Plants* as being 'by far the noblest species of oak known, whether for the size of the foliage or acorns, their texture and colour, or the imposing appearance of the tree, which has a tall, straight solid trunk, forty to sixty feet high'.

It was a short walk to Pemiongchi monastery enjoying, according to Hooker, one of the finest views of the Snowy Mountains, 'the eye surveying at one glance the vegetation of the Tropics and the Poles'.[16] Fig trees, plantain and palms choked the depths of valleys; then followed a zonal succession of laurels, magnolias, oaks, chestnuts, birches, and pines with rhododendrons at the top.

The two friends separated on 1 January 1849, Campbell to keep an appointment at the great annual fair at Titalya (Titalia), and Hooker, despite winter conditions, determined to continue exploring. 'It is quite impossible for any one who cannot from experience realise the solitary wandering life I had been leading for months, to appreciate the desolate feeling that follows the parting from one who has heightened every enjoyment, and taken far more than his share of every annoyance and discomfort'.[17] He bought enough rice to last his party of twenty-five men until they got to Jongri about four or five marches to the north. At the picturesque village of Yoksum (Yuksom) he saw two ruined temples with their sentinel weeping cypresses. No moss

16. *Himalayan Journals*, 1891, p. 231.
17. Ibid., p. 233.

Lengths of bamboo were used to ascend steep slopes. (*Royal Geographical Society, London.*)

adhered to their smooth trunks but their branches supported epiphytic orchids and pendulous lichen. At the neighbouring temple at Doobdi (Dubdi) he found a massive cypress about sixteen and a half feet in girth and ninety feet high, perhaps the oldest in Sikkim.

He followed a precipitous path 1,000 feet above the Ratong river, climbing its steep sides by the now familiar notched poles and tree roots, cautiously negotiating unstable landslips, and crossing torrents by vestigial bamboo bridges. In a letter to George Bentham he nonchalantly dismissed these perils. 'One often progresses spread-eagled against a cliff some way and crosses narrow planks over profound abysses with no hold, but as my head never gets giddy, there is no more fear of falling than in the main roads'.[18] They camped on Mon Lepcha, a particularly steep mountain spur. Its summit afforded an extensive view to the south 'from the deep valleys choked with tropical luxuriance to the scanty yak pasturage on the heights above'. To the north Pundim (Pandim) rising to just over 20,000 feet, dominated the middle distance with Kangchenjunga as a backdrop.

He camped at Jongri where four of his men took several hours to make a hole sixteen inches deep in the frozen soil to enable him to record the ground

18. Hooker to Bentham.
1 April 1891. *J.D. Hooker. Indian Letters, 1847-51*, f. 148.

temperature. Among numerous lichens he recognised 'many as natives of the wild mountains of Cape Horn, and the rocks of the stormy Antarctic ocean'. The pervasive smell of a dwarf rhododendron, probably the resinous scent of the leaves of *Rhododendron setosum,* offended the entire party. Snow fell relentlessly: 'large, soft and moist flakes' in the south wind, 'small, hard and dry' in the wind from the north. Its cumulative weight on his tent caused him some anxiety, but having propped it up with a tripod, he slept soundly, his dog at his feet. When his Lepchas complained of snow glare he cut Mrs Campbell's crepe veil into pieces to protect their eyes. On this journey to Jongri he collected ten species of rhododendrons, a couple of them new, and forty-six species of ferns.

On his way to Catsuperri (Kechepari) he gathered another thirty-five ferns and numerous grasses. Sphagnum moss bordered the sacred lake and *Rhododendron barbatum* and *Berberis insignis* lined its banks. Its two insignificant temples failed to tempt him but the restoration of one at Changachelling (Sangacholing) caused him to linger. There among the newly-painted murals he recognised himself. 'I was depicted in a flowered silk coat instead of a tartan shooting jacket, my shoes were turned up at the toes, and I had on spectacles and a tartan cap, and was writing notes in a book. On one side a snake king was politely handing me fruit, and on the other a horrible demon was writhing'.[19] The ridge on which the monastery stood could be seen from Darjeeling only four marches away. At Lingcham he met up again with the still inebriated headman who had accompanied him to Bhomsong. Hooker gave him money to buy a pair of spectacles, not because his sight required them, but because they were a coveted status symbol. He returned to Darjeeling on 19 January. Apart from strenuous marching when they frequently managed only one mile an hour, forcing a way through dense forest or climbing valleys and ridges, the trek had been relatively uneventful. His collections, amounting to eighty loads, were transported by cart and river boat to Calcutta for shipment to Kew.

Hooker had already written about his experiences in eastern Nepal to Charles Lyell who was instructed to let Darwin see the letter. He now wrote to Darwin about the final stages of the journey through Sikkim.[20] Much of this letter described the country's physical geology. Meridianal and lateral spurs intersected Sikkim in rythmical 'ridge and spur' pattern. Two great rivers (the Teesta and Rungeet) were conduits for melting snow from the Snowy Mountains and tropical vegetation followed their sinuous courses. A 'uniform deposit of red clay' covered the country, reaching a depth of thirty feet on plateaux where villages were built. He suspected the flat ground around Yoksum to be glacial deposits. 'I am now more than ever alive to the fact that any *flat* in Sikkim might be an object of suspicion to the geologist'. But dense forest cover up to 12,000 feet frustrated accurate geological investigation. However, he had enjoyed an unimpeded view of Mount Pundim's

19. *Himalayan Journals*, 1891, p. 260.
20. 3 February 1849. *Correspondence of Charles Darwin*, vol. 4, 1988, pp. 194-202.

Hooker graciously receiving a tribute of flowers. Watercolour copy by Fitch of a whimsical composition by William Tayler. Hooker complained to his father of Fitch's errors. 'The stream of water and *fruits of Hodgsonia* which Fitch has brought into the foreground are doubtless improvements, though the latter are anachronisms when coupled with *Rhododendron flowers*, the one being the offspring of May and the other of September.' (Letter of 30 January 1850.) (*Collection of Rachel Lambert Mellon, Oak Spring Garden Library*.)

'stupendous precipice', the lower part of which looked like 'shot or watered silk from the contortion of the gneiss & other strat. rocks, which are twisted & coiled together like snakes; they are red grey & black, & broad veins of plutonic rock are shot through the mass in all directions'.

He followed this letter the same day with another to Darwin about a matter that clearly embarrassed him.[21] His father had been publishing a digest of his son's letters in his *Hooker's Journal of Botany*. The first instalment covering Joseph Hooker's arrival at Calcutta and his excursion in Bengal was described by the *Athenaeum* as being 'about as interesting as a voyage to Gravesend would be'. Although he protested to Darwin that it had never been his wish to publish his correspondence, he, nevertheless, wanted the public to know about his scientific discoveries. He wondered whether Darwin or Lyell would extract from his letters any facts worthy of the attention of the *Athenaeum*.

21. Hooker to Darwin. 3 February 1849. *Correspondence of Charles Darwin*, vol.4, 1988, pp. 203–05.

A more restrained version by Frank Stone. Mezzotinted by W. Walker.

While Darwin appreciated Hooker's concern for his reputation, he advised against this proposal, arguing that an article, specifically written for publication, would be preferable. He consoled his friend by revealing that he kept all his letters, dispersing them among his portfolios, 'but half-an-hour's work will get them all together'.[22]

22. Darwin to Hooker. 9 April 1849. Ibid., pp. 232-34.

In an earlier letter to Darwin,[23] Hooker had mentioned that during December when the risk of malaria was not so great, he and Hodgson hoped to explore the terai. But before the trip he posed for his portrait by William Tayler, the Postmaster-General of Bengal. An amateur painter of some ability, Tayler was using his artistic talents to pay off some debts. He persuaded Hooker to be the subject of a sylvan composition with mountains in the background, attended by his loyal Lepchas and Ghurka escort. Seated on a log, Hooker is seen graciously receiving a spray of *Dendrobium nobile* from his headman. Even his dog got into the picture. This exotic theme was accentuated by Hooker's dress: a native cloak of blue, green, white and red stripes with a scarlet lining. 'Enough is thrown back to show English pantaloons, and my lower extremities cased in Bhotea boots. My shirt collar is romantically loose and open, with a blue neckerchief, which and my projecting shirt wrists, show the Englishman'.[24] As a symbol of rank, a long peacock feather drooped from a rather fetching Tibetan hat. When Fitch made a copy of this large canvas, he unfortunately included both the flower and the fruit of the rhododendron. Another artist, Frank Stone, corrected this error, improved the composition, and modified Hooker's costume in a version which was subsequently engraved.

Hooker escaped from Darjeeling on 27 February to meet Hodgson at Titalya in the Bengal plains. The forest below the town which had so impressed him on his arrival ten months earlier now seemed insignificant after the giant trees of the Himalayas. The cacophony of birds and insects contrasted with the stillness of the mountains. The two men rode east to where the Teesta river flowed into the plain. At Jeelpigoree (Jalpaiguri) they were received by the Dewan, the elderly adviser to the local Rajah, a boy of ten, who invited them to his residence. Unfortunately they arrived during the festival of Holi when everybody, and especially visitors, were energetically bombarded with red powder.

Eight miles to the north lay Rangamelly on the banks of the Teesta, now a broad, quiet river. In later life the two men would no doubt recall with pleasure gliding along its waters in canoes. 'Fresh verdure on the banks, clear pebbles, soft sand, long English river-reaches, forest glades, and deep jungles', occasionally shooting a rapid. They would remember, too, Sillagoree which they next visited, as rich breeding grounds for many birds. Claw scratches on tree trunks and tiger footprints on mud paths and sand banks had cautioned alertness as they botanised. *Bombax* and *Erythrina* were in full flower, racemes of starkly white blossoms hung from *Lagerstraemia reginae*, and the climber *Beaumontia grandiflora* smothered trees indiscriminately with its huge funnel-shaped flowers. Hooker and Hodgson were caught in a violent storm of conically-shaped hailstones. Icy evidence that the same storm had passed over Darjeeling lay in sheltered spots when they returned to the hill station on 24 March.

23. Hooker to Darwin. 13 October 1848. *Correspondence of Charles Darwin*, vol.4, 1988, p. 173.
24. Hooker to Frances Henslow. *J.D. Hooker. Indian Letters, 1847-51*, f. 162.

Chapter 9

EXPLORATION OF SIKKIM

During April 1849 Hooker planned and organised a more ambitious and a much longer excursion into Sikkim. He wanted to trace the Teesta river to its headwaters in the mountain range close to the Tibetan border north east of Kangchenjunga. Campbell wrote three times to the Rajah for authorisation before it was grudgingly granted. Hooker mustered a party of forty-two, mostly dependable Lepchas and some Bhutias. Only two or three had been anywhere near the Snowy Mountains but all readily accepted the challenge. His personal servant was a half-caste Portuguese from Calcutta. A Bhutia interpreter, fluent in Lepcha and Tibetan, had charge of food supplies. Four Hill Ranger sepoys and a havildar provided an escort to 'inspire confidence in my people & that is all I want'. Snow boots and thick blankets would in due course be issued to those in his party chosen to climb with him to the passes.

He had allowed for up to thirty marches to reach the Tibetan border and Campbell undertook to despatch rice and other provisions every fourteen days together with any mail. With this back-up Hooker felt optimistic about the success of his expedition though he knew that the Rajah's permit did not necessarily guarantee co-operation from local governors and headmen.

Before he left Darjeeling on 3 May, he supervised the packing of boxes of items for the Kew museum: native fabrics, string made from fibres, brick tea, a bamboo fishing basket, weapons, musical instruments, two attractive Bhutia cups, a hookah, and a small comb with an elephant pattern. This cargo also included the roots of several species of rhododendrons which he hoped would survive the long voyage to England. He promised his father frequent despatches of rhododendron seedlings and anticipated a good haul of alpines.

A monk tried to detain him at Namtchi (Namchi) until he had received the Rajah's permission for him to proceed. When shown the Rajah's permit, he then made the bad state of the road ahead an excuse for delay. Hooker received instant help from the Tchebu Lama who arrived at his tent with an escort of armed Lepchas. They had previously met at the Rajah's court at Bhomsong and had been attracted to each other by a mutual dislike of the Dewan. Before continuing to Darjeeling as Sikkim's official representative, he arranged for a guide to be allocated to Hooker.

Hooker climbed Mount Tendong at just over 8,600 feet to reach the valley

Plate 1

HODGSONIA HETEROCLITA, Hook.fil.et Thoms.

MALE PLANT.

J.D.H.del., W.Fitch,lith.

Vincent Brooks imp.

Hand-coloured lithograph by Fitch of *Hodgsonia macrocarpa*, based on a sketch by Hooker (Hooker. *Illustrations of Himalayan Plants*, 1855). Hooker named it after B.H. Hodgson 'in whose hospitable residence my examination of this splendid plant was conducted'.

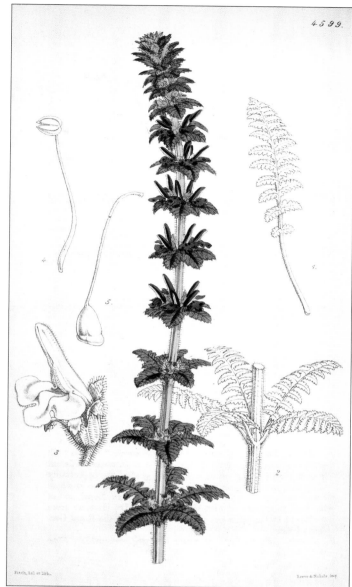

(Above left) Hand-coloured lithograph of *Inula hookeri* drawn by Anne Barnard, Hooker's sister-in-law. (*Curtis's Botanical Magazine*, 1879, plate 6411). Hooker collected its seeds in the valleys in Sikkim's interior at heights of between 7,000 and 10,000 feet. It flowered at Kew Gardens in 1851.

(Above right) Hand-coloured lithograph of *Pedicularis mollis* by Fitch. (*Curtis's Botanical Magazine*, 1851, plate 4599). Kew Gardens raised this plant from seeds collected by Hooker in Sikkim.

of the Teesta where *Houttuynia cordata* covered the river banks and the climbers *Aristolochia saccata* and *Hodgsonia macrocarpa* enveloped trees. The latter which Hooker named after his friend had 'immense yellowish-white pendulous blossoms whose petals have a fringe of buff-coloured curling threads, several inches long'.[1] Lepchas ate its nuts and the leaves of the other climber. The giants among the vegetation were the tropical oaks and *Terminalia* whose leaves Hooker could get at only by shooting down one of its high branches.

1. *Himalayan Journals*, 1891, p. 292.

He usually reserved the personal and more intimate details of his travels for letters to his fiancée, his mother and numerous aunts. He thought his mother would like to know about his clothes. 'I go dressed nearly as I did in Scotland, with the addition of an umbrella to keep off the sun as much as the rain, & I use a linen coat in the hot weather. I always wear long worsted stockings, & my trousers tucked up to the knees, on account of . . . leeches which get all over one's person, & of which I have sometimes taken off a hundred in a day: & they work quite through the clothes.[2]

At Bhomsong his porters wove waterproof covers of bamboo and *Phrynium* leaves to protect their loads. Hooker sheltered from the rain, depressed by the relentless downpour, the threat of malaria, acutely aware of his isolation, the hostility of the chief minister, and his vulnerability. One of the Dewan's supporters, the Lama at Gorh, had instructions to block his progress: a bamboo bridge was dismantled, crossing-stones were removed from streams, and the path was strewn with branches of trees. More seriously, a swinging bridge over the Teesta had been sabotaged with the intention of pitching any unsuspecting traveller into the river. With the timely arrival of Meepo who had been sent by the Rajah to assist Hooker, the party moved on.

Prudence dictated that they should cross the river by another bridge two days' march away. Once over the Teesta, their route took them to Singtam where the governor or soubah whose jurisdiction extended to the Tibetan frontier politely received him but failed in his promise of supplies. He was yet another of the Dewan's allies conspiring to thwart Hooker's plans. In order to save his dwindling stock of food Hooker dismissed his sepoy escort. He moved slowly along an unstable path on the steep slope of the valley, often delayed by landslips and deep channels gouged by broad mountain streams. Large leeches clung to his legs, smaller ones clustered on the instep of his foot. He obtained some relief by wrapping tobacco leaves around his feet within his stockings and liberally dusting his legs with snuff. Sandflies caused intolerable itching. 'We daily arrived at our camping-ground streaming with blood, and mottled with the bites of peepsas, gnats, midges, and mosquitos, besides being infested with ticks'.[3] At night the light in his tent attracted swarms of nocturnal insects.

At Chakoong (Chakung) the vegetation appeared to be in a transitional state. Here were European genera of the temperate Himalayas co-existing with tropical ones: birch, willow, alder and walnut competed with plantain, palm and giant bamboo; figs, balsams, peppers and vigorous climbers consorted with brambles, speedwell, forget-me-not and nettles; the Himalayan moss *Lyellia crispa* had the English *Funaria hygrometrica* as a neighbour.

There was, unfortunately, no time to linger. Hugging the river, the party pressed on to Choongtam (Chunthang), a mountain 10,000 feet high, separating the Lachen and Lachoong (Lachung) rivers. The village where he camped had orders not to sell any food to his party though Hooker himself

2. Hooker to his mother. 24 May 1849. *J.D. Hooker. Indian Letters, 1847-51*, f. 168.
3. *Himalayan Journals*, 1891, p. 300.

Pencil and watercolour drawing by Fitch of *Potentilla cuneata,* subsequently lithographed by him in *Curtis's Botanical Magazine,* 1851, plate 4613. Hooker found this plant growing in woods at 12,000–13,000 feet.

was excluded from this prohibition. He bought chicken, eggs and milk for himself while his men subsisted on half rations, supplemented by whatever edible plants they could find growing wild. He believed that the Rajah, or rather the Dewan, hoped this tactic would starve him into submission. Messages from the court transmitted to him through Meepo urged him to return to Darjeeling but Hooker could be very stubborn. He refused to leave and by giving presents to the monks and village elders and by treating their ailments he hoped to win their sympathy and support. Campbell's provisions when they eventually arrived gave him enough rice for another eight days. The porters from Darjeeling had eaten part of their load when rains which had washed away paths had lengthened their journey. He immediately despatched some of his men to Darjeeling for more rice. There was one small consolation. This enforced delay had allowed Hooker to botanise much more intensively in the neighbourhood. On the heights above the village he found ten species or varieties of rhododendron – 'scarlet, white, lilac, yellow, pink, maroon' – and nine primulas gave him a foretaste of what he hoped to collect at higher altitudes.

He was determined to reach the passes leading to Tibet but in deference to political sensitivities decided to refrain from crossing the frontier. He had a choice of two routes; one to the north west up the Lachen valley to the

Kongra Lama pass, the other to the east up the Lachoong valley to the Donkia (Donkya) pass. He chose the former before the rains made it inaccessible. There he hoped to discover a plateau with different populations of plants and animals. On 25 May he headed for Lamteng on the Lachen river with fifteen men; the rest of his party stayed behind with instructions to forward any food supplies from Darjeeling.

He crossed the narrow, thickly-wooded sides of the Lachen river by cane bridge or rocky promontaries. His unreliable guide pronounced one bridge unsafe clearly expecting Hooker to turn back. To prove him wrong, Hooker took off his shoes and slowly edged across. The 'tremor of the planks was like that felt when standing on the paddle-box of a steamer, and I was jerked up and down as my weight pressed them into the boiling flood, which shrouded me with spray. I looked neither to the right nor to the left, lest the motion of the swift waters should turn my head, but kept my eye on the white jets d'eau springing up between the woodwork, and felt thankful when fairly on the opposite bank'.[4] His loaded porters strolled nonchalantly across. Shortly afterwards the bridge was swept away.

A plateau encircled by mountains sheltered the lilac-painted houses of the small village of Lamteng 1,000 feet above the river. Its flora, a community of plants from Europe, North America and Asia convinced Hooker of the pivotal role of Sikkim in the global distribution of plants.

> This is a subject of very great importance in physical geography; as a country combining the botanical characters of several others, affords material for tracing the direction in which genera and species have migrated, the causes that favour their migration, and the laws that determine the types or forms of one region, which represent those of another.[5]

Friendly villagers secretly gave him food but his supplies were now almost exhausted. Porters sent from Darjeeling with another consignment of rice had been compelled to turn back when landslides made paths impassable.

The headman volunteered to take Hooker to the frontier which Hooker knew was close. He was taken to a wooden bridge across a river and shown two sticks linked by a thread. Refusing to believe that this represented a national boundary, Hooker threw the sticks into the river and defiantly crossed to the other side where he saw a ruined building, probably a frontier post before the Tibetans withdrew to the north. Hooker camped near this spot to indulge in several days' frantic collecting.

Two days' marches brought him to the junction of the Thlonok (Lhonak) river where he camped on a broad terrace at nearly 11,000 feet. On the heights of the north flank of Tukcham (Lama Amden) his floral finds averaged ten a day: blue, pink and violet primulas and new rhododendrons – one with thirty to forty flowers in each cluster of blossoms: 'it is an awful pest, its long

4. *Himalayan Journals*, 1891, p. 310.
5. Ibid., p. 313.

Hooker's sketch of a cane bridge with Tukcham mountain in the background, improved by Fitch. (Wood engraving in *Himalayan Journals*.)

branches covering the ground in inextricable confusion and impervious'. They came back from these daily trips 'tired, with torn clothes and cut feet and hands, returning to a miserable dinner of boiled herbs'.

He and a few of his party tried to ascend the Thlonok river (in actual fact it was the Zemu).[6] They trudged through snow, followed the river up to their waist in icy water, and supported themselves on rocky projections. Meepo tried to hack a passage through the rhododendron scrub which eventually became an impenetrable barrier. It had taken them all day to cover just four miles. Only a man of Hooker's stamina and determination could have withstood the severity of the terrain and the weather. Brian Hodgson told Sir William Hooker that his son was the 'first botanist who has himself ventured to bide the pelting of the rainy season'.[7] Sir Richard Temple who also explored the northern regions of Sikkim some years later vouched for the hardships imposed by the weather. 'The mist and rain are provoking beyond my power of description. You have to march in the wet, to unpack your tent in the wet, to lie down to sleep in the wet, to pack-up in the wet'.[8]

When Hooker returned a day or so later from a successful trip to discover a path above the Thlonok river (which he mistakenly called the Zemu), he found his men frightened by reports that Tibetan soldiers were approaching to take them into slavery as a reprisal for Hooker's crossing of the fictitious border. When that failed to alarm Hooker, a rumour was circulated about the presence of robbers in the neighbourhood. He told his father that 'I kept them together & stuck diligently to my drawing & collecting & having at length pacified them moved on this morning up a steep gulley which I hope leads to

6. According to Freshfield, Hooker confused the two rivers. See also *Bengal Past and Present*, vol. 14, 1917, p. 264.
7. Hodgson to W.J. Hooker. 20 June 1849.
J.D. Hooker. Indian Letters, 1847-51, f. 182.
8. *Proceedings of Royal Geographical Society*, vol. 3, 1881, p. 325.

Tibet and Lake Cholamoo from Donkia pass. Sketch in Hooker's notebook.

Thibet'.[9] He camped above the river where, in a blanket tent with a fire to warm him, he wrote a long letter to Darwin:

> I am above the forest region, amongst grand rocks & such a torrent as you see in Salvator Rosa's paintings, vegetation all a scrub of rhodods. with pines below me as thick & bad to get through as our Fuegian Fagi [beeches] on the hill tops, & except the towering peaks of P.S. [Permanent snows] that here shoot up on all hands there is little difference in the mt scenery – here however the blaze of Rhod. flowers & various coloured jungle proclaims a differently constituted region in a naturalists eye & twenty species here, to one there, always are asking the vexed question, where do we come from?[10]

As the flowering season advanced so it became easier to locate and identify alpines: primroses, cowslips, polyanthus, gentians, saxifrages and poppies. 'The handsomest herbaceous plant' in Sikkim, a large rhubarb (*Rheum nobile*) lodged itself on black rocks. Shaped like a slender pyramid, three feet high, it had yellow bracts edged with pink, flowers overlapping like tiles, and basal leaves tipped with red. Villagers ate the stems and made a sort of tobacco out of its dried leaves.

On his return to the village with his plants, he found his men still being intimidated. On 28 June a gang from outside the village ejected his party from their shed, removing at the same time Hooker's plants, boards and papers. Hooker, his gun at his side, ignored them as they gathered around his tent, 'ragged Bhoteas, with bare heads and legs, in scanty woollen garments sodden with rain, which streamed off their shaggy hair, and furrowed their sooty faces'.[11] He agreed to confer with three representatives provided the rest dispersed. He even promised to leave if it were proved that he had actually crossed the frontier. Some letters he received from Campbell and the Tchebu Lama on 1 July vindicated his refusal to be coerced. Campbell had protested about the treatment of Hooker to the Rajah who assured him that Hooker would be given provisions and conducted to the frontier, whereupon the Tchebu Lama despatched an order to the headman to take Hooker to the pass. Three days later the governor of Singtam turned up, professing friendship and bearing gifts of Tibetan cloth and Chinese silk from the Rajah and dried fruit from the Rani. He directed Hooker to Tallum, a day's march away, the last village in Sikkim he declared.

9. Hooker to his father.
22 June 1849. *J.D. Hooker.
Indian Letters, 1847-51*, f. 184.
10. Hooker to Darwin.
24 June 1849. *Correspondence of
Charles Darwin*, vol. 4, 1988,
p. 242.
11. *Himalayan Journals*, 1891,
p. 331.

Fitch's interpretation of the same view.

Hooker, aware that the elusive pass was at Kongra Lama, refused to be fobbed off with Tallum where he resolved to stay until he received directions from Campbell in about twenty days' time. 'The Singtam Soubah behaved courteously to me; but, to draw me away from my purpose of entering Thibet, he expressed the Rajah's affection for me as boundless; – nothing but extreme solicitude for my safety possessed his breast and actuated his conduct; – and if I were to be lost in a stream – if evil of any kind befell me, – a shrine at Lhassa and annual worship were the least honours that would be decreed to my memory; therefore he implored me to consult my own security and return to Darjeeling'.[12]

The governor knew that his adversary's supplies were very low but Hooker had also learned that the Governor's provisions would run out in six days. So they played a cat and mouse game, chatting amiably every morning, assessing each other's obstinacy with growing respect. Having made a good collection of plants and rocks, the governor really could not understand why Hooker did not return to the comforts of Darjeeling. He capitulated, however, when Hooker treated his severe bout of colic. He, shamefacedly, admitted that he knew the way to Kongra Lama and volunteered to take Hooker there. *En route* they were entertained to a meal by a family of Tibetans who had brought their yaks to summer pastures. Their temporary home was a black yak-hair tent. Rice and wheat flour, curd and roasted maize were served, and wooden cups were constantly refilled with salted and buttered tea. They rode and walked through the mist, the valley below echoing with the sound of avalanches to 'a high blue arc of cloudless sky' framed between the shoulders of the Kongra Lama pass.

In the afternoon of 24 July they stood near a cairn on the boundary between Sikkim and Tibet. In the face of a bitterly cold wind Hooker spent nearly two hours measuring the height which he calculated to be 15,745 feet with his barometer, and 15,694 feet with a boiling water test.

> So here, at last, after three months of obstacles, I stood at the back of the entire Himalaya range, and at its most northern trend in the central Himalaya; for this spot is far north of Kinchin-Junga and Chumalari, or the Nipal passes which I visited last winter. It opens directly upon the Thibetan plateau, without crossing a snowy ridge to be succeeded by another and still other snowed spurs, as is the case at Kanglachem and Wallonchoong.[13]

12. Hooker to his father. 25 July 1849. *Hooker's Journal of Botany*, vol. 1, 1849, p. 338.
13. Hooker to his father. 25 July 1849. Ibid., p. 341.

Pen and pencil sketch of Lamteng village; reproduced as wood engraving in *Himalayan Journals*. The winter quarters of the inhabitants of the valley. The houses 'are painted lilac, with the gables in diamonds of red, black and white; the roofs are either of wood or of the bark of *Abies brunoniana* held down by large stones'. (Hooker. *Himalayan Journals*.)

He noticed that the snowline on the Indian face of the Himalayan range terminated at 15,000 feet whereas on the northern or Tibetan face it climbed to 16,000 feet. Enduring altitude sickness he quickly sketched this aerial view on four sheets of folio paper. He examined and sampled isolated tufts of vegetation – a *Potentila, Ranunculus, Morina, Cyananthus*, a grass and a carex which he added to the score of more interesting specimens he had collected on the way up. The weather cleared as they descended. The views of the mountains 'rising almost perpendicularly, excelled anything I ever beheld. For 6,000 feet they rise sheer up, and loom through the mist overhead, their black wall-like faces patched with ice, and their tabular tops capped with a bed of green snow'.[14] Hooker reflected that he was 'returning laden with materials for extending the knowledge of a science which had formed the pursuit'[15] of his entire life.

The headman at Tungu (Thanggu), now eagerly attentive to Hooker's comforts and interests, invited him to a Tibetan camp at the base of Kinchinjhow (Khangchenyao), the most easterly of the great peaks. The men and women, 'indescribably filthy', and their children half-naked, were accompanied by a Lama who was participating in an annual festival in honour of the mountain. Assisted by a local guide, Hooker reached the source of the Chachoo (Shako Chhu) river in a deep ravine to examine several small glaciers which terminated there. A week was spent at Tungu enjoying local hospitality.

14. *Hooker's Journal of Botany*, vol.1, 1849, p. 342.
15. *Himalayan Journals*, 1891, p. 346.

Hooker/Fitch drawing of Lachoong valley and village. (Wood engraving in *Himalayan Journals*). 'Grassy flats of different levels, sprinkled with brushwood and scattered clumps of pine and maple, occupy the valley, whose west flanks rise in steep, rocky, and scantily wooded grassy slopes'. (Hooker. *Himalayan Journals*.)

Rain had washed away the snow on the lower slopes of the mountain tempting Hooker to climb Chomiono (Chomo Yummo) in order to reach the bottom level of the perpetual snows. It took him two days to return to Lamteng with frequent stops to gather those plants which had not been in flower on the way up. He continued his descent to Choongtam where he rested for ten days drying his plants before despatching them to Darjeeling. He complained to his father about Campbell's circumspect diplomacy in dealing with the Rajah and in believing the excuses of Sikkim's officials. 'I got Campbell's answer ordering me to accept the Soubah's word for what was or was not the pass! ordering me not be so distrustful & suspicious of impediments & deceit! . . . he would have me stoop to any amount of insolence & overbearance, & this I will not'.[16] And now Campbell was reassuring the Rajah that Hooker would return to Darjeeling as soon as he had visited the Lachoong pass, his next objective.

He had to stay at Choongtam for ten days until the Singtam governor, his escort for the trek to the Lachoong (Lachung) pass, recovered from leg ulcers inflicted by leeeches and sandflies. The journey began inauspiciously when his dog Kinchin, now fully grown, fell into the river. The creature had been in the habit of dashing ahead, and several times had to be rescued from swaying bamboo bridges. On this occasion he slipped before help arrived and within seconds was carried away by the torrent below.

The river of the Lachoong valley meandered through grassy plateaux and clusters of maple and pine and the peaks of the Tunkra (Tankar) mountain framed its eastern end. Umbelliferae and Compositae and the terrestrial orchid, *Satyrium nepalense*, were in flower. Hooker identified eight or nine balsams, some eight feet tall. Dock, nettles, shepherd's purse and other English weeds choked poorly tended fields. Here his party camped and, as the governor was still disabled, Hooker seized this opportunity to explore on his own the Tunkra pass whose existence was not known to the British.

A severe headache limited any botanising on the way up but after he had camped at 15,000 feet, Hooker compensated for this lapse with about fifty

16. Hooker to his father.
6 August 1849. *J.D. Hooker. Indian Letters, 1847-51*, f. 194.

151

The lichen *Lecanora miniata* on quartz conglomerate. Herbarium specimen collected by Hooker in Sikkim. (See p.80 for his drawing of the same lichen collected in Antarctica.)

Pencil sketch by Hooker of *Abies webbiana* at Lachen. He found the Himalayan silver fir at elevations between 10,000 and 13,000 feet 'forming dense black forests along the slopes and crests of innumerable ranges'.

new species – alpines such as gentians, saxifrages and primulas. He left the snow, and crossed a glacier to reach the pass, 'a gentle sloping saddle' beyond which lay a verdant valley grazed by yaks, with the Machoo river flowing into Tibet. The few plants growing beyond 16,000 feet were different from those he had noted on the Palung and Kongra passes, the most conspicuous being miniature primroses, a pink-flowered *Arenaria*, the cottony *Saussurea*, and two species of *Corydalis*. He could not find a single grass or sedge. This brief but profitable excursion had taken four days and the pass he had surveyed provided a convenient route to Lhassa for a British mission years later.

After leaving Lachoong his destination was Yeomtong (Yumthang), a summer base for cattle. Hot springs about a mile below the village were used as medicinal baths. The Singtam governor, resentful at having to accompany Hooker, was again uncooperative and villagers in turn were reluctant to sell any produce to Hooker. 'The Sikkim Rajah has done everything in his power, short of violence, to harass or oppose me, & his standing order is that I am not to be treated as a sahib. The insults to which this exposes me & the degree of patience & resolution required I may talk of to my parents who know how short of temper I am in trifles. To my face I am told by a ragged rabble that if I were a gentleman, the S.S. [Singtam Soubah] would give different instructions to his people'.[17] Another former adversary, the Lachen headman,

17. Hooker to his mother. 2 September 1849. *J.D. Hooker, Indian Letters, 1847-51*, f. 204.

Watercolour of *Cassiope selaginoides* by Gerald Atkinson, botanical artist at Kew. Subsequently appeared in *Curtis's Botanical Magazine,* 1924, plate 9003B. Hooker collected it above Zemu Samdong in the Lachen valley in June 1849.

learning that the Tibetan authorities were not perturbed by Hooker's proposed visit to the Donkia pass, offered his services as a guide. With a month's provisions for ten men from Darjeeling, Hooker left on 8 September for Momay Samdong (Yume Samdong), the highest yak grazing grounds in Sikkim. He climbed through successive vegetational zones to bleak and stony terrain at 14,000 feet. At just over 15,300 feet he pitched his tent on minute creeping willow and dwarf rhododendrons.

When he found a reasonably weather-proof hut in an enticing habitat of alpines, grasses and sedges, his decision to lodge there for some time, letting his porters forage for extra supplies in the village below, provoked the governor's irritable departure after the ascent to the pass. Now on his own in a spectacular landscape Hooker could examine plants at leisure. Some shallow lakes at 17,500 feet added aquatic plants to his collections. From the top of the Donkia pass at 18,466 feet Lake Cholamoo (Chho Lhamo) below contributed a sheet of blue, three to four miles long, to a kaleidoscopic display: white snow, black mountains, red quartz hills, and two miles to the west, the wall of Kinchinjhow 'a glacier 4,000 feet nearly perpendicular, to all appearance a great blue curtain, reaching from earth to heaven, except where a small black rock appears, and then icicles 50 feet long in lines like organ-pipes'.[18]

In this 'terrible desolation & sterility' where the wind never dropped he discovered a grass (*Festuca*), a fern (*Woodsia*), and a *Saussurea* near the summit. In the pass itself he gathered a species of *Arenaria* and several lichens including one he had first seen during the *Erebus* and *Terror* voyage.

> I was greatly pleased with finding my most Antarctic plant, *Lecanora miniata* at the top of the pass and today I saw stony hills at 19,000 feet stained wholly orange-red with it, exactly as the rocks of Cockburn Island were in 64° South; is not this most curious and interesting? To find the identical plant forming the only vegetation at the two extreme limits of vegetable life is always interesting; but to find it absolutely in both instances painting a landscape, so as to render its colour conspicuous in each case five miles off, is wonderful.[19]

Seemingly indifferent to the vagaries of the atrocious weather, he made several attempts to climb Kinchinjhow and Donkia[20] where he traced moraines from 19,000 down to 12,000 feet, examined the stratification and foliation of rocks, and compared his theories on glaciation with those in Darwin's *Geological Observations on South America* (1846).

The view from the summit of Sebolah (Sebu La) encompassed the castellated façade of Kinchinjhow, the flank of Donkia, distant Kangchenjunga and the plains of Tibet. As traders passed through Momay Samdong he questioned them about the course of rivers he had distantly seen in their country.

On 28 September the governor of Singtam struggled up from Yeumtong to tell Hooker that he was leaving to look after his sick wife. His presence was no longer required since Campbell and the Tchebu Lama who had left Darjeeling to seek an audience with the Rajah would meet Hooker at Choongtam.

It took Hooker three swift marches to get there and while he was waiting for Campbell he wrote to his father.[21] He assured him that despite the appalling weather and paths he was wasting no time in collecting. 'The tardy advance of the whole flora is most remarkable, and many plants actually ripening their seeds, and uniformly past flower at 15–16,000 feet are still in full flower at 7–10,000. The reason plainly is, the further north you go the more sunshine there is'. He met Campbell on 4 October. The Political Officer hoped to establish better relations with the Rajah but suspected that his Dewan was really responsible for any resentment towards the British. This mission also gave him an opportunity to see more of the country, and so he welcomed Hooker's proposal to visit the

18. Hooker to his father.
13 September 1849. *J.D. Hooker, Indian Letters, 1847-51*, f. 207.
19. Ibid.
20. On some later maps Donkia has been renamed Pauhunrhi.
21. Hooker to his father.
3 October 1849. L. Huxley. *Life and Letters ...*, vol. 1, 1918, pp. 307-09.

154

Kongra Lama pass. The Tchebu Lama raised no objection and the governor of Singtam reluctantly accompanied them to clear roads, repair bridges and organise local co-operation.

They travelled through the Lachen valley along the route Hooker had taken in July. This time he wanted to get round the Donkia pass and Lake Cholamoo to complete his survey of the river Teesta. Accompanied only by the Tchebu Lama they rode to the top of the Kongra Lama pass where a Tibetan border guard detained them. While Campbell and the Lama conferred with the officer in charge, Hooker galloped on up the Lachen valley into Tibet, outstripping the soldiers who tried to stop him, determined not to return until he had followed the river to Lake Cholamoo. He took his bearings from landmarks he had earlier observed from the Donkia pass and rounding a spur of Kangchenjunga saw the lake. 'My pony was knocked up, and I felt very giddy from the exertion and elevation; I had broken his bridle, and so led him on by my plaid for the last few miles to the banks of the lake; and there, with the pleasant sound of the waters rippling at my feet, I yielded for a few moments to those emotions of gratified ambition which, being unalloyed by selfish considerations for the future, became springs of happiness during the remainder of one's life'.[22] He thought nothing could compare with the serenity of this smooth stretch of water, flanked by mountains, waterfowl speckling its surface, deer and antelope quietly drinking from its banks.

On his return he met a search party alarmed by his sudden disappearance, fearful he might be lost and would not survive a night in exceedingly low temperatures. While Hooker had been absent an armed band of Tibetans had appeared but through the intervention of the Tchebu Lama had agreed to escort them to the Donkia pass. Their commanding officer, a short, plump man, heavily pock-marked, greeted them next morning after a night's rest, wearing a white cap with a green glass button indicating his rank. He formally expressed his willingness to conduct them back into Sikkim by the Donkia pass. The agreement was ratified by rum for him and a basin of weak grog for his comrades.

He led them across the valley and up the rocky slopes of Bhomtso (Bam Chho) to its summit at nearly 18,600 feet where only lichens grew. The prospect embraced mountain ranges across Sikkim, Bhutan and Tibet. 'The transparency of the pale-blue atmosphere of these lofty regions can hardly be described, nor the clearness and precision with which most distant objects are projected against the sky'.[23] There were no signs of habitation in this empty landscape; a yellow lichen and a small beetle, probably blown there by the winds, were the only signs of life. Fires made of dried yak dung hardly warmed the party in the intense cold and some of the porters collapsed in the thin air, requiring Hooker's medical skills to revive them. His own powers of endurance during these alpine treks were impressive. He climbed up Donkia

22. *Himalayan Journals*, 1891, pp. 400-1.
23. Ibid., p. 409.

155

Page of Hooker's *Indian Journal* (f. 360v) for 5–7 November 1849. At the bottom he records his imprisonment: 'I [was] seized, guarded & interrogated with intimidation – won't answer. Sent to separate tents'.

again on his own to take other bearings of the mountains in Tibet; rejoined Campbell at Momay Samdong and together descended to Yeumtong. Again he noticed variations in flowering patterns at different altitudes; rhododendron seeds were still immature but those of *Viburnum* and *Lonicera* were fully ripe.

Sepia drawing by Fitch of Rajah's residence at Tumloong. In the foreground is the thatched hut in which Hooker and Campbell were held. Passing it is a procession carrying the Dewan to the Court. This scene appears as a wood engraving in *Himalayan Journals*.

At Lachoong his Lepchas killed an old yak, devoured its flesh and entrails, fried the skin, made soup of the bones, and only discarded its horns and hooves. Hooker always praised their loyalty and his journal gives an instance of this at Lachoong. A thermometer had slipped out of a hole in a bag carried by one of his porters. As it had last been used at the hot springs on the Kinchinjhow glacier, the porter who blamed himself for its loss set off on his own to find it, taking a few handfuls of rice to sustain him. It was evening when he reached the springs at 16,000 feet where he passed a cold night sitting in the hot water to keep warm. After a futile search next day he was on his way back when he spied the thermometer's brass case glistening between two planks on a bridge at Momay!

They returned once again to Choongtam where Hooker harvested the seeds of six rhododendrons before he and Campbell set off with Meepo who had been authorised by the Rajah to take them to the Chola and Yakla passes in eastern Sikkim. They followed the Teesta to Singtam to pick up supplies from Darjeeling: buckwheat loaves, butter, ham and yak bull meat. Hooker, who always had a good appetite, tucked into mince pies and a bottle of pale sherry while dinner was being prepared.

Denied an audience with the Rajah at his court at Tumloong, they pressed on to the Chola pass which they reached on 7 November. At the top they

Watercolour of Tchebu Lama by Lieutenant H.M. Maxwell. Reproduced as wood engraving in *Himalayan Journals*.

157

were politely turned back by a Tibetan guard who insisted that there was no road beyond to Yakla. Near the frontier they were jostled by some Sikkimese soldiers, one of whom pointed his bow at Campbell who defended himself with a stick. Leaving the pass behind them they found the governor of Singtam waiting for them. He greeted Hooker but ignored Campbell. The Tchebu Lama looked distinctly ill at ease. When they received a hostile reception in a traveller's hut, Hooker heard him shout 'Hooker! Hooker! the savages are murdering me'. Without any provocation he had been attacked, brought to the ground, and tightly bound. Hooker, who went to his assistance, was forced back into the hut but no violence was used against him. The Tchebu Lama was arrested or at least put under restraint, and the rest of the party made prisoners.

Campbell was being used as a political hostage to win concessions from the Government of India concerning the nomination of Sikkim's representative at Darjeeling, the settlement of the frontier with Nepal, and the right to detain fugitive slaves. He was tortured by twisting cords round his wrist with a bamboo wrench in an attempt to make him write a dictated letter to his government. Apprehensive about British reaction to their action, the governor asked Hooker what the Governor-General might do. Still he refused to let Hooker see his companion although he assured him that he bore no ill-feeling to Hooker himself. In fact, he was free to go and could even visit Yakla or any other pass, an offer Hooker declined unless Campbell was also freed. Both were taken to Tumloong, Hooker collecting rhododendron seeds on the way and keeping as close as he could to his friend. He refused the offer of a pony while Campbell was forced to walk.

At Tomlong the governor brought Hooker conciliatory presents, reminding him that he was not a prisoner. Hooker pitched his tent near the small thatched hut where Campbell was confined, and they communicated with each other by the simple expedient of placing notes in a teapot which passed unchecked between unsuspecting guards. On 12 November Hooker wrote a reassuring letter to his father which Meepo promised to smuggle to Darjeeling. 'I have made you a fine collection of seeds & am in excellent health & spirits too', he told him. 'The weather is wretched, fog & rain, but this place is low (about 6,000 feet), & the climate delicious at this season'.[24] The next day Hooker joined Campbell in his hut and a few days later the Dewan arrived from Tibet. He entered the court in style, carried in an English chair, ironically an earlier present from Campbell, ceremonially dressed in a blue silk gown lined with lambskin, an enormous straw hat with a red tassel and black velvet butterflies attached to its brim. He feigned sickness to avoid meeting his captives, and despatched a letter to the Governor-General declaring that they would not be released until the Rajah had received an official response to his requests. Campbell heard a disquieting rumour that should British troops invade Sikkim, he would be killed and his body thrown into the Teesta river.

24. Hooker to his father. 12 November 1849. *J.D. Hooker. Indian Letters, 1847-51, f. 228.*

A meeting held on 22 November with the Dewan, clearly the perpetrator of their detention, and the Rajah's council revealed that the Sikkimese had no idea of the likely consequences of their behaviour. But now made aware of them by Campbell, they were anxious to negotiate a settlement and, with this in mind, allowed their captives to write letters. Hooker told his mother that as soon as his prospective trip to Nepal was over he would come straight home and marry Frances. To his father he lamented the imprisonment and dispersal of his party, the loss of much of his collections, and the theft or destruction of his equipment. Brian Hodgson informed Sir William Hooker that his son was no longer in danger; ' . . . the real grievance [of the Rajah] is, that not merely your son, a traveller, but that a representative of Government [Campbell] goes north, exploring the frontier & entering Thibet, against the wish and remonstrance of Sikkim'.[25] This violation of the frontier had now become Sikkim's justification for imprisoning the two men.

Captain Byng who had taken charge of Darjeeling during Campbell's absence, asked for reinforcements to defend the settlement in the event of any attack. The Government of India which disapproved of his placatory correspondence with the Rajah, replaced him with a special commissioner, C.H. Lushington, with instructions to warn the Rajah that unless he released his hostages, British troops would invade his country and 'exact a severe retribution'. The Rajah capitulated, blaming his Dewan who, in turn, accused other members of the court. Presents were showered on Hooker and Campbell when they departed on 9 December under escort for Darjeeling with many unnecessary stops as if to delay their release for as long as possible. They rode into Darjeeling in the evening of 23 December.

The elderly and ineffectual Rajah was punished by the withdrawal of his British pension and the annexation of territory in the south of his country. At least one official in the Government of India thought he had been too severely treated. 'The infringement by Dr Campbell of the Chinese regulations prohibiting the entry of strangers to their territory was an act of grave indiscretion . . . It was more – it was an act certain to embroil the Sikkim Raja with the Chinese. A weak power between great powers must doubly suffer. We seem to have punished the Sikkim Raja far too heavily for his offence'.[26] Major General Sir J.H. Littler considered Campbell's attitude towards the Rajah as 'unnecessarily harsh', displaying an insensitivity to the reasonable suspicions of hill people towards any Europeans surveying their land. Hooker who had always wanted Campbell to adopt a more aggressive posture now felt he had let his friend down. 'If anyone is to blame I am, who at Kongra Lama rode ahead of Campbell, and at Chola went on an hour after him against Meepo's entreaties'. Only the Tchebu Lama came out of the affair with an unblemished reputation. He was awarded an estate of 75,000 acres near Darjeeling in appreciation of the sympathetic support he had given Campbell and Hooker.

25. Hodgson to W.J. Hooker. 1 December 1849. *J.D. Hooker, Indian Letters, 1847-51*, f. 223
26. 30 July 1851. Government of India. Political Department. *Indian and Bengal Despatches.*, f. 1269, E/4/810. British Library: India Office Library and Records.

Watercolour and pencil drawing by Hooker of *Rhaphidophora affinis*, one of the plants he collected at Churra in Assam during September 1850.

Vanda coerulea. Hooker and Thomson collected 360 panicles of this orchid, 'each composed of from six to twenty-one broad pale blue tesselated flowers, three and a half to four inches across; and they formed three piles on the floor of the verandah, each a yard high'. (Hooker. *Himalayan Journals.*) (*P. Cribb.*)

Chapter 10

ASSAM

Hooker passed January and February 1850 mainly writing up his journal and scientific observations, putting the finishing touches to his map of Sikkim, and sorting his collections. He was trying to replace as many as possible of the specimens lost on the last excursion in Sikkim. Some were particularly bulky, palms twelve feet long, for instance, and tree-ferns needing four porters to carry each one; a large *Pandanus* presented similar transportation problems. Everything was wrapped securely in gunny – coarse jute sacking – for shipment to Kew.

Now that his trip to Borneo had been cancelled, he had to consider an alternative bearing in mind his father's wishes that he remained in the Himalayas. He had been invited to join the British punitive force to Sikkim but had no desire to revisit the country. Neighbouring Bhutan was just as unfriendly. 'I would not go there for the world, let the Rajah promise as fairly as he would, without 500 men in front of me and as many in the rear'.[1] With

1. Hooker to his father. 18 March 1850.

161

Thomas Thomson (1817–1878) by George Richmond, the fashionable portrait painter.

the North West Himalayas being explored, it left Nepal of which he had briefly seen the eastern region. On a quick visit to Calcutta in March he had been urged by Lord Dalhousie and Hugh Falconer at the Calcutta Botanic Garden to choose Nepal 'as the finest prospect opened to a scientific man in India or elsewhere'.[2] He hoped Thomas Thomson would be his companion and share the expenses of the expedition.

Thomson had been a fellow student and friend at Glasgow University. Both had graduated in 1839 when Thomson went to India as an assistant surgeon in the East India Company and Hooker joined Captain Ross's expedition to Antarctica. Thomson was captured during the Afghan war and taken to Bokhara to be sold into slavery, when he and some other British prisoners bribed their captors to release them. He served with the Army of the Indus during the Sutlej campaign, and as one of three commissioners appointed in 1847 to determine the precise boundary between Ladakh and Tibet, climbed the Karakoram range of mountains on his own. Whenever possible he collected plants. He took leave due to him in order to botanise with Hooker in Nepal. His friend was delighted. 'To say nothing of private friendship, the being associated in Indian botany with so eminent, enthusiastic & laborious a man, is not a prospect to be willingly relinquished'.[3]

A snag arose, however, regarding Nepal. Jung Bahadur, the Nepalese Prime Minister, then about to lead a delegation to England, insisted that the expedition be deferred until his return. He had sanctioned Hooker's trek in eastern Nepal but would not accept responsibility for Hooker's safety during his absence. Hooker who, on the other hand, could not wait that length of time, chose Sylhet and the Khasia (Khasi) Hills in Assam, fully aware that their

2. Hooker to his father.
7 April 1850. *J.D. Hooker. Indian Letters, 1847-51*, f. 277.
3. Hooker to his father.
2 January 1850. Ibid., f. 242.

The roots of *Ficus elastica* and other species linked together to form a 'living bridge' in Khasia Hills. (Wood engraving in *Himalayan Journals*.)

flora had already been investigated by William Griffith, Francis Jenkins and other competent collectors. Nevertheless, what the plants lacked in novelty might be compensated for in their richness and variety.

The two men left Darjeeling on 1 May on an expedition that was to last nine months. They sailed down to Mahanuddy (Mahanadi) river to the Upper Gangetic Delta in the Bay of Bengal, and Thomson's thorough searching of the river banks located 400 to 500 'weeds' during the first month. The Brahmaputra and Surmat rivers brought them close to the foot of the Khasia Hills where they transferred to elephants. The hills were a mere 4,000 to 6,000 feet, covered with lush tropical vegetation: glossy-leaved evergreen trees, species of palms and bamboos, laurel, nutmeg, and a dense ground cover of balsams, ferns and much else, a flora with pronounced Malayan characteristics. At a temporary base, a rented bungalow, they employed four natives as collectors and another six to stoke fires to dry herbarium specimens and papers. During their trek they had as many as twelve to fourteen collectors at work, who, despite the fact that they were less alert and willing than the Lepchas, could gather about 1,000 species in a week within a five mile radius of the camp. The only hindrance to collecting on this prodigious scale was the rain, much heavier and more prolonged than anything Hooker had experienced in Sikkim. They recorded in excess of 500 inches during the seven months they were there.

The climate and the protean character of the terrain – tropical jungles, deep valleys, dry slopes, rock faces, moor-like uplands – bred a profusion of plants, 'the richest in India, and probably in all Asia'.[4] Within ten miles of their base at Churra they collected about 2,000 flowering plants, 150 ferns and many mosses, lichens and fungi. Screwpines (*Pandanus*) dominated the landscape; balsams presented a variety of shapes, sizes and colour; orchids formed the largest family – epiphytic on trees and terrestrial in woods and on grassy slopes. (Some of the attractive orchids introduced into cultivation by Thomas Lobb, a collector for the Veitch nursery at Exeter, came from the Khasia

4. *Himalayan Journals*, 1891, p. 490.

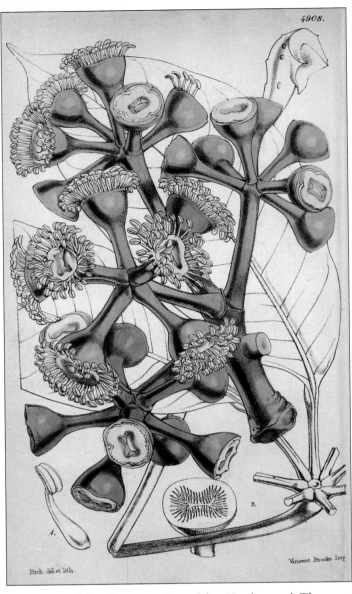

Four of the flowers collected by Hooker and Thomson which were reproduced in *Curtis's Botanical Magazine* as hand-coloured lithographs.

(*Above left*) *Schefflera pueckleri* by Fitch (1856, plate 4908). Collected in the humid tropical forests of the Khasia Hills.

(*Above*) *Agapetes acuminata* by Fitch (1857, plate 5010). W. Griffith and N. Wallich had collected it before Hooker and Thomson who found it at elevations of 3,000–4,000 feet, usually as epiphytes on trees.

Hills.) Hooker watched with some dismay collectors from the Calcutta Botanic Garden recklessly filling hundreds of baskets with these exotic blooms. 'I assure you for miles it sometimes looks as if a gale had strewn the road with rotten branches and Orchideae'.[5] He refused to participate in this indiscrimate plunder, preferring to seek less fashionable genera in families such as Palmae and Scitamineae. Unwilling to risk his health in the malarial swamps of Assam's terai, he engaged six Indians to collect there.

Still with Churra as their headquarters, they explored to the north in the sandstone region of Kala-Panee and on the banks of the largest river in the Khasia Hills, the Boga-panee. At Shillong at nearly 5,000 feet, the entire

5. Hooker to his father. 23 August 1850. L. Huxley. *Life and Letters ...* , vol. 1, 1918, p. 337.

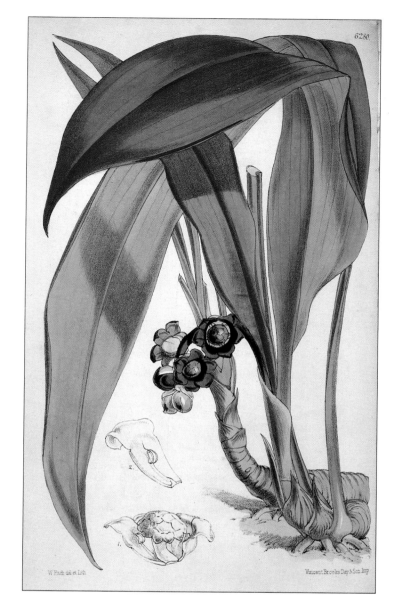

(*Above*) *Hedychium gardnerianum* by Matilda Smith (1887, plate 6913). Wallich rated it 'the queen of the genus, if not of the whole order'.

(*Left*) *Tupistra tupistroides* by Fitch (1877, plate 6280). Collected at elevations of 2,000–4,000 feet.

Assam valley, about seventy miles across, lay before them; contours of receding hills led the eye to the distant Himalayas; the Gangetic Delta sprawled to the south west. Hooker reckoned, perhaps extravagantly, that the visible horizon encompassed an area of about 30,000 square miles. At Myrung they glimpsed the Himalayas again, and they could distinguish Chumalari's (Chomalari) peak. A bungalow at Nunklow, ten miles distant, sheltered them while they botanised in the tropical forest below right down to the river at the bottom of the valley. Balsams populated wet ravines; tree-ferns, ferns, the dwarf phoenix palm and a cycad (*Cycas pectinata*) were common; and *Rhododendron formusum* grew at 2,000 feet. Their last three weeks at Churra were spent packing and despatching their collections: thirty bales of dried plants, seven Wardian cases packed with living plants, separate packages for palms and bamboos, and many bottles of plants preserved in spirits.

The purple orchid, *Pleione praecox*, covered rocks at Nonkreem; *Mesona palustris* whose crushed leaves had a scent similar to that of patchouli oil grew

In the sketch:
Dipterocarpus turbinatus
Gurjon oil tree
Chittagong.
90 feet high

Book XIV

Pen and ink sketch of
Dipterocarpus turbinatus by
Hooker, January 1850.
The pencilled comment
was probably intended for
Fitch who redrew it for
Himalayan Journals.

6. 26 November 1850.
Correspondence of Charles Darwin,
vol. 4, 1988, p. 370.
7. *Himalayan Journals*, 1891,
p. 538.

on the slopes of Mooshye; *Loropetalum chinense* at Nurtiung was a reminder of the proximity of the flora of East Asia. At last even Hooker succumbed to orchidomania when he collected seven men's loads of the blue *Vanda coerulea* for Kew Gardens. Few survived the voyage but another collector had better luck when one load reached England in poor condition but still sold for £300 at Stevens auction rooms in London. Hooker reckoned that a good collector could easily make between £2,000 and £3,000 in a single season through the sale of Khasia orchids.

In a letter to Darwin written from Cachar,[6] Hooker expressed great delight in identifying a familiar peak in distant Tibet from the Khasia Hills, a symbolic farewell. Their trek was now in its final stages. At Sylhet they inspected tree-ferns, some forty feet tall, in shallow valleys. On 9 December they paid off their Khasia collectors and loaded their plants on boats. The Megna river on which they were sailing gradually widened, becoming muddier as it got closer to the delta in the Bay of Bengal. Two days before Christmas they stepped ashore at Chittagong, a busy seaport and important shipbuilding centre. Here they were reminded of the Malayan element in the Indian flora by the ubiquitous Gurjan tree (*Dipterocarpus turbinatus*), 'the most superb tree we met with in the Indian forests'.[7] Straight branchless trunks soared to about 200 feet, terminating in a display of glossy leaves. On the road to Comilla Hooker had another chance to admire the splendid climber, *Hodgsonia macrocarpa*. The boat that bore them to Calcutta steered a careful passage through the swamps of the Sunderbunds to the Hoogly river. They disembarked at the Botanic Garden on 28 January 1851 and ten days later boarded a steamer for England.

Hooker's three years in India had cost £2,200 of which £1,000 were contributed by his father and himself, but the results more than justified this expenditure. He had collected over 3,000 species in Sikkim and Bengal and many more when he botanised with Thomas Thomson in Assam. During his study of the flora from the terai above the Indian plains to the snows of the Himalayas, he had explored three zones of vegetation: a tropical zone ascending to 6,500 feet, followed by the temperate zone to 11,500 feet, and then an alpine zone to the snow-line. He discovered that some herbaceous plants grew at 18,000 feet and that cryptogams survived even higher. Few collectors, if any, had climbed so high in search of plants.

His equipment for his expeditions was confined to essential items: scientific instruments for navigating and surveying; brush, pen, pencil and paper for sketching; a small collection of reference books; and the normal accoutrements of a travelling botanist – vasculum, small tin boxes, glass bottles, boards and straps for pressing specimens, and cutting implements. A small writing desk was an excusable indulgence.

It has to be remembered that for much of his time in India he travelled through unmapped jungles and mountains; add to this monsoon conditions, few roads, and difficulties in getting supplies, and one can sympathise with his lament that 'the fatigues of travelling are not light here, and I am often so tired that I cannot even sleep at night'.[8] Like most collectors he found that it was not always possible to be at a particular site when seeds were ripe for picking. 'It is one thing to explore & find species & another to get them in all seasons of their growth'.[9] He complained to George Bentham that 'I fear my father does not think I do well as to seeds and roots but as I tell him it is one thing to find these things and another to collect them alive'.[10] As he told his father, locating specific plants for their seed could be frustrating. 'I saw the seed of [Rhododendron] Dalhousiae nearly ripe . . . & am trying to get it now but this is difficult for you cannot see the plant on the limbs of the lofty oaks it inhabits except it be in flower & groping at random in these woods is really like digging for daylight'.[11] He responded rather curtly to Sir William's insistent demands for more rhododendrons. 'If your shins were as bruised as mine with tearing through the interminable Rhod. scrub of 10–13 ft you would be as sick of the sight of these glories as I am'.[12] He made sure his father realised the discomfort in harvesting seeds at very high altitudes: 'with cold fingers it is not easy at the ripening season to collect them from the scattered twigs generally out of reach'.[13]

Fortunately Hooker was a very fit young man and, apart from altitude sickness, coped remarkably well with the rigours of botanising in the Himalayas. This he attributed to abstinence (although he liked the occasional glass of wine), a diet of meat and potatoes, and never over-eating.

His problems as a plant collector did not cease with the boxing and parcelling of plants and seeds. Sometimes they were lost or dropped into rivers on the journey to Calcutta; often they died before they reached the port. When absolutely nothing had survived out of one particular assignment of 150 rhododendron shoots, Hooker ordered four Wardian cases to be sent to Darjeeling.

This case had been invented by Nathaniel Ward, a physician in London's East End. Quite by chance he discovered in 1829 that some plants had grown

8. Hooker to Bentham. 28 May 1849. *Letters from J.D. Hooker.*
9. Hooker to his father. 4 December 1849. *J.D. Hooker. Indian Letters, 1847-51*, f. 226.
10. Hooker to Bentham. 28 May 1849. *Letters from J.D. Hooker.*
11. Hooker to his father. 5 June 1849. *J.D. Hooker. Indian Letters, 1847-51*, f. 153.
12. Hooker to his father. 23 June 1849. Ibid., f. 184.
13. Hooker to his father. 27 March 1849. Ibid., f. 146.

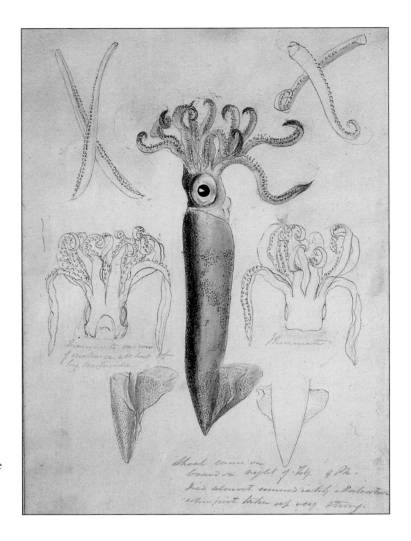

Watercolour of a squid, probably the common South Atlantic species *Loligo gahi*, by Hooker. (*Natural History Museum, London.*)

14. Hooker to his father. 9 November 1840. *J.D. Hooker. Correspondence, 1839-45, from Antarctic Expedition,* f. 47.

in damp soil in a sealed bottle. A combination of sunlight, evaporation and transpiration had filled it with water vapour which, condensing on the glass, had run back into the soil in a continuous cycle. He designed a glass case as an ornamental feature in which plants could be displayed in Victorian drawing-rooms. From this prototype he developed a Wardian case (as it became known) to transport plants over long distances. A trial consignment of plants in such a case survived a four months' journey to Australia in 1833. By the late 1830s a number of nurserymen and botanic gardens, including the one at Calcutta, were using them. They were never an infallible means of transport but they certainly reduced plant fatalities. Unfortunately most sailors detested having them cluttering the decks of their ships, as Hooker explained to his father when he served on H.M.S. *Erebus.* 'Ward's cases are sadly ticklish things to take to sea . . . they are sad annoyance to the First Lieut who is luckily a great friend of mine. One good sea breaking over us demolished the glass . . . out of the 18 plants I brought from Kerguelen's Land only 5 survived that 3 days; the [Kerguelen's Land] cabbage is among them'.[14] Hooker himself usually packed any important shipments for Kew. For instance he bedded some New Zealand plants in a Wardian case in the following manner. 'I filled the bottom of the box with billets of wood, covered them with sandy soil & then put in

Pagothenia phocae. Hooker's drawing of a fish 'taken from stomach of a seal 15 January 1842'. Several of his fish sketches were reproduced in *Zoology of the Voyage of H.M.S.* Erebus *and* Terror *(1844–75)* by J. Richardson and J.E. Gray. These marine drawings demonstrate his artistic competence with non-botanical subjects. (*Natural History Museum, London.*)

the clay soil in which these plants grow; with some vegetable mould watered them until the water ran freely from the plug hole, let it drain, corked it up & put on the covers'.[15]

From time to time his father complained that seeds had not been ripe when collected; on one occasion he objected to their being left in their pods. This petulance irritated his son. 'I did not shell them & perhaps am sorry in not so

15. Hooker to his father. 23 November 1841. *J.D. Hooker. Correspondence, 1839-45, from Antarctic Expedition*, f. 80.

One of the Wardian cases in regular use at Kew Gardens before the last war. They were superseded by plastic bags and air transport during the 1950s.

Hooker sometimes embellished his letters, and even envelopes, with rapid sketches. This one to his father in 1848 depicts the boat which took him along the Ganges, an acorn of *Quercus lamellosa*, and the profiles and vegetation of some of the mountain ranges. (Hooker. *Indian Letters, 1847–51*, f. 101v.)

doing but I thought they took care of themselves throughout winter in the pods & rather took care to keep them in the latter'.[16] Always conscious of the uncertain viability of seeds, Hooker tried different methods of packing them: tins, oilcoth wrapping, paper packets. Sometimes he posted them in letters. But whatever the material, too often they reached their destination damp or rotting or eaten by insects. When they were sown in an apparently healthy condition, Kew's gardeners often failed to germinate them. Out of the very first batch of forty packets of seeds collected by Hooker on his journey from Calcutta to Darjeeling, only a few seedlings were produced at Kew.

In March 1850 Hooker saw an ice-ship from North America deliver a box of frozen live fruit trees and bushes to the Calcutta Botanic Garden. As soon as they thawed out, 'the leaves sprouted and unfolded, and they were packed in Ward's cases for immediate transport to [experimental gardens] in the Himalaya mountains'.[17] This novel method was never a threat to the Wardian case although it was occasionally revived. In 1930 the Himalayan alpine,

16. Hooker to his father. 27 March 1849. *J.D. Hooker. Indian Letters, 1847-51*, f. 146.
17. *Himalayan Journals*, 1891, p. 468.

Primula sonchifolia, was transported through Burma in ice-packed bamboo stems to the cold storage compartment of a homeward-bound steamer.

Sir William Hooker prized his son's drawings almost as much as the plants he collected. He owed his accomplishment as an amateur artist to his father's encouragement and guidance, and to the inspiration he had derived from his grandfather's magnificent collection of pictures. He also claimed that colouring plates in a copy of his father's *Musci Exotici* during the summer of 1837 taught him 'how to lay on colour'.[18]

Captain Ross used his assistant surgeon's talent to record marine life, often micro-organisms, dredged up by the *Erebus*. Hooker also drew a selection of the plants collected on the voyage, adding dissections in the style of Francis Bauer, Kew Gardens' late botanical artist. Some of these floral analyses were 'almost worthy, my husband says, of Bauer's pencil', Lady Hooker told a friend. But her son had reservations about the quality of his drawings. 'There is some danger, however, that inaccuracies may have crept into my work due to the pitching of H.M.S. *Erebus* at sea'.[19] His apparent lack of progress in sketching landscapes also troubled him; 'my talent for sketching is, however, far below par and without colours it would be nothing', he tells his father; 'miserably done' is the verdict of another letter. Ross who got him to sketch coastal features presumably thought otherwise; indeed he reproduced a few of Hooker's drawings in his *Voyage of Discovery and Research*. Whatever his shortcomings, real or imagined, Hooker enjoyed sketching. 'Were it not for drawing', he wrote to his father, 'my sea life would not be half so pleasant to me as it is'. When J.E. Gray of the British Museum supported Hooker's candidature for the chair of botany at Edinburgh, he made a point of praising his Antarctic voyage drawings, and Charles Darwin wanted to know whether the plates in the *Flora Antarctica* were based on Hooker's drawings – 'they strike me as excellent'.

Quickly realising the value of instant sketches, Hooker tied a small notebook and a pencil to his jacket in India. 'It is impossible to begin observing too soon, or to observe too much'.[20] Never intended to be more than an *aide-mémoire*, they served to recall a place, a plant or a feature when he wrote up his journal at the end of a long day's trek. From the numerous species he saw or collected, he selected a few for larger plant portraits, usually an outline with a colour wash of a leaf or inflorescence. Herbarium-size sheets of paper suited most flower drawings but some of the rhododendrons needed larger sheets and a gigantic plant like the Himalayan rhubarb (*Rheum nobile*) was spread over eight sheets. Some of the imperfections in his drawings he attributed to eye

18. Hooker to D. Turner. 14 November 1837. *Letters from J.D. Hooker.*
19. Hooker's *London Journal of Botany*, vol. 2, 1843, p. 264.
20. Hooker to his father. 2 April 1849. *Letters from J.D. Hooker.*

A marginal flourish in his *Indian Journal*, f. 45: a weaver bird and its nest.

One of several sketches Hooker made of *Rheum nobile* showing the colour of its leaf and a cross-section of the stem.

Himalayan Journals, 1891, p. xvii.

strain or to hands made less nimble by minor injuries or intense cold. He persevered on a panoramic sketch on the Tibetan frontier while a 'keen wind blew a gale & we were quite wet'. The grandeur and scale of such vast vistas tested his interpretative skills. 'I have always endeavoured to overcome that tendency to exaggerate heights, and increase the angle of slopes, which is I believe the besetting sin, not of amateurs only, but of our most accomplished artists . . . My drawings will be considered tame compared with most mountain landscapes, though the subjects comprise some of the grandest scenes in nature'.[21]

(Opposite) From such sketches and dried specimens Fitch produced a composite drawing for *Illustrations of Himalayan Plants*, 1855.

The view from above Momay Samdong in Sikkim. A watercolour impression in one of the small notebooks Hooker always carried with him.

Sal trees (*Shorea robusta*) and other vegetation in the neighbourhood of the Great Rungeet river. Pencil drawing by Hooker who clearly drew plants with a greater competence than he did people.

He returned from India with drawings of over 700 plants plus many sketches of views, geological features, buildings and also maps, evidence not only of his industry but also of his conviction that drawings provided a valuable record. When his son was eleven he reminded him that 'you should always be trying to draw whatever comes in your way'

He sketched the profiles of mountains during his surveying of Sikkim. When he went to India he already knew how to use barometers, chronometers, sextants and an artificial horizon. Using a military theodolite he calculated the height of inaccessible mountains 'with perfect ease & rapidity'. Other heights were measured barometrically by comparing the temperatures of boiling water which vary with the pressure of the atmosphere. Naturally he was always anxious about the careful packing and transport of these delicate instruments. One potentially disastrous accident occurred as he was surveying near the Tibetan border at 17,500 feet. A gale blew his barometer set on a tripod down a hill, the only one he had for measuring great heights. 'I really could have cried with vexation. I have carried it two years nearly on my own back & the thermometers [which were also dislodged] were the identical & only ones with which, since leaving England, I have taken several thousand observations. Down hill I went & there was the tripod lying with the barometer on its back between its legs, like a free mason's sign, the thermometers so smashed that my curious Lepchas could not find a scrap of glass'.[22] Incredibly, the barometer was undamaged!

He had few opportunities for using his instruments effectively during his brief excursion in East Nepal. 'The real great difficulty of the country I have lately travelled through [Nepal] is the impossibility of grasping your position, elevation or the direction even in which you are travelling; and it is extremely rarely that you see a known height or object to get a bearing of. This requires the constant use of compass, sextant and a good watch, which are terrible

22. Hooker to his father. 18 September 1849. *J.D. Hooker. Indian Letters, 1847-51,* f. 207.

174

The Encampment of the Officers Ships Company of the French frigate L'Uranie — Berkeley Sd. Falkland Isd. April 30th. 1820.

While Hooker was in the Falklands the Governor lent him a drawing of the encampment of the stranded crew of the French frigate *L'Uranie* in April 1820. This copy by Hooker again shows his difficulty with human figures. (*Family of the late R.A. Hooker.*)

bores to work out though the using is simple enough'.[23] In Nepal and Sikkim he found it difficult, and occasionally impossible, to discover the local names of prominent landmarks.

Gradually he constructed a map of Sikkim. Obviously those parts he never visited remained blank; he also admitted that some routes, rivers and places were approximations and needed verification. 'As a topographical map I hope it will do me credit, it is as full as I could make it with accuracy, and I have the materials for working the elevations of 5 or 600 places over the surface, as also full ones for making it geological, botanical, and meteorological from the plains to 19,000 feet of elevation in one direction, and to 16,000 feet along the northern, N.E. and N.W. frontiers'.[24] The Surveyor General's Office in Calcutta copied it in May 1850 and it formed the basis of a map eventually prepared by the Indian Trigonometrical Survey.[25] Hooker also made a map of the Khasia Hills for inclusion in the General Atlas of India.

As he surveyed, Hooker examined geological formations as well. When, for example, he calculated the height of a prominent precipice on the south face of Pundim, he took notes of its structure.

> . . . black stratified rocks sloping to the west, and probably striking north-west; permeated from top to bottom by veins of white granite, disposed in zigzag lines, which produce a contortion of the gneiss, and give it a marbled appearance . . . The summit of Pundim itself is all of white rock, rounded in shape, and forming a cap to the gneiss, which weathers into precipices.[26]

His eighteen months in the Geological Survey in England had introduced him to another discipline which he put to good use in India. In his *Himalayan Journals* and in letters to Darwin he identified rock types, described geographical features, and commented on glaciers and moraines. Meteorology, entomology, ornithology and zoology came within his purview. This diversity

23. Hooker to Bentham. 1 April 1849. *J.D. Hooker, Indian Letters, 1847-51.*
24. Hooker to his father. 11 July 1850. Ibid.
25. *Map of Sikkim & Eastern Nepal by J.D. Hooker ... exhibiting the Routes of that Traveller copied in the Surveyor General's Office from the Original.* Calcutta, 28 May 1850. X/1288/1. *Independent Sikkim from a Sketch by J.D. Hooker based on the Operations of the Great Trigonometrical Survey 1850.* X/1287. Both maps in British Library.
26. *Himalayan Journals,* 1891, pp. 242-43.

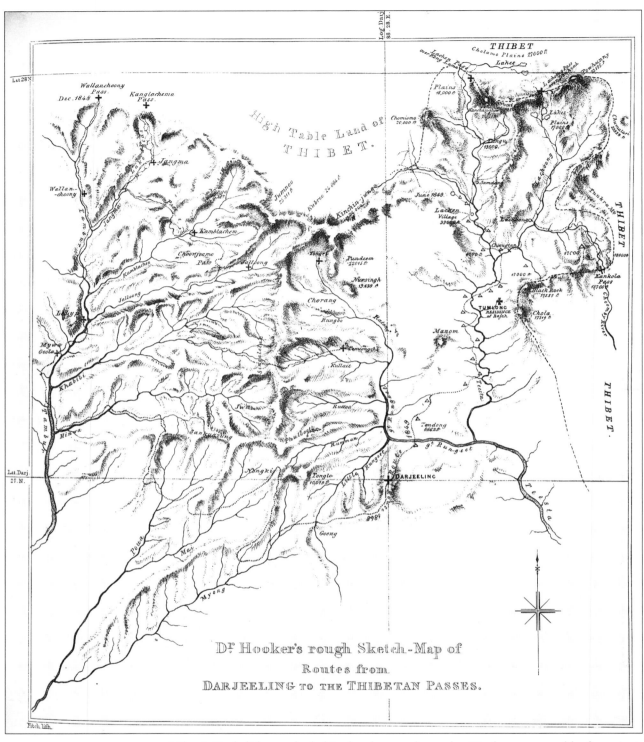

Dr Hooker's rough Sketch-Map of Routes from DARJEELING TO THE THIBETAN PASSES.

(*Above*) Fitch lithographed this sketch map drawn by Hooker, presumably for private distribution.

(*Opposite*) The Surveyor General's Office 1850 map of Sikkim with an acknowledgement to Hooker. (*Oriental Collections, The British Library.*)

27. Humboldt to W.J. Hooker. 11 December 1850. *Hooker's Journal of Botany*, vol. 3, 1851, p. 21. Humboldt urged W.J. Hooker to publish his son's letter (to Humboldt) on the physical geography of Sikkim. This appeared in *Hooker's Journal ...*, pp. 23–31.

of interests impressed the polymath Baron von Humboldt. 'What a notable traveller is Joseph Hooker! What an extent of acquired knowledge does he bring to bear on the observations he makes, and how marked with sagacity and moderation are the views that he puts forward'.[27]

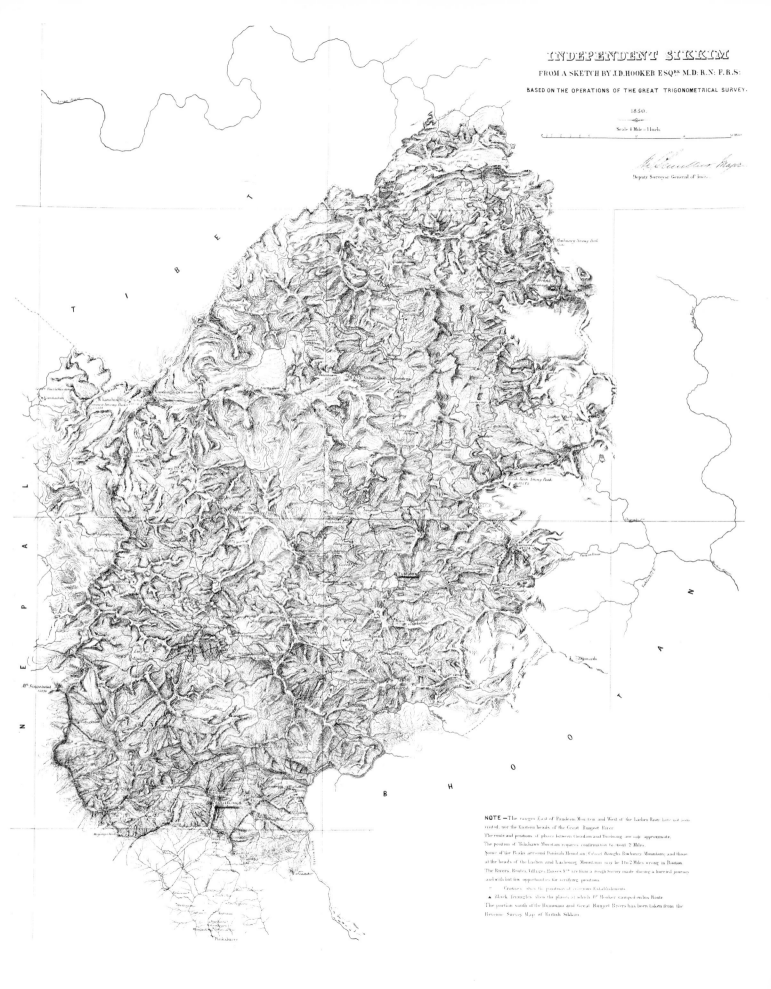

INDEPENDENT SIKKIM

FROM A SKETCH BY J.D.HOOKER ESQ.RE M.D: R.N: F.R.S:

BASED ON THE OPERATIONS OF THE GREAT TRIGONOMETRICAL SURVEY.

1850.

Scale 4 Mile = 1 Inch

Deputy Surveyor General of India.

T I B E T

N E P A L

B H O O T A N

NOTE—The ranges East of Pundecin Mountain and West of the Lachen River have not been visited, nor the Eastern heads of the Great Runjeet River.

The route and positions of places between Tiradam and Tumloong are only approximate.

The position of Tukchawo Mountain requires confirmation to about 2 Miles.

Some of the Peaks around Donkiah Mountain, Colonel daughs Rowhunry Mountain, and those at the heads of the Lachen and Lachoong Mountains may be 1 to 2 Miles wrong in Position.

The Rivers, Routes, Villages, Passes &c are from a rough Survey made during a hurried journey and with but few opportunities for rectifying positions.

— Crosses show the positions of various Establishments.

▲ Black Triangles show the places at which Dr Hooker camped on his Route.

The portion south of the Runnman and Great Runjeet Rivers has been taken from the Revenue Survey Map of British Sikkim.

Chapter 11

PUBLICATIONS BASED ON HIS INDIAN TRAVELS

Hooker's Indian travels are commemorated in print by two slim folio volumes of flower drawings, his journals, and his first attempt to compile a comprehensive flora of the sub-continent. *Rhododendrons of Sikkim-Himalaya* appeared in three parts, the first in 1849 while he was still in India, with ten lithographic plates executed by W.H. Fitch, based upon Hooker's field sketches and dried specimens. The publisher was Lovell Reeve who had undertaken *The Botany of the Antarctic Voyage*. Two more parts in March and December 1851 completed the portrayal of thirty-one species on thirty plates. These flamboyant blooms had an ideal interpreter in Fitch who drew them freely, vigorously and with bold colouring. Sir William Hooker edited his son's descriptive notes and supervised the book's publication. The plates alone guaranteed appreciative reviews. The speed of its production impressed the *Athenaeum*.

> That he should have ascended the Himalaya, discovered a number of new plants and that they should be published in England in an almost unequalled style of magnificent illustration, in less than eighteen months – is one of the marvels of our time. But it is not every botanist who has such a father at home as Sir W. Hooker.

Joseph Hooker, basking in this universal praise, admitted to his father that 'The work makes me feel three inches taller, but I feel I owe it all to you'. He apologised for a few misidentifications due to having seen only single specimens of some species, and to not having any reference books. Those in an alpine habitat could look different from the same species growing in woodland at a lower altitude. Altitude could produce colour variations in flowers of the same species. He corrected some errors of nomenclature in an article in the *Journal of the Horticultural Society of London* [1] but nurserymen and gardeners, undismayed by such flaws, endorsed the optimistic forecast of the *Literary Gazette* 'that all the species but one have a fair chance of being successfully introduced into our gardens and pleasure grounds'. Of all the plants introduced to Britain during the nineteenth century the rhododendrons of the Himalayas, many hardy and easy to hybridise, made the greatest impact on the British landscape.

Only about fifty species of rhododendrons were known when Hooker's book came out. Today well over a thousand species have been identified,

1. *Journal of the Horticultural Society of London*, vol. 7, 1852, 69-131.

ranging from large trees to miniature shrubs growing at high altitudes. Between 400–500 species are now in cultivation, the majority from the Sino-Himalayas. The earliest gardening manual to recommend rhododendrons was John Parkinson's *Paradisi in sole Paradisus Terrestris* (1629). During the eighteenth century they were being imported from North America. The first Asian rhododendron made its appearance early in the nineteenth century.

When Thomas Hardwicke found *Rhododendron arboreum* in the Siwalik Hills in northern India in 1796 he sent a drawing and a description of it to Sir James Edward Smith who featured it in his *Exotic Botany* (1804). Nathaniel Wallich, the enthusiastic Superintendent of the Calcutta Botanic Garden, sent seeds of it to the botanic gardens at Kew and Edinburgh in 1818 and 1819, confident that it would be hardy in Britain, but only Endinburgh succeeded in germinating those particular consignments. Several attempts had been made to hybridise the genus but a cross between *arboreum* and *ponticum* species was the first successful one. By 1835 the Veitch nursery at Exeter had several hybrid Nepalese rhododendrons in their new conservatory. In 1847 Veitch presented Sir William Hooker with 'one of the finest things ever introduced to our gardens' – *Rhododendron javanicum*, collected in Java by Thomas Lobb. When Joseph Hooker sailed to India in November 1847 rhododendrons with horticultural potential were high on his desiderata list.

The cream of his introductions were illustrated and described in *Curtis's Botanical Magazine*, edited by Sir William Hooker. This periodical, founded in 1787, published brief accounts of plants, usually novelties from abroad, likely to interest professional and amateur gardeners. Fourteen of Hooker's finds appeared in its issues between 1852 and 1866. The very first one to flower at Kew had to be included, the dwarf *Rhododendron ciliatum* (plate 4648 (1852)) which Hooker had collected in a valley at about 9,000 to 10,000 feet. The size and fragrance of the epiphytic *R. dalhousiae* (plate 4718 (1853)) which grew effortlessly in a cool, moist glasshouse qualified it for inclusion. *Curtis's Botanical Magazine* rated *R. maddenii* (plate 4805 (1854)) 'the noblest of the Sikkim Rhododendrons' after *R. dalhousiae*. 'The large delicate flowers contrast well with the ample dark-green foliage, which is rusty beneath, and has red petioles'. *R. campylocarpum* (plate 4968 (1857)), collected in East Nepal, had flowers 'of surprising delicacy and grace'. Long, broad leaves, with silvery undersides, distinguished *R. argenteum* (plate 5054 (1858)), now merged in *R. grande*. Hooker described the flowers as 'pink in bud, gradually whitening as they expand, and having at the base of the tube within, a rich dark, blood-purple spot surrounding the stamens'. *R. griffithianum* (plate 5065 (1858)) had been collected by William Griffith in Bhutan, but it was Hooker who introduced it into cultivation. He compared it to a 'fine lily', its individual flowers occasionally measuring as much as seven inches across. The accolade, however, was awarded to *R. fulgens* (plate 5317 (1862)) in this lyrical passage by Joseph Hooker:

> The foliage is perennial, of a bright-green hue, and gives a singular hue to the bleak snowy mountain faces, immediately overhung by the perpetual snow, contrasting in August with the bright scarlet of the Barberry, the golden yellow of the fading birch and the Mountain-Ash, the lurid green of the Juniper, and the brown of the withered grass. Whether, then, for the glorious effulgence of its blooms, which appear to glow like fire in the few sunny hours of the regions it inhabits, or the singular tints its foliage assumes at other seasons, it is one of the most striking plants of the inhospitable regions it inhabits.

R. hodgsonii (plate 5552 (1866)) when it flowered in Kew's Temperate House was admired as much for 'its pale brown papery bark which flakes off in patches as broad as the hand' as for its blossom. One of the most hardy of the genus, *R. falconeri* (plate 7317 (1893)), flowered freely in gardens as far apart as Cornwall, Surrey and Lancashire. Some of them had been grown from seed sent by Colonel W.H. Sykes in 1830.

So thoroughly did Hooker search Sikkim that no rhododendron of any significance has since been found there. A number of his twenty-five new species have become the progenitors of vigorous hybrids. *R. thomsonii* was grafted by Messrs Methven of Edinburgh on to *R. ponticum*. Another nurseryman, Isaac Davies of Ormskirk crossed *R. ciliatum* and *R. dauricum*. Messrs Standish and Noble of Sunningdale saw the Sikkim introductions as 'material for giving new features to succeeding crosses . . . from *fulgens* and *thomsonii* we shall obtain brilliancy of colour, rivalling even *arboreum* itself; while *wightii* will contribute a yellow tint, and *hodgsonii* the beautiful form of its individual flowers, as well as that of its fine compact truss'.[2] *R. griffithianum* was the parent of over 100 hybrids; even the hybrids were crossed to produce a bewildering choice of attractive and reliable plants.

Kew's hardy species were planted in Hollow Walk, a miniature valley created in the mid-eighteenth century by 'Capability' Brown, a transformation that justified its new name of Rhododendron Dell.

Kew distributed seeds to institutions and individuals including any subscriber to the reprint of *Rhododendrons of Sikkim-Himalaya* who requested them: botanic gardens at Belfast, Dublin, Edinburgh and Hull; London and provincial nurseries; botanists and gardeners. Charles Darwin received twelve specimens, two of which flowered a decade later. Owners of large estates begged seeds: Belvoir Castle, Bury Hill, Carclew, Castle Kennedy, Denbies, Doneraile, Heligan, Highclere, Killerton and Stoke Edith. Hooker's seeds also went to applicants in Europe, Australia, New Zealand, U.S.A. and Jamaica. Not all those fortunate recipients succeeded in germinating them. For their

2. *Gardeners' Chronicle*, 1855.

Rhododendron Dell. Hooker's rhododendrons considered to be hardy were planted in this dell and in the grounds of the Queen's Cottage at Kew.

benefit Hooker described their native habits as a guide to the conditions which they should emulate.[3] Epiphytes thrived best in a humid atmosphere; 'rich vegetable mould of loam and peat with good drainage' were essential. He included climatic tables of the three altitudinal zones in which Sikkim's rhododendrons grew.

Hooker's enthusiasm for this genus helped to create a new floral fashion in Britain. Impressed by the splendid illustrations in his book, Thomas Nuttall of Nutgrove near Liverpool sent his nephew, Thomas J. Booth to India to collect them. It was fortunate that he was unable to get into Sikkim since he discovered new species in Assam. *Curtis's Botanical Magazine* hailed his *R. nuttallii* (plate 5146 (1858)) as 'the Prince of Rhododendrons' and in commending his *R. calophyllum* (plate 5002 (1857)) wondered 'if the lofty mountains of the Malaya Archipelago were as well explored, an equally extensive harvest would be reaped'. News of the floristic discoveries of missionaries and other Europeans in China prompted Hooker in 1890 to predict that 'the Chinese empire may contain more species than the rest of the world beside', a prophecy amply confirmed by the plant hunting expeditions in the twentieth century of E.H. Wilson, George Forrest, Reginald Farrer and Frank Kingdon Ward who between them garnered more than 600 new rhododendrons.

3. 'On the Climate and Vegetation of the Temperate and Cold Regions of East Nepal and the Sikkim Himalaya Mountains'. *Journal of the Horticultural Society of London*, vol. 7, 1852, pp. 69-131.

Rhododendrons brought splashes of brilliant colour to woodland gardens in those estates with a suitably acidic soil. They surrounded Lord Armstrong's house at Cragside in Northumberland. James Bateman at Biddulph Grange in Staffordshire created a Himalayan ravine and built a glasshouse for tender species from that region. Rhododendrons too tender for out-of-doors at Kew, flourished in many Cornish gardens. As a grateful tribute, Menabilly called its collection 'Hooker Grove'. Gardens on the west coat of Scotland and in parts of Ireland also boasted fine collections.

John Ferguson Cathcart, formerly a judge in the Bengal Civil Service, intended to use *Rhododendrons of Sikkim-Himalaya* as a model for an illustrated book on lesser-known plants of the Himalayas. Hooker had met him when he was recuperating at Darjeeling and employing Lepchas to collect every plant in flower in the neighbourhood up to 8,000 feet. Two Indian artists, later increased to five, drew the specimens under their employer's supervision.

Indian artists, some of whom had been trained in the fastidious technique of miniature painting and to use flowers as stylised patterns, had to abandon traditional methods when they worked for foreigners. With the disintegration of the Mughal empire in the eighteenth century, they sought the patronage of Europeans who expected them to paint in a naturalistic manner, to renounce opaque gouache for transparent watercolours, to modify their palette with more subdued colours, and to draw in ink and pencil. Botanists demanded that they adopted the discipline of scientific accuracy and eschewed the decorative appeal of line and colour. Some artists found it difficult to convey the fragility of petals and the texture of leaves. After the appointment of William Roxburgh as Superintendent in 1793, the Calcutta Botanic Garden employed Indian artists to record its stock of interesting plants. Cathcart asked Hooker to teach his artists perspective and floral dissections, and in return Hooker had access to all the drawings. Following Cathcart's death in Switzerland in July 1851, his sister presented about a thousand drawings to Kew Gardens.

Joseph Hooker selected a few of them for inclusion in *Illustrations of Himalayan Plants*, published by Lovell Reeve in 1855. He chose those that combined 'scientific interest with reasonable beauty in form or colour, or some other qualification that would render them eminently worthy of cultivation in England'. Fitch who lithographed the plates corrected 'the stiffness and want of botanical knowledge displayed by the native artists' (Introduction). In his inimitable style he transformed the aura of static repose in the originals into fresh and dynamic plant portraits. Hooker added floral analyses and included a few of his own drawings which Fitch made presentable for publication.

The title-page is a bravura composition, a wreath of rhododendrons, orchids, alpines, bamboo, palm and magnolia, a typical virtuoso performance

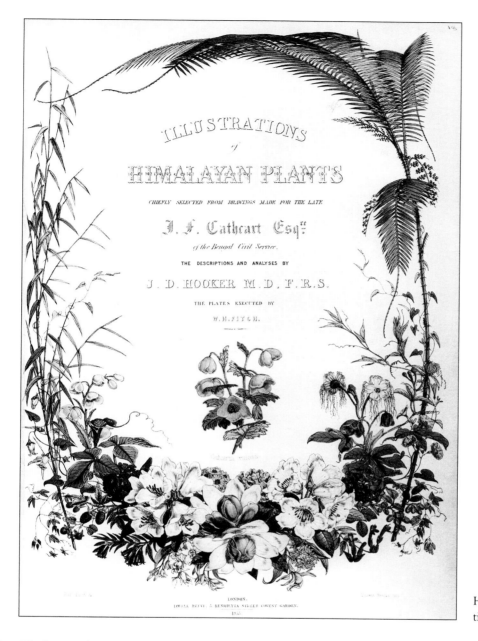

ILLUSTRATIONS
of
HIMALAYAN PLANTS
CHIEFLY SELECTED FROM DRAWINGS MADE FOR THE LATE
J. F. Cathcart Esqre
of the Bengal Civil Service.
THE DESCRIPTIONS AND ANALYSES BY
J. D. HOOKER M.D. F.R.S.
THE PLATES EXECUTED BY
W. H. FITCH.

LONDON.
LOVELL REEVE, 5 HENRIETTA STREET COVENT GARDEN.
1855.

Hand-coloured lithographed title-page by Fitch.

by Fitch. *Hodgsonia macrocarpa* with long spiralling fringes to its petals is a wonderfully theatrical introduction to the following twenty-three plates. Another impressive drawing, *Magnolia campbellii*, commemorates the Political Officer at Darjeeling. Hooker also found *Magnolia globosa* but British gardeners never saw it until George Forrest collected it in 1919. As Cathcart's collectors never reached the alpine zone, Hooker used his own drawing of *Meconopsis simplicifolia*, 'the most beautiful and conspicuous of all the alpine flowers of Sikkim, if not the whole Himalaya'. Hooker collected another species, *Meconopsis napaulensis* and again his sketch was polished by Fitch. Hooker could not resist including *Rheum nobile*, 'the most striking of all the many fine alpine plants of Sikkim'. The rather drab *Begonia gemmipara* was chosen because it was 'one of the most curious and anomalous that I met in Mr Cathcart's drawings'.

Hooker assessed the suitability of his selection for cultivation in Britain either in the open or under glass. He judged *Magnolia*, *Meconopsis*, *Decaisnea insignis* and *Buddleja colvilei* to be hardy; *Hodgsonia*, *Talauma hodgsoni*, *Duabanga grandiflora* and *Codonopsis inflata* would need a heated glasshouse.

Sikkim was as much renowned for primulas as for rhododendrons, most of them growing at high altitudes. *Primula sikkimensis* with a range from Nepal to western China was one of Hooker's most popular introductions. He collected it above 11,000 feet at Lachen and Lachoong where it carpeted acres of ground with its yellow cowslip-like flowers. He also found *P. scapigera* and *P. uniflora* but neither was introduced into cultivation until much later.

Nathaniel Wallich found *Meconopsis simplicifolia* and *M. napaulensis* but Hooker brought them to the attention of gardeners. For H.J. Elwes who visited Sikkim years later, *M. napaulensis* was 'the most beautiful herbaceous plant in the world'.

> Imagine a large rosette of leaves clothed with long golden hairs, which, when covered with raindrops, glisten in the sunshine, running up into a branching spike of golden green buds covered with similar hairs, and opening from the top downwards into large poppy-like flowers, normally of a bright pale purple, whose centre is filled with a mass of golden anthers.[4]

Hooker also collected *M. paniculata*. Another, *M. villosa*, had been originally classified by Hooker as *Cathcartia villosa* in honour of J.F. Cathcart.

Hooker was expected to collect orchids for Kew which received its first consignment in October 1848, and others followed at intervals. In 1850 Kew got twenty-one baskets of them but many were dead on arrival. The same fate awaited *Arachnis cathcartii* and none of the seed of *Galeola lindleyana* germinated at Kew. Both these orchids were figured in *Illustrations of Indian Plants*.

Quercus lamellosa, considered by Hooker to be the noblest of India's oaks, was awarded a place in the book. Again the seeds he sent home failed to germinate. His luck changed with *Larix griffithiana*. When readers first saw this Himalayan larch in his book, Kew had already produced young saplings three to four feet high. Kew distributed hundreds of young plants but since it easily succumbs to frost or larch aphids, it is now rarely found in Britain. Hooker had hoped that *Exbucklandia populnea* and *Acer campbellii* would adorn English gardens but they turned out to be too tender. The Himalayan birch, *Betula utilis*, which he collected in 1849, was less hardy than the Chinese form collected by E.H. Wilson and George Forrest.

This random sampling of the plants Hooker collected and described could easily be expanded. Several are illustrated in *Curtis's Botanical Magazine*: three of his *Berberis* species, for instance − *B. concinna*, *virescens* and *wallichiana* − *Buddleja colvilei*, *Cassiope selaginoides*, *Lonicera tomentella*, etc. A serendipitous search of Hooker's multi-volume *Flora of British India* gives some idea of the riches he delivered to botanists and gardeners.

4. H.J. Elwes. *Memoirs of Travel, Sport and Natural History*, 1930, p. 113.

The publication of *Rhododendrons of Sikkim-Himalaya* and *Illustrations of Himalayan Plants* had not been anticipated by Joseph Hooker, the former having been conceived by his father, and the latter prompted by the presentation of Cathcart's drawings. Nor did Hooker originally propose publishing a journal of his Indian tour. 'As to writing a book of travels . . . I have no thought of it'.[5] Those of his friends who had read the letters he wrote on the Antarctic voyage thought differently. Darwin believed that 'if he will but write as well from India, what a capital book he will make'.[6] Sir William Hooker had published generous extracts from his Antarctic correspondence but his son had declined an invitation from the publisher, John Murray, to expand it into a narrative to complement Darwin's *Journal of Researches* (1839). He confined himself to botanical notes in Ross's *A Voyage of Discovery and Research* (1847) and a long piece on cattle hunting in the Falklands which Ross inexplicably chose to treat as an anonymous contribution.[7] Darwin had enjoyed it tremendously. 'I at first thought it must have been you, but then why was it not given under your name. Whoever the officer was, to my taste he is a first-rate describer – you & he together would indeed have made a first rate book'.[8] In conveying the excitement of the chase, and his revulsion at the slaughter of the wild cattle which he, nevertheless, described graphically, Hooker displayed considerable narrative skills. It is, therefore, not surprising that he yielded to the persuasion of friends. Much of his Indian travels had already been reported in the *Journal of the Asiatic Society of Bengal* and Hooker's *London Journal of Botany*, and his young wife lightened his task by sorting his diaries and notes.[9]

5. Hooker to Wallich. 12 June 1850. L. Huxley, *Life and Letters ...* , vol. 1, 1918, p. 339.
6. Darwin to Henslow. 26 September 1849. *Correspondence of Charles Darwin*, vol. 4, 1988, p. 257.
7. *A Voyage of Discovery and Research*, vol. 2, 1847, pp. 245-53.
8. Darwin to Hooker. 6 October 1848. *Correspondence of Charles Darwin*, vol. 4, 1988, pp. 168-71.
9. Lady Thiselton-Dyer (née Harriet Hooker) to Sir Arthur Hill. 2 September 1835. File 4/T/1.

Hooker's sketch of hunting wild cattle in the Falklands. (Wood engraving in J.C. Ross. *A Voyage of Discovery and Research*, 1847, vol. 2.

RHODODENDRON BARBATUM, Wall.

Rhododendron barbatum
(*Above*) Hand–coloured lithograph by Fitch.   (*The Rhododendrons of Sikkim-Himalaya*, 1849–51.)
(*Opposite*) Watercolour and pencil sketch by Hooker.

He had written most of it by September 1853 when he discussed a tentative title for it with Darwin who dismissed his choice of 'Journal of a Naturalist in the East' as being somewhat imprecise, recommending the inclusion of the word 'Himalayas' in the title. *Himalayan Journals* was published in two volumes in January 1854, and dedicated to Darwin as a mark of gratitude for the pleasure and inspiration his friend's journal of the *Beagle* voyage had given him: ' . . . you do not know how from my earliest childhood I nourished & cherished the desire to make a creditable journey to a new country & with such a respectable account of its natural features as should give me a niche amongst the scientific explorers of the globe I inhabit, & hand my name down as a useful contributor of original matter'.[10] That ambition now realised, Hooker was content 'to go on jog-trot at botany till the end of my days'.

Darwin was touched by this dedication and impressed by the work itself – 'a first-class book', he called it. It had ninety-two illustrations, mostly by the author, twelve of them coloured lithographs, all reworked by Fitch, with maps based on Hooker's surveying – 'the best I have ever seen', said Darwin. As a scientist he welcomed Hooker's observations and speculations; as a general reader he enjoyed his impressions of the people of northern India and their

10. Hooker to Darwin.
26 February 1854.
Correspondence of Charles Darwin,
vol. 5, 1989, pp. 177-78.

(*Above left*) *Rhododendron edgworthii*. Watercolour and pencil sketch by Hooker.
(*Opposite*) Hand-coloured lithograph by Fitch of *Rhododendron edgworthii*.
(*The Rhododendrons of Sikkim-Himalaya*, 1849–51.)

(*Above right*) Watercolour of *Rhododendron griffithianum* by Fitch prior to lithographing it
in *Curtis's Botanical Magazine*. Hooker found it in great abundance in wooded valleys
and on mountain spurs at 12,000–14,000 feet.

11. Darwin to Hooker.
10 March 1854. *Correspondence of
Charles Darwin*, vol.5, 1989,
p. 182.

culture. Hooker's resilience in these uninviting regions astonished him.
Inevitably the book precipitated a flow of observations and questions from
Darwin. Did the moraines suggest a remote glacial period? How did the
tropical vegetation of Brazil and the lower Himalayas compare? His evidence
on the geographical distribution of plants was 'curious'. If Hooker had
ignored vegetation entirely, Darwin declared that the book would still have
been 'a very remarkable undertaking for its geology, meteorology, zoology &
geography'.[11] Certainly any geologist would find much to interest him, and a
zoologist would be entertained by anecdotes on animal behaviour and such
titbits of information as the flesh of the musk-deer being sweet and tender, far

Tab. XXI

J.D.H. del. Fitch, lith.

Reeve & Nichols, imp.

RHODODENDRON EDGEWORTHI, Hook. fil.

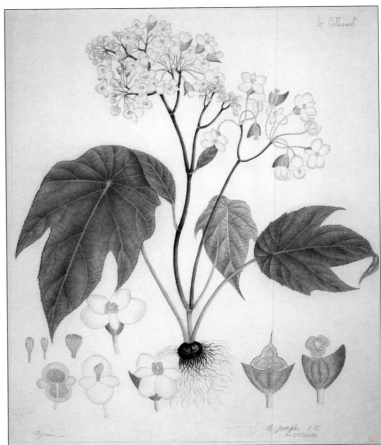

Flower drawings by Cathcart's team of Indian artists.
(*Above left*) *Rubus wardii*. (*Above right*) *Begonia josephii*. (*Opposite left*) *Toricellia tiliifolia*.
(*Opposite right*) *Cucumis sativus*.

Sketch of a Lepcha porter sheltering beneath his plaited bamboo hood. In a letter from Hooker to his father, 30 August 1848.

12. *Himalayan Journals*, 1891, p. 306.

better than Indian venison. Since he collected insects, Hooker frequently commented on them:

> An enormous hornet (*Vespa magnifica* Sm.), nearly two inches long, was here brought to me alive in a cleft-stick, lolling out its great thorn-like sting, from which drops of a milky poison distilled; its sting is said to produce fatal fevers in men and cattle, which may very well be the case, judging from that of a smaller kind, which left great pain in my hand for two days, while a feeling of numbness remained in the arm for several weeks. It is called Vok by the Lepchas, a common name for any bee; its larvae are said to be greedily eaten, as are those of various allied insects.[12]

His style, it has to be said, is sometimes turgid and his narrative impeded by a density of facts. Even Darwin thought the first two chapters rather dull and recommended condensing them in any future edition. Yet there are memorable phrases that encapsulate an image or a moment: Lepcha porters running in the rain 'look like snails with their shells on their backs'; butterflies poised with erect wings on the sand reminded him of 'a crowded fleet of yachts on a calm day'. He responded both emotionally and aesthetically to the grandeur of nature and picturesque scenery. Spectacular sunsets recalled Turner's watercolours. Occasionally he invoked the name of the Italian

Watercolour of *Magnolia campbellii* by one of Cathcart's Indian artists. 'The purple-flowered kind again (*M. campbellii*) hardly occurs below 8,000 feet, and forms an immense, but very ugly, black-barked, sparingly branched tree, leafless in winter and also during the flowering season, when it puts forth from the ends of its branches great rose-purple, cup-shaped flowers, whose fleshy petals strew the ground'. (Hooker. *Himalayan Journals*.)

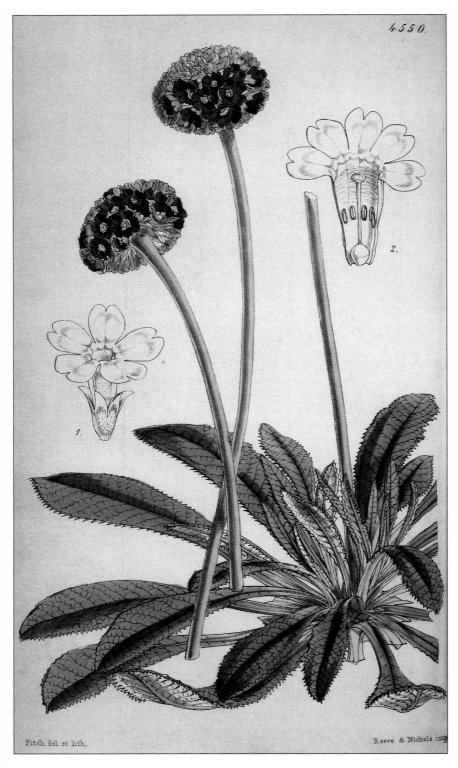

4550.

1.

2.

Fitch del et lith.

Reeve & Nichols imp

(Above) Primula scapigera by Stella Ross-Craig. (*Curtis's Botanical Magazine,* 1950, N.S., plate 120). Hooker found this primula in 1848 but it remained unnamed for over 30 years.

(Left) Hand-coloured lithograph of *Primula capitata* by Fitch. (*Curtis's Botanical Magazine,* 1850, plate 4550). Hooker gathered its seed at Lachen at 10,000 feet. It flowered in Kew Gardens' rockery.

(Opposite) Watercolour of *Primula Sikkimensis microdanta* by Lilian Snelling. (Subsequently figured in *Curtis's Botanical Magazine,* 1930, plate 9210). Hooker discovered it in Sikkim in 1849; it was later found in Nepal, Bhutan and China.

romantic painter Salvator Rosa. 'The scenery is as grand as any pictured by Salvator Rosa; a river roaring in sheets of foam, sombre woods, crags of gneiss and tier upon tier of lofty mountains flanked and crested with groves of black firs, terminating in snow-sprinked rocky peaks'.

2 X

193

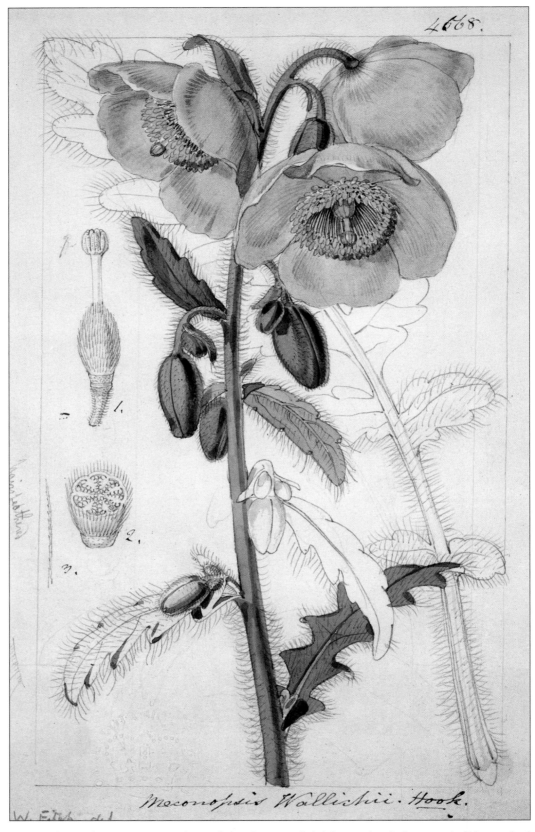

4668.

Meconopsis Wallichii. Hook.

W. Fitch del

Watercolour of *Meconopsis napaulensis* (formerly *M. wallichii*) by Fitch. (Subsequently lithographed in *Curtis's Botanical Magazine*, 1852, plate 4668). Wallich's collectors found it in Nepal and Hooker in Sikkim at elevations of 9,000–10,000 feet. It flowered at Kew Gardens in 1852.

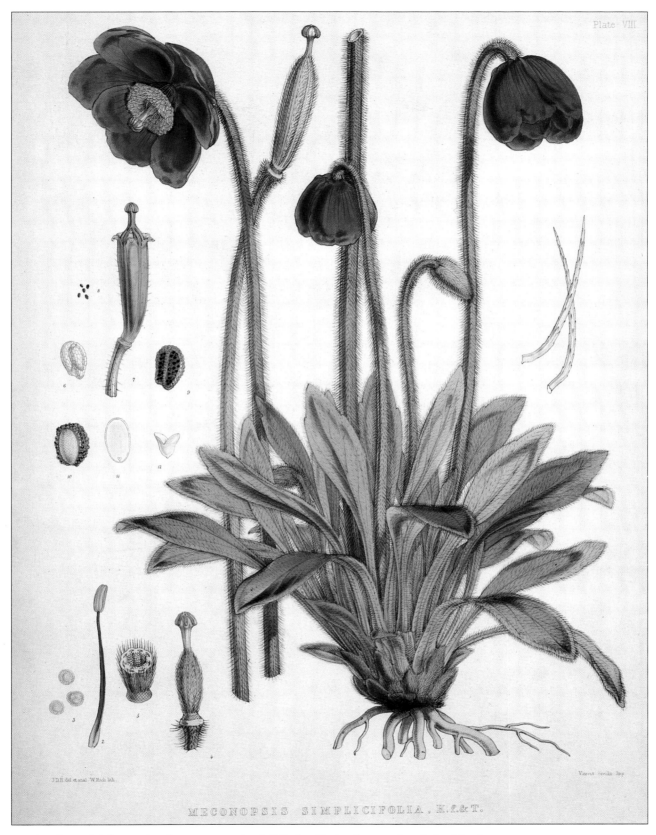

Plate VIII

MECONOPSIS SIMPLICIFOLIA, H.f.&T.

Hand-coloured lithograph of *Meconopsis simplicifolia* by Fitch, from a sketch by Hooker. (*Illustrations of Himalayan Plants*, 1855). Both *Meconopsis* and *Primula* are abundant in Sikkim, often covering the ground in spectacular patches of colour.

Watercolour of *Dendrobium hookerianum* by Fitch. (Reproduced in *Curtis's Botanical Magazine*, 1873, plate 6013). This epiphytic orchid was discovered by Hooker in 1848 in humid valleys at elevations of 1,000–5,000 feet.

Berberis concinna, Hook. fil.

Rosa sericea. Lindl.

(Above left) Watercolour and pencil drawing of *Berberis concinna* by Fitch. (Reproduced in *Curtis's Botanical Magazine*, 1853, plate 4744). Hooker harvested its seeds in the Lachen valley in Sikkim at elevations of 12,000–13,000 feet.

(Above Right) Watercolour of *Rosa sericea* by Fitch. (Reproduced in *Curtis's Botanical Magazine,* 1860, plate 5200). Discovered by Wallich but introduced to British gardens by Hooker and Richard Strachey.

(Right) *Cymbidium hookerianum*. Collected by Hooker in Sikkim. Like *Vanda coerulea* it is a parent of successful and popular hybrid orchids. (*P. Cribb*.)

The illustrations in *Himalayan Journals* are lithographs and wood engravings based on Fitch's interpretation of Hooker's sketches. This view of Kangchenjunga viewed from Singtam demonstrates a typical progression from artist's sketch to publication: (*Above left*) Hooker's sepia drawing. (*Above right*) Fitch's watercolour. (*Opposite*) Lithograph.

Himalayan Journals which went into a second edition in 1855, and was reprinted in 1891, is now recognised as a minor classic of travel literature. Army officers on active duty as well as armchair travellers praised it. An officer with a British force in Sikkim in 1861 called it 'a most perfect staff officer's report, containing accurate information on every point that would be useful to a commander of an expedition'.[13]

In February 1849, intimidated by the prospect of having to complete the *Botany of the Antarctic Voyage*, Hooker had vowed he would never tackle a similar one for India. Yet within six months he had changed his mind and had discussed its presentation with his father.[14] This ambition became a resolve when he and Thomson botanised together in Assam. 'It is easy to talk of a *Flora Indica*, and Thomson and I do talk of it to imbecility'.[15] Nathaniel Wallich, the former Superintendent of the Calcutta Botanic Garden, now in retirement in London, offered to help using the Indian herbarium he had deposited at the Linnean Society of London. They had even decided upon its format, calculated it would fill twelve octavo volumes, and take about

13. L. Huxley. *Life and Letters* ..., vol. 1, 1918, p. 322.
14. Hooker to his father. 23 June 1849. *Letters from J.D. Hooker*.
15. Hooker to his father. June 1850. L. Huxley. *Life and Letters...* , vol. 1, 1918, pp. 340-42.

eighteen years to complete. As their enthusiasm was tempered by an awareness that it depended on adequate financial backing, they never contemplated anything as lavish as the *Flora Antarctica*. Hooker cautioned 'extreme simplicity of form & mode of publication & such an arrangement as shall effectually counteract the possibility of an abrupt imperfect termination'.[16] When the two men left India their combined collections, gathered in north-west and eastern India, amounted to about 150,000 specimens representing 6,000–7,000 species, an excellent basis for their project.

16. Hooker to his father. 18 June 1850. *Letters from J.D. Hooker.*

A selection of the many objects, mainly of vegetable origin, acquired in India by Hooker for the Kew Gardens Museum: dyed native cloth (*Symplocos racemosa*), wooden teacups (*Balanophora involucrata*), snuff box (*Lagenaria vulgaris*), and bellows (*Bauhinia vahlii*).

Chapter 12

AN UNCERTAIN FUTURE

Hooker's wanderlust having abated, his immediate goal was to find a job, something congenial and preferably salaried. He had declined the vacant post of Director of the Botanic Garden at Peradeniya in Ceylon when the incumbent, George Gardner, died in March 1849, although it was well paid and, so Hooker fervently believed, preferable to a university professorship or to lecturing. He had resolutely set his sights on Kew Gardens. 'A position like my father's is the only thing I am cut out for except travelling', he confided to Bentham.[1] His father, anxious to see his son settled, submitted a report on his Indian tour to Lord Seymour, Chief Commissioner of Woods and Forests, extolling his achievements. He had acquired living plants and seeds for Kew, objects for its museum, dried specimens for the herbarium, and had presented all his drawings and sketches. As his son was the obvious person to sort, name and arrange these collections, he requested that he be engaged for a specified period. He also asked that the house of the late W.T. Aiton, the former Director at Kew, be made available to him both as a residence and as a place to work on the collections. In May 1851 eight eminent botanists petitioned Lord Seymour to employ Joseph Hooker at Kew, a plan supported by the Royal Society, the Geological Society, the Zoological Society and the Royal Geographical Society. Sir William Hooker's tactful and deferential approach

1. Hooker to Bentham. 28 May 1849. *Letters from J.D. Hooker.*

200

irritated his son, impatient for a speedy and positive decision. He begged Professor Henslow to persuade his father to act more assertively. 'You again might fairly demand that he exert himself towards getting me into the Garden permanently, on Frances' account [his fiancée and Henslow's daughter] and into Aiton's house. The latter will be necessary for the vast Indian collections'.[2] He complained, perhaps unreasonably, to Bentham about his father's 'excess of modesty', his diffidence in seeking a salary and accommodation for him.[3] In a subsequent letter to Bentham he expressed his determination to have Aiton's house, seeing it and a salary as the route to an established post at Kew. 'My father is all for asking too little, I am not sure that is good policy so long as I have a claim to demand something'.[4] He never got Aiton's house but the Treasury awarded him £400 a year until 1854 to sort his Indian specimens and to distribute duplicates to other herbaria. The Admiralty agreed to keep him on half-pay as a naval surgeon for the same period in order to complete *The Botany of the Antarctic Voyage*. A permanent appointment still eluded him but his marriage to Frances Harriet Henslow in August 1851 no doubt consoled him.

Thomas Thomson had less luck with his employers, the East India Company. In April 1851 he sought their permission to put into order the vast accumulation of Indian herbaria in their India Museum in London, reminding the Company that these were inaccessible until they had been sorted and named. Citing the precedent of their treatment of another employee, Hugh Falconer, whose pay and allowances had not been suspended while he was in England cataloguing their Siwalik Hills fossils, he requested a similar dispensation for himself. He had hoped that this task could go in tandem with the compilation of an Indian flora about to be undertaken by Joseph Hooker. The Company raised no objection to this collaboration but refused to pay his salary although it offered to consider some financial recompense on the completion of the flora. Neither did the support of the Ipswich meeting in July of the British Association for the Advancement of Science for Thomson persuade the Company to change its mind, now close to bankruptcy. With the death of his father in 1852, Thomson magnanimously devoted his legacy to the project.

Denied the use of Aiton's house, they stored their dried specimens in the Temple of the Sun and in a shed behind the Orangery at Kew where they examined them. Hooker's Indian sketches and drawings, in excess of a thousand, were lodged in the Museum. Competent volunteers were needed to help in the compilation of the flora. Bentham agreed to describe Leguminosae, and William Munro, an amateur botanist serving with the army in India, was asked to deal with Gramineae. Hooker and Thomson made a start with Ranunculaceae. United by a love of Indian botany, the two men were divided by temperament – Thomson lethargic and pernickety, Hooker a workaholic exasperated by his companion's frequent absence through ill-

2. Hooker to Henslow. 14 April 1851. *Letters from J.D. Hooker.*
3. Hooker to Bentham. 20 April 1851. Ibid.
4. Hooker to Bentham. May 1851. Ibid.

health. Because of Thomson's 'excessive scrupulosity, his natural slowness, and his matchless procrastination', Hooker despaired of the *Flora Indica* ever appearing in print. He had difficulty in getting Thomson to write about the plants of Tibet and North West India for the Introductory Essay. With Munro's return to India and Thomson's inactivity, Hooker occupied himself with the distribution of duplicate Indian plants to public and private herbaria in Europe, U.S.A. and India.

No one was probably more surprised, certainly no more relieved, than Hooker when eventually the first volume of the *Flora Indica* was published in July 1855. It described the species of fifteen plant families with an Introductory Essay of 280 pages occupying nearly half the volume. A perceptive and broad appraisal of Indian botany, both past and present, this Essay was also available separately. In 1908 when Hooker had forgotten his earlier resentment towards Thomson, he told J.S. Gamble that the Essay would never have been written without Thomson's input. It was an exposition of their objectives, a manifesto of their botanical beliefs, and an explanation of their methodology. Believing that no national flora should be undertaken without an awareness of the vegetation of contiguous countries, they included territories from 'Persia to the Chinese dominions', dividing the region into phytogeographical zones. A special study was made of the influence of soil and climate on the geographical distribution of plants.

They had not anticipated so much synonymy. New names had been concocted by botanists unaware that in many cases scientific names already existed. Hooker and Thomson also deplored the 'prevailing tendency to exaggerate the number of species and to separate accidental forms by trifling characters'.[5] As 'lumpers' rather than 'splitters' of species, they set out to reduce the number of existing specific names consistent with taxonomic criteria. Too often botanists had been misled by the 'protean habit' of a plant which could, for example, be a tall tree in deep forests or a shrub on open slopes, and accordingly described as different species. They came to the conclusion that 'more than one half of the recorded species of Indian plants are spurious'.[6]

Still reluctant to adopt Darwin's radical concept of a species, Hooker preferred for practical purposes to follow orthodox opinion that species were 'definite creations'. He judged 'variability' in a species rather than 'mutability' as being 'a part of the scheme of nature'. Nevertheless the following passage indicates a shift towards the Darwinian concept of natural selection.

> Plants, in a state of nature, are always warring with one another, contending for the monopoly of the soil – the stronger ejecting the weaker – the more vigorous overgrowing and killing the more delicate. Every modification of climate, every disturbance of the soil, every interference with the existing vegetation of an area, favours some species at the expense of others.[7]

5. *Flora Indica*. Introductory Essay, p. 12.
6. Ibid., p. 39.
7. Ibid., p. 41.

MUSEUM.

Interior of the Principal Room.

Wood engraving of the interior of the Museum established in Kew Gardens by Sir William Hooker. (*Museum of Economic Botany*, 1855.)

Their own collections which they estimated to be about 8,000 species including cryptogams, had formed the nucleus of their research material. This they supplemented by consulting the personal herbaria of Sir William Hooker, Nathaniel Wallich and John Forbes Royle. Notwithstanding their hope that future parts of the *Flora Indica* might be issued as monographs prepared by specialists, nothing further appeared. If the joint authors had continued to provide the same density of detail, someone had calculated it would have required about 12,000 pages to complete it. An anonymous reviewer in *Hooker's Journal of Botany and Kew Garden Miscellany* preferred a general flora to 'a learned study of a few natural orders'.[8] Thomson's appointment as Superintendent of the Botanic Garden in Calcutta and Hooker's as Assistant Director at Kew, postponed its continuation in the foreseeable future.

Flora Novae-Zelandiae, the second part of *The Botany of the Antarctic Voyage* appeared in instalments between 1852 and 1855. The first volume, completed in 1853, listed flowering plants with the concluding volume in 1855 listing the cryptogams. Altogether 1,767 species of which 731 were flowering plants and 119 ferns and fern-allies were described, and 313 were illustrated by Fitch. Hooker could never have tackled this first published account of the New Zealand flora without access to the specimens of more than thirty botanists and collectors. One notable collector, David Lyall the naturalist on an official survey of New Zealand in 1847, had been assistant surgeon on H.M.S. *Terror*. Hooker dedicated this *Flora* to his former colleague and two other distinguished collectors – William Colenso and Andrew Sinclair. He doubted that many new species of flowering plants would be discovered in New Zealand where collectors could be more profitably engaged seeking fungi, mosses and other cryptogams.

His Introductory Essay to the first volume summarised botanical research in New Zealand from the time of Captain Cook's voyages. Hooker used its flora to elaborate his theories on the affinities, limits and origin of plants and their geographical distribution. His opinions on 'species' anticipated those delivered in his *Flora Indica* two years later, but still gathering evidence, he adopted a pragmatic approach:

> Although in the Flora I have proceeded on the assumption that species, however they originated or were created, have been handed down to us as such, and that all the individuals of a unisexual plant have proceeded from one individual, and all of a bisexual from a single pair, I wish it to be distinctly understood that I do not put this forward intending it to be interpreted into an avowal of the adoption of a fixed or unutterable opinion on my part.[9]

Darwin congratulated him on a well-argued presentation of his thesis, 'though parts take the wind very completely out of my sails',[10] and thanked him for a generous tribute: ' . . . Mr Darwin not only directed my earliest studies in the subjects of the distribution and variation of species, but has discussed with me all the arguments, and drawn my attention to many of the facts which I have endeavoured to illustrate in this Essay'.[11]

Soon after the publication of the first volume, the Executive Council of Tasmania in 1854 voted to give Hooker £350 towards the writing of *Flora Tasmaniae*, the final part of *The Botany of the Antarctic Voyage* and, furthermore,

8. *Hooker's Journal of Botany*, vol. 7, 1855, p. 256.
9. *Flora Novae-Zelandiae*. Introductory Essay, p. viii.
10. Darwin to Hooker. 25 September 1853. *Correspondence of Charles Darwin*, vol 5, 1989, p. 155.
11. *Flora Novae-Zelandiae*. Introductory Essay, p. xxii.

Joseph Hooker in middle age. Compare this photograph with George Richmond's portrait executed about the same time.

placed an order for six copies. Any financial assistance was welcomed by Hooker whose income from government sources ceased at the end of 1854. His future was still undecided. The Royal Institution wanted him as a lecturer in January 1854 but he disliked public speaking. He told Asa Gray in March that he was considering writing for a living but with a young family to support that was never a serious option and, besides, his father would have objected strongly. The stress caused by this uncertainty manifested itself in a stomach complaint. Darwin who suffered from flatulence recommended a cold bath and a walk before breakfast; 'be careful of your stomach', he cautioned, 'with which, as I know full well, lie intellect, conscience, temper & the affections'.[12] Ever fearful about his own state of health, Darwin later that year nominated Hooker as his literary executor in the event that he might not live to finish his *magnum opus.* 'Hooker is by far the best man to edit my species volume'.

With no other job in sight Hooker accepted that autumn the position of examiner in botany for candidates entering the medical branch of the East India Company. Early in November he learned he was to receive the Gold Medal of the Royal Society for his botanical researches during the Antarctic voyage and in India. The flora of Tasmania now absorbed every spare moment. Having failed to get a house at Kew, he moved to 3 Montagu Villas on the top of Richmond Hill in December.

12. Darwin to Hooker. 29 May 1854. *Correspondence of Charles Darwin*, vol. 5, 1989, pp. 194-6.

1855 was a productive year: *Illustrations of Himalayan Plants* and *Flora Indica* published, *Flora Novae-Zelandiae* finished, several palaeobotanical papers printed in the *Journal of the Geological Society*, others in the *Philosophical Transactions of the Royal Society*, *Proceedings of the Linnean Society* and *Hooker's Journal of Botany*. The first number of *Flora Tasmaniae* came out in October. Darwin applauded his intention to tackle the geographical distribution of the entire Australian flora; 'this is ambitious', conceded Hooker, 'but it is really the most extraordinary thing in the world'.[13] He believed the flora of south western Australia to be quite distinct from that of New South Wales.

What he had always desired and what his father had schemed for was at last realised in 1855. In May he was appointed Assistant Director to Sir William Hooker at an annual salary of £400, and in October he moved into an official residence on Kew Green. Now a contented man, he assured his friend W.H. Harvey some months later that 'Daddy and I get on famously in Garden matters'.[14]

Hooker brought to casual commissions as much scholarship and thought as he gave to more ambitious enterprises. What need not have been more than a modest review of Alphonse de Candolle's *Géographie Botanique Raisonnée* in 1856 became an important statement on plant geography spread over seven issues of *Hooker's Journal of Botany*.[15] He dismissed de Candolle's belief in the permanence of species – 'there is not a show of proof of this'.

He joined forces with George Bentham to compile a *Genera Plantarum*, an ambitious attempt to list and describe all seed-bearing genera. No matter how busy he was he always found time to promote Indian studies. For many years he worried about the deplorable state of the vast collections of plants gathered by officials of the East India Company, without question the finest repository of the Indian flora in the whole of Europe. They lay neglected in the Company's notorious cellars, many still in their packing cases, others only partially sorted. When Hooker inspected them in January 1858 he found William Griffith's specimens mixed with plants from Abyssinia; some collections had lost their provenance labels. He impetuously offered to take the lot to Kew Gardens, optimistically thinking he might be able to identify and list them in a couple of years. In return the Company allowed Kew to transfer some of them to its herbarium and also to borrow their folios of flower drawings by Indian artists. The East India Company which jumped at the chance to rid themselves of this encumbrance promptly sent eleven waggon loads of chests, bundles and packages to Kew and, moreover, contributed £200 towards the project. Hooker and Thomson collaborated in a series of articles published in the *Journal of the Linnean Society* between 1858 and 1861, entitled *Praecursores ad Florum Indicum*, a synopsis of Indian plant families intended as an interim substitute for a continuation of the *Flora Indica*. At the same time Hooker resolved problems in plant identity and synonymy

13. Hooker to Darwin before 7 March 1855. *Correspondence of Charles Darwin,* vol. 5, 1989, p. 277.
14. Hooker to Harvey. 3 February 1857. *Letters from J.D. Hooker.*
15. *Hooker's Journal of Botany,* Vol. 8, 1856, pp. 54-64, 82-88, 112-21, 151-57, 181-91, 214-19, 248-56.

for George Thwaites, the Director of the Botanic Garden at Peradeniya who was compiling a list of Ceylonese plants called *Enumeratio Plantarum Zeylaniae* (1858–1864).

1858 is a particularly memorable year, not so much for research and curatorial activities but rather for a meeting that Hooker and the geologist, Charles Lyell, organised at the Linnean Society of London on behalf of Charles Darwin and Alfred Russel Wallace. For years Hooker had been a sounding-board for Darwin's maturing thoughts on the origin of species, always supportive, yet often critical. Occasionally Darwin resented his friend's ruthless interrogation. 'I generally believe Hooker implicitly, but he is sometimes, I think, & he confesses it, rather over critical & his ingenuity in discovering flaws seems to me admirable'.[16] He realised, however, his indebtedness to Hooker for his botanical expertise, for his evidence on geographical distribution, and for his exceptional knowledge of relevant literature, especially obscure articles in scientific journals. The accumulation and evaluation of data became almost an end in itself for Darwin while his friends waited impatiently for the publication of his researches. Fearing, however, a hostile reception to his radical, even blasphemous theories, Darwin hesitated to publish them. Surprisingly he failed to recognise a rival in the author of an article 'On the Law which has regulated the Introduction of New Species' in the *Annals and Magazine of Natural History* in 1855. It had been written by Alfred Russel Wallace, then collecting natural history specimens in Borneo, who, quite independently, was reaching similar conclusions to Darwin's. Urged by Lyell to be the first to get into print, even with incomplete research, Darwin began organising a plethora of notes into chapters and pondering the best method of publication.

In June 1858, out of the blue, a letter came from Wallace, outlining his theories on evolution and natural selection. It read like an abstract of Darwin's own work, a blow to any claim of originality, and a deterrent to continuing with his book. Anxious not to be seen to be dishonourable to Wallace, he, nevertheless, desired credit for so many years' labour. He reminded Hooker that in strictest confidence he had shown him and Lyell early in 1847 his 1844 manuscript essay, some 230 pages long, as evidence of his early researches. Completely at a loss to know what action to take, he placed the matter in the hands of Hooker and Lyell who wasted no time writing to the Secretary of the Linnean Society of London on 30 June. They enclosed extracts from Darwin's 1844 essay, an abstract of a letter in 1857 to Asa Gray summarising his views on the origin of species, and also Wallace's essay 'On the Tendency of Varieties to depart indefinitely from the Original type', urging that they should be brought to the attention of the Society's members. The opportunity to submit these papers came at a meeting of the Linnean Society on 1 July. Neither protagonist was present – Darwin was attending his son's funeral and

16. Darwin to Gray. 21 February 1858. *Correspondence of Charles Darwin*, vol. 7, 1991, p. 27.

Wallace was far away in the Moluccas. The thirty or so members who attended had no advanced notification of the agenda. There was no discussion because, according to Hooker, 'the subject was too novel and too ominous for the old school to enter the lists before armouring'.[17] The President had no idea that he was chairing an historic occasion. His subsequent review of the Society's activities from May 1858 to May 1859 blandly declared that it had not been 'marked by any of those striking discoveries which at once revolutionize, so to speak, the department of science on which they bear'.[18] And likewise the publication of the papers of Darwin and Wallace in the Society's *Journal* in August made little immediate impact on the scientific world. Darwin had intended presenting a longer abstract of his researches in the *Journal* but unable to condense it he ended up writing a book which was published on 24 November 1859 as *On the Origin of Species and Varieties by means of Natural Selection*.

When booksellers bought the entire edition of 1,250 copies on the first day of publication, a reprint speedily appeared early in January 1860. The country's leading anatomist and palaeontologist, Richard Owen, a militant defender of orthodoxy, led a vociferous opposition but younger scientists, including Joseph Hooker, responded sympathetically to its revolutionary pronouncements. Hooker had been privy to the development of Darwin's views for some fourteen years through correspondence and frequent meetings. During the course of his own researches, Hooker had questioned traditional belief in the immutability of species, and by April 1859 Darwin was convinced that he had converted him. He gleefully informed Wallace that Hooker intended declaring his 'confession of faith' in the Introductory Essay which he was then writing for the *Flora Tasmaniae*. This Essay, published in December 1859, was the distillation of two years spent in patient sifting through a vast accumulation of data, of methodically digesting and evaluating the evidence.[19] Darwin congratulated him for 'the grandest and most interesting essay on subjects of the nature discussed I have ever read'.[20]

Apart from a passing reference to plants being in constant conflict, 'the more vigorous overgrowing and killing the more delicate', in his *Flora Indica*, this Essay was Hooker's first published acknowledgement of Darwin's influence, an unequivocal acceptance of the premise that 'species are derivative and mutable'.[21] He devoted about a fifth of its 128 pages to discussing the species concept and the remainder to speculation on the origin and distribution of plants in Australia, treating the subject mainly from the perspective of a plant geographer.

Nothwithstanding the title of his work, Hooker considered Tasmanian vegetation within the context of the flora of Australia which he described as being one of the most remarkable in the world. He calculated a high level of endemism — two-fifths of its genera and seven-eighths of its species were confined to Australia. Since he had personally seen very little of the

17. Hooker to F. Darwin. 22 October 1886. L. Huxley. *Life and Letters ...* , vol. 2, 1918, 301.
18. A.T. Gage. *A History of the Linnean Society of London,* 1938, p. 56.
19. It was also published separately: 'On the Flora of Australia, its Origin, Affinities and Distribution'.
20. Darwin to Hooker. 3 January 1860. *Correspondence of Charles Darwin,* vol. 8, 1993, p. 6.
21. *Flora Tasmaniae.* Introductory Essay, p. ii.

continent's vegetation, he relied heavily on the discoveries and observations of other plant collectors such as Robert Brown, the naturalist on Captain Flinders's Australasian expedition, 1801–05, the Kew gardener, Allan Cunningham, based at Sydney, 1816–26, 1837–39, and generous help from local colonists – competent botanists like William Archer and Ronald Gunn to whom he dedicated *Flora Tasmaniae*. His father's private herbarium was particularly rich in Australian material. Through such resources Hooker became acquainted with some 7,000 plants. When George Bentham compiled his monumental *Flora Australiensis* (1863–1878), he found himself in agreement with much of the pioneering work of his predecessor.

Flora Tasmaniae completed the series entitled *The Botany of the Antarctic Voyage*, begun in June 1844 with the first number of *Flora Antarctica*. This impressive work in six quarto volumes described 5,340 species with 528 coloured lithographic plates by W.H. Fitch. Much of the text was written by Hooker but specialists dealt with the majority of the cryptogams. In the *Flora Tasmaniae* M.J. Berkeley considered fungi, W.H. Harvey algae, C. Babington and W. Mitten lichens and W. Wilson most of the mosses.

In addition to three years' half-pay as a naval surgeon, the Admiralty showed its appreciation of his 'zeal, perseverance and scientific ability in his botanical services' with an award of £500. The colonial governments of New Zealand and Tasmania each contributed £350 towards publication costs, supplementing the £1,000 advanced by the British Treasury.

The world's botanical fraternity congratulated Hooker. The praise of Asa Gray in the United States was typical. 'Young as he still is, no living botanist has investigated on the spot so many and so widely separated floras, and few like him have had constant access to the largest and best determined herbaria in the world'.[22]

The publication of the final parts of *The Botany of the Antarctic Voyage* coincided with solving the mystery surrounding the disappearance of Sir John Franklin, the Arctic explorer who had been Governor of Tasmania when Hooker explored the island. After the *Erebus* and *Terror* returned to England in 1843, they were refitted for yet another attempt to find the North West Passage, the hypothetical link between the Atlantic and the Pacific oceans which navigators since Elizabethan times had vainly sought. Franklin was commander of the expedition with Francis Crozier, the second in command on Captain Ross's Antarctic voyage, fulfilling a similar role under Franklin. The two ships sailed in May 1845 and were never seen again. Several searches were made, but it was not until 1859 that an expedition, financed by Lady Franklin, found a cairn containing a terse note written by the captain of H.M.S. *Erebus* in April 1848 reporting that Franklin had died in June 1847, and that the two ships were being abandoned. Had Franklin's expedition needed a naturalist, Hooker might well have been tempted to join it.

22. *American Journal of Science and Arts*, vol. 17, 1854, p. 252.

Chapter 13

VISIT TO THE MIDDLE EAST

It was inevitable that Darwin's book would be discussed at the annual meeting of the British Association for the Advancement of Science at Oxford in 1860. Professor Charles Daubeny in his paper 'On the Final Causes of Sexuality in Plants, with special reference to Mr Darwin's Work in *The Origin of Species*' cautiously welcomed Darwin's hypothesis as a means of reducing the number of existing species but stressed the limitations of its application. Sir Richard Owen responding 'in the spirit of the philosopher' rejected it outright as he had done in his review in the April issue of the *Edinburgh Review*. An authority on the brains of apes, he confidently asserted that they were different from those of humans. T.H. Huxley, who was present, curtly refuted this statement, promising a carefully considered answer which duly appeared in the *Natural History Review* in 1861. He had declined to be embroiled there and then in a confrontation since 'a general audience, in which sentiment would unduly interfere with intellect, was not the public before which such a discussion should be carried on'. This skirmish was a prelude to a hostile attack by the Bishop of Oxford the following day, 30 June.

Between 700 and 1,000 people, far too many for the lecture hall, crowded into the unfurnished new library of the University Museum. The clergy were there in force eager to see the heresy savaged. Darwin's former tutor and Hooker's father-in-law, Professor J.S. Henslow, was in the chair flanked by the speaker Professor Draper of New York, Bishop Wilberforce, Sir John Lubbock, Sir Benjamin Brodie, T.H. Huxley and Joseph Hooker. Sickness prevented Darwin's attendance. Professor Draper initiated the debate with a paper on the 'Intellectual Development of Europe considered with reference to the Views of Mr Darwin'. The audience impatiently endured his hour-long address, asked few questions, and loudly called for Bishop Wilberforce.

The Bishop, an accomplished and urbane speaker, spoke fluently for about half an hour; 'in such dulcet tones, so persuasive a manner, and in such well-turned periods', according to one eyewitness. This suave performance did not blind Hooker to the 'uglyness & emptyness & unfairness' of his attack, obviously well rehearsed under Owen's tutelage. Wilberforce relished the criticisms in unfavourable reviews of *The Origins*. His onslaught was received with acclamation; ladies in the audience decorously waved their handkerchiefs in approval.

It was brilliant oratory compared with T.H. Huxley's restrained but quietly eloquent defence of Darwin who, he said, had attempted an explanation of all the facts he had assembled, and in the process had formulated a reasonable concept of the origin of species. Wilberforce is reported as having asked Huxley whether it was through 'his grandfather or his grandmother that he claimed his descent from a monkey'. Huxley riposted that if he had to choose between 'a miserable ape for a grandfather or a man highly endowed by nature and possessed of great means and influence and yet who employs those faculties for the mere purpose of introducing ridicule into a grave scientific discussion – I unhesitatingly affirm my preference for the ape'.[1] No one appears to have remembered the famous retort exactly, possibly because Huxley's words were partly drowned by the applause.

Because Hooker had some reservations about Huxley's performance – he did not exploit Wilberforce's weaker points nor did his voice carry well in the crowded chamber – he took on Wilberforce himself. 'I smashed him amid rounds of applause', he told Darwin.[2]

> I hit him in the wind at the first shot in 10 words taken from his own ugly mouth – & then proceeded to demonstrate in as few more (1) that he could never have read your book, and (2) that he was absolutely ignorant of Bot. Science – I said a few more on the subject of my experience, & conversion & wound up with a very few observations on the relative position of the old & new hypotheses ... Huxley ... praised me to my face, told me it was splendid, & that he did not know what stuff I was made of – I have been congratulated & thanked by the blackest coats & whitest stocks in Oxford ... & plenty of ladies have flattered me.

Hooker later regretted this lack of modesty, and persuaded Francis Darwin to omit the letter from his father's *Life and Letters* which he was editing. The principal protagonists believed they had given a good account of themselves. Huxley thought himself 'the most popular man in Oxford for full four & twenty hours afterwards', and Wilberforce never doubted that he had trounced his opponent. The audience judged the contest a draw. When Darwin read Hooker's account of the event he was relieved not to have been there. 'I sh^d have been overwhelmed, with my stomach in its present state'. He admired Hooker's 'audacity ... I had no idea you had this power'.[3]

Hooker's visit in the autumn of 1860 to Syria and the Lebanon where a civil war was raging provided Darwin with another instance of his friend's 'audacity'. 'For God's sake do not go & get your throat cut. Bless my soul, I think you must be a little insane'.[4] A conflict between Druses and Maronite Christians which had broken out in 1841 had culminated in the summer of 1860 in the massacre of thousands of Christians.

Hooker had accepted an invitation from Captain John Washington, a hydrographer in the Royal Navy to accompanying him to Syria in order, among other tasks, to locate the celebrated cedar grove on Mount Lebanon

1. *Correspondence of Charles Darwin*, vol. 8, 1993, pp. 271-72.
2. Hooker to Darwin, 2 July 1860. Ibid., pp. 270-71.
3. Ibid., p. 272.
4. Darwin to Hooker. 2 September 1860. Ibid., p. 342.

and to investigate its history. In the brief time available it could be no more than a superficial reconnaissance which, if proved promising, might lead later to a thorough topographical survey. One of Hooker's friends, the pharmacist Daniel Hanbury, was also in the party.

They left Trieste by steamer on 15 September bound for Beirut via Smyrna where they had a few hours ashore. The local flora rich in genera belonging to the Leguminosae family compensated for the squalor of a 'most wretched town'. Rhodes, their next stop, was more to Hooker's liking. At daybreak on 25 September, Lebanon appeared as a long, mountainous ridge on the eastern horizon. Beirut was swarming with soldiers of a French expeditionary force sent by Napoleon III to restore order. As they had requisitioned most of the horses, Hooker's party rode out of the town next day in a cavalcade of rejected horses and mules, escorted by five Christian Maronites, through lanes of *Saccharum*, *Donax*, *Rosa*, *Asclepias* and *Rubus* towards the bay. They camped that night at the village of Zuc, their sleep disturbed by the competing clamour of crickets and convent bells. Their rocky route ascended through pine woods and ragged limestone cliffs. At 3,000 feet pervasive *Poterium spinosum* gave way to maple, *Pistacia*, cultivated mulberries and vineyards. Higher still the vegetation thinned to small trees and shrubs in a red, rocky landscape, reminding Hooker of Tibet. *Rhododendron ponticum* was in flower. They climbed another ridge to reach Afké at the head of a valley, now partially destroyed by Christians, then descended to the Kedisha valley which ran from Tripoli to undulating hillocks on which a clump of Cedars of Lebanon stood, appearing like a 'black speck' in a great, shallow amphitheatre of bare, red, rounded hills. As they approached Hazrun Hooker noted the familiar deep green leaves and white undersides of *Populus alba* and the immense roots of large walnut trees.

Their first ascent of Mount Lebanon took them by a winding road to the head of a valley; below lay many moraines, some with scattered cedars; the purple flowers of tufts of silvery *Vicia* relieved the gauntness of barren hill sides; there were few grasses. The plateau on the summit at about 9,000 feet was a desolate spot, predominantly pale red and white with scarcely any turf. Hooker found *Oxyria reniformis* sheltering under stones or in deep rock fissures, a remnant, he conjectured, of the Arctic-type flora belonging to Lebanon's glacial period. He told Darwin that the absence of alpine plants on the mountains of Asia Minor was a characteristic shared with Algeria's mountains. Old moraines were evidence of former glaciers, another observation duly passed on to Darwin.

A moraine at about 6,000 feet provided sanctuary for a grove of Cedars of Lebanon (*Cedrus libani*). Many of the trees were obviously very old and two of the party counted and measured them and plotted their location. Nearly 400 trees in nine groups congregated there, the largest forty feet in girth and the smallest about twenty-seven inches. It was assumed that the sanctity of the site

An old photograph of cedars on Mount Lebanon.

had ensured their preservation. Hooker salvaged a fragment of the tree's hard, close-grained wood for the Kew Museum.

Following his visit to India Hooker had argued a relationship between the *Cedrus deodara* of the Himalayas, Lebanon's *Cedrus libani* and the *Cedrus atlantica* of North Africa; that they were, in fact, varieties of the same species.[5] He raised the matter again in his *Flora Indica* [6], and in the Introductory Essay to *Flora Novae-Zelandiae*.[7] He suggested that the Lebanon and Himalayan cedars were extreme forms of the original cedar which was now extinct.[8] On his return to England from the Middle East Hooker consolidated what he had learned on Mount Lebanon with his earlier hypotheses in an article 'On the Cedars of Lebanon, Taurus, Algeria, and India' in the *Natural History Review* for January, 1862.[9] He dismissed the traditional belief that the Cedar of Lebanon had been used to build Solomon's temple since better timber trees were more accessible. He also rejected the proposition that *C. atlantica* was a variety of *C. libani* whereas *C. deodara* was another species. He still believed that they should be regarded as 'three well-marked forms, which are usually very distinct, but which often graduate into one another... Each will yield varieties after its own kind'. At some time in the past when perpetual snows covered Lebanon, its cedars formed a belt with those in the Cilician Taurus in Turkey which, in turn, had links with the cedar forests in the Himalayas. Another form of the Cedar of Lebanon was discovered by Samuel Baker in Cyprus in 1879 which Hooker classified as a variety: *C. libani* var. *brevifolia*.[10]

On a second ascent of Mount Lebanon Hooker fell off his horse, broke his barometer and burst a large boil on his thigh, the only accident of the entire trip. They wandered through the ruined splendours of Baalbeck as the sun was setting and the plains below turned to purple. As they drew near to Damascus, it appeared as 'a winding stream' of clay-coloured houses, punctuated by minarets and low domes. They entered the city on 4 October under escort

5. *Himalayan Journals,* 1891, pp. 179-80.
6. *Flora Indica*, pp. 30-31.
7. *Flora Novae-Zelandiae,* p. xvii.
8. Hooker to Gray. 26 January 1854. L. Huxley. *Life and Letters* ... , vol. 1, 1918, p. 476.
9. Vol. 2, 1862, pp. 11-18.
10. *Journal of Linnean Society,* vol. 17, 1879, pp. 517-19.

Hooker's sepia sketch of the country around Baalbeck. 'Camped in the hexagon of the great temple. Astonishing ruins – beauty of moonlight. Views of plains and camels, dust and caravans. Splendid purple of Lebanon in setting sun, and orange of Antilebanon' (Hooker. *Indian, Moroccan and Syrian Journals*, f. 669 et seq.). *(Family of the late R.A. Hooker.)*

Pen and ink sketch of Abraham's Oak, *Quercus calliprinos*, by Hooker. It was then 90 feet high with a girth of 23 feet. *(Family of the late R.A. Hooker.)*

11. *J.D. Hooker, Indian, Moroccan and Syrian Journals*, f. 669 et seq.

with Christians fleeing from a massacre. The Christian quarter had been reduced to 'ruins piled 4 feet deep in every lane, heaps of mutilated corpses, bones – stench'.[11] Hooker's party, however, were never in any danger.

After three days in Damascus they headed back to Beirut collecting whatever they could find in a barren landscape. Their best discovery was a purple crocus in an Arab village. The richest concentration of vegetation grew on the ridges and precipices of the seaward side of Lebanon. Clearly autumn was not a good season for collecting as Hooker's meagre specimens testified. A quick visit to Jerusalem and its neighbourhood concluded their five weeks' tour.

Sepia pen and ink sketch
of Hebron by Hooker.
(*Family of the late
R.A. Hooker.*)

Years later Hooker succinctly sketched the flora of Syria, Lebanon and
Palestine in Sir William Smith's *Dictionary of the Bible* (1893).[12] He identified it
as being essentially Mediterranean mixed with many familiar wild and
cultivated European plants. He divided the country, once thickly forested, into
three floristic regions. In the western or seaward half of Syria and Palestine
Leguminosae, Compositae, Labiatae and Cruciferae were the most prolific
plant families. *Astragalus*, for example, was represented by about fifty species
and numerous thistles covered the plains and hills. In eastern Syria and
Palestine Hooker confined his listing to the valley of Jordan, the Dead Sea and
the country around Damascus. In the middle and mountainous regions of
Syria oaks predominated below about 3,000 feet. Oaks were the commonest
tree in the entire country followed by *Pistacia* and the carob or locust-tree
(*Ceratonia siliqua*).   Hooker and Hanbury made a diagnostic study of three
species of oak.[13] *Quercus calliprinos* clothed the hills with a dense brushwood up
to twelve feet high but reckless destruction prevented it from reaching its full
height. At Mamre near Hebron Hooker drew Abraham's Oak, a venerable
specimen revered by Jews, Christians and Muslims as the tree where Abraham
had pitched his tent.[14] A portion of a branch that had broken off during the
winter of 1856–57 was dated by Kew from a count of its annual rings to be
about 700 years old, that is about the mid-twelfth century. Hooker met
Q. infectoria, a gall oak widely distributed in Asia Minor, on Lebanon's eastern
slopes, the hills of Galilee and on top of Mount Carmel. The Valonia oak,
Q. aegilops, was used as timber and fuel and its large acorns eaten.

Besides studying the flora, Hooker had requests from Darwin to fulfil: to
seek beetles under stones on the summit of Mount Lebanon; to examine the
microscopic life of any brine lakes; to look out for asses with double or treble
shoulder stripes or any trace of forked shoulder stripes.[15] Hooker noted in his
diary that he saw '4 asses with banded legs both fore and hind down nearly to
hoof' and 'two asses with forked end to shoulder stripe'.[16] Hooker was
commanded to compare the 'state of vigour' of the first plant species he

12. pp. 683-89.
13. 'On Three Oaks of
Palestine'. *Transactions of the
Royal Irish Academy*, vol. 23,
1861, pp. 381-87.
14. *Kew Bulletin*, 1919,
pp. 233-36; 1920, pp. 257-64.
15. Darwin to Hooker.
2 September 1860.
Correspondence of Charles Darwin,
vol. 8, 1993, p. 342.
16. L. Huxley. Life and
Letters ... , vol. 1, 1918,
p. 530.

encountered on any mountains with the last as instances of the 'struggle for life'. He was also to note 'the degree of abruptness of limitation of the species'.[17] Darwin carefully filed away Hooker's comments on glacial moraines in Lebanon for future use.

Safely back at Kew, Hooker resumed work on the *Genera Plantarum*. The *Gardeners' Chronicle* for 3 March 1860 announced that a start had been made on it. Its botanical editor, John Lindley, commented that 'no work in natural history is more needed' since the discovery of many new plants had made existing natural classifications out of date. Relying largely on Sir William Hooker's personal herbarium and that of George Bentham who had generously presented it to Kew, Hooker and Bentham adapted de Candolle's system, giving concise Latin descriptions of the genera of all the seed-bearing families of plants, synonymy, geographical distribution, and other facts. The first part of this monumental work appeared in April 1862.

Hooker was temporarily diverted from this project when he accepted an invitation from the Government of New Zealand late in 1862 to compile another flora of New Zealand. Its Government voted £500 to publish it, guaranteed to purchase 100 copies, and paid the author a fee of £100. The intense botanical activity in New Zealand during the decade since the publication of *Flora Novae-Zelandiae* justified a general – and portable – manual for both professional and amateur botanists. Hooker's *Handbook of the New Zealand Flora*, published between 1864 and 1867, met this requirement, and was not superseded until T.F. Cheeseman's *Manual of the New Zealand Flora* in 1906.

Its layout followed the style recommended by his father for a series of floras of the British colonies. Kew Gardens was already playing an active role in advising the British Government on improvements in colonial agriculture and horticulture – identifying indigenous plants of commercial value and introducing new crops – when Sir William Hooker submitted a proposal to the Colonial Office in May 1857, outlining the publication of regional floras for the benefit of colonists and travellers. He reminded the Secretary of State for the Colonies that his office had sanctioned and financed the *Flora Boreali-Americana* (1829-40), a flora of North America, written by Sir William himself. His son's *The Botany of the Antarctic Voyage* incorporated the floras of Australia, Tasmania, New Zealand and the Falkland Islands. These, however, were costly publications intended solely for professional botanists. What Sir William had in mind was a series of cheap octavo volumes, without any expensive plates, 'scientific yet intelligible to any man of ordinary intelligence'. He nominated the British West Indies as the first territory in the series since a knowledgeable botanist, Professor A. Griesbach of Göttingen University, was willing to undertake it. No objection was raised to this proposal probably because it had the support of his friend and keen botanist, John Ball, then Under-Secretary of State at the Colonial Office. George Bentham completed the *Flora Hongkongensis* in 1861 and started the *Flora*

17. Darwin to Hooker.
6 September 1860.
Correspondence of Charles Darwin,
vol. 8, 1993, p. 345.

Australiensis two years later. Joseph Hooker was compiling a popular account of New Zealand's vegetation. This progress encouraged Sir William Hooker to petition the Colonial Office in 1863 to take on the remaining territories in the British Empire. One conspicuous omission was India.

The preoccupation of Joseph Hooker and Thomas Thomson with official duties and the demise of the East India Company in 1858 had prevented a continuation of the *Flora Indica*. But Hooker had not abandoned it, and when Thomson returned to England on sick leave in 1861, they talked about resuming it. Hooker wondered whether the Indian Presidencies of Calcutta, Bombay and Madras could be persuaded to emulate the example of the Government of Australia which had offered a subsidy towards the publication of the *Flora Australiensis*. Having spent some fourteen years on the flora of India, either writing about it or sorting the accumulation of specimens he had acquired from the East India Company, Hooker was willing to 'give up [supervising] examinations and all other emoluments but Kew for 8 years'[18] to finish off the *Flora Indica*. He had hoped that Thomas Anderson at the Calcutta Botanic Garden might have been able to engage the co-operation of the Government of India but only Sir William Denison, the Governor of Madras, showed any interest. When Denison received a copy of Sir William Hooker's memorandum on colonial floras, he urged Sir Charles Wood, then Secretary of State for India, to involve India in the scheme. Thomson who had resigned his post as Superintendent of the Botanic Garden at Calcutta and settled at Kew, was keen to start work on it but Joseph Hooker was beginning to have doubts about his own involvement. Lack of free time was one impediment, but the *Handbook of the New Zealand Flora* had been such a chore that he dreaded (his word) the more challenging task of taking on India. It was only the knowledge that Thomson and possibly Anderson, lately retired from India, would share the burden that ensured his collaboration. Meanwhile Sir William Hooker had converted the Secretary of State for India, whose Finance Committee in October 1863 accepted his proposition to publish a ten-volume flora of India, and his nominating his son and Thomas Thomson as joint authors. They would receive £150 a volume. It was the fee that finally decided Joseph Hooker as he confessed to Darwin. 'Pay would tempt me, but only because it would hold out a prospect of early retirement from the struggle of scientific work for one's livelihood, and shaking the dust off my feet at the Govt. and Kew Gardens – but for God's sake let this go no further, I regard succession to my father with horror. Not that a better scientific place exists in the world, except my own'.[19]

The *Flora of British India*, as it was to be called, incorporated material for the unfinished *Flora Indica* but rejected the detailed presentation of the pioneering work in favour of more concise descriptions of plants. The joint authors had at their disposal the riches of many European herbaria but none could rival that of Kew, and in London, only a few miles away, the resources of the

18. Hooker to Anderson. 18 August 1861. L. Huxley. *Life and Letters* ... , vol. 2, 1918, p. 13.
19. Hooker to Darwin. No date. Ibid., p. 68.

Hand-coloured lithograph of *Biarum angustatum* by Fitch. (*Curtis's Botanical Magazine,* 1878, plate 6355). Common on dry ground in both Syria and Palestine. Found by Hooker 'but I cannot tell exactly where, for the tubers were collected in Sept., without flowers, and put into a bag with many other roots that I dug up as I journeyed along, and to whose generic name even I had then no clue'.

20. Hooker to Anderson. 19 February 1860. *Letters from J.D. Hooker.*

Botany Department of the British Museum and N. Wallich's herbarium in the Linnean Society. They were so committed to Indian botany that they were now hypersensitive to any slight. When Anderson submitted to Hooker a draft of an article for possible publication he was mildly rebuked for failing to acknowledge their research. 'I have given your paper on Sikkim palms to Thomson who will see to it. Neither of us feels very complimented by there being no notice of his or my being the discoverers of most of the species, and no allusion to 'Herb.Ind.' of which the best set went to Calcutta [Botanic Garden]'.[20] Despite this oversight Hooker hoped to enlist Anderson as a collaborator on the *Flora of British India* project. 'In two years you might make a good stroke into the Flora Indica [*Flora of British India*] which Thomson will never do a stroke of – and as for me, my share is done in the 7 years of hard work I had in naming and arranging the whole Indian collections of ourselves, Jacquemont, Griffith, Falconer, Helfer, Wight and all the others, and

Watercolour by Hooker of distant Damascus: 'immense valleys carpeted with bright green, trees, mulberries, figs, walnuts, aspens, poplars, vines and cypresses'. (Hooker. *Syrian Journal*.) (*Family of the late R.A. Hooker*.)

incorporating with the old Wallichian etc, etc at Kew. That and the praecursores must stand as my contribution'.[21]

Hooker had become disenchanted with his joint author and wished to sever connections with the work. Thomson's frequent bouts of illness and his habitual dilatoriness resulting in little progress on the *Flora of British India* had reduced Hooker to despair, eventually leading to a confrontation with his friend. Their first serious disagreement which surfaced in January 1870 concerned the geographical limits of the flora. Hooker wanted to incorporate Afghanistan, Burma, Malaya and Ceylon; Thomson insisted it should be confined to the three British Presidencies of India, the Sind, Punjab and the Himalayas. Furthermore, Thomson protested that the text he had ready for the press could not be used as it stood if this proposed editorial change of policy was implemented. If Hooker persisted he would print his contribution separately.[22]

When the India Office demanded to know why not a single volume had appeared during the seven years since they had agreed to undertake its compilation, Hooker was at a loss to know how to reply. 'I am heartily ashamed of my position in connection with it', he told Bentham.[23] He did not mince words with Thomson.

> 'Where I feel myself most to blame is in not writing to the Board [i.e. India Office] years ago, & calling off the work, feeling sure as I long have, that you never wd be up to it. But you continued buoying up your own hopes at intervals, though you never could mine, & I really did not like to dispel an illusion that gave you pleasure... After 15 years with no published results, under our circumstances, it is clearly hopeless to expect anything from our joint action. I have had no influence whatsoever in procuring a result, & feel I have no wish left to urge you further'.[24]

He proposed tendering Thomson's ill-health as the reason for the lack of progress. Thomson resented the tone of this letter and, while agreeing with Hooker that this matter should not provoke a quarrel, warned his friend that 'if your course of action be such as to deprive me of my only source of active interest in life I shall undoubtedly be much distressed'.[25] Hooker replied the

21. Hooker to Anderson. 20 May 1868. *Letters from J.D. Hooker*.
22. Thomson to Hooker. 28 January 1870. *Flora of British India (correspondence)*, f. 42.
23. Hooker to Bentham. 30 July 1870. *Letters from J.D. Hooker*.
24. Hooker to Thomson. 30 July 1870. *Flora of British India (correspondence)*, f. 43.
25. Thomson to Hooker. 2 August 1870. Ibid., f. 45.

same day more in sorrow than in anger. He now regretted that he had ever abandoned the *Praecursores* in favour of a revised flora of India. He had done so, he informed Thomson, 'in deference to your wishes, with loyalty to you, & against my own judgement'. He told Bentham that Thomson's addiction to morphine and sherry were partly to blame. Bentham bluntly replied that the desultory *Praecursores* were no substitute for a systematic flora that the entire botanical world now eagerly awaited. To this end many collections had been forwarded to Kew which thereby had assumed a responsibility for its publication. The stark choice was a rupture with Thomson or an admission that Hooker was unable to meet the commitment he had entered into.[26]

Hooker marshalled all the extenuating circumstances he could think of when he answered the India Office's peremptory letter: his father's death, his own succession to the directorship at Kew, a temporary illness, and Thomson's chronic state of health. He assured the Secretary of State that drafts for several plant families had already been prepared and that he had no intention of abandoning the project. Thomson petulantly refused to discuss the flora although he still worked on it. According to Hooker, he refused to write shorter entries and delayed returning his proofs. Hooker could take no more. On 31 July 1871 he notified the India Office that ill-health had necessitated Thomson's resignation. He offered himself as sole editor supervising the work of competent botanists who would be paid for their contributions.

Sir William Hooker who had negotiated with the India Office the publication of the *Flora of British India* had died on 12 August 1865. The transformation of a neglected royal estate at Kew into a botanic garden of international repute was his memorial. Under his management the grounds had been landscaped, the Palm House and other glasshouses built, a museum of economic botany created and a herbarium and library formed. But it has to be said that a personal motivation lay behind these reforms, a belief that the enhancement of Kew's reputation might improve the chances of an additional senior post being established which his son might fill. Shortly after his appointment he disclosed this aim to his father-in-law Dawson Turner. 'The more important the Garden becomes in the eyes of the Government, the better chance I think there may be for an opening for Joseph at some future day'.[27] He never hesitated to draw attention to his son's activities and progress. He even offered to present his precious herbarium and library to the nation provided he received an assurance that his son would succeed him as director. When this offer was declined, his collections formed part of his son's patrimony. Joseph Hooker also inherited from his father his remarkable energy, his capacity for sustained hard work, his talent with pencil and paintbrush. There existed a rapport between the two men that transcended the normal bonds of filial affection. Joseph Hooker publicly acknowledged his indebtedness to his father in 1898 when the Linnean Society of London awarded him a gold medal.

26. Bentham to Hooker. 4 August 1870. *Flora of British India (correspondence)*, f.43, f. 8.
27. W.J. Hooker to D. Turner. 5 August 1843. Kew file 88.

I inherited from him my love of knowledge for its own sake, but this would have availed me little were it not for the guiding hand of one who had himself attained scientific eminence; who by example, precept and encouragement kept me to the paths which I should follow, launched me in the fields of exploration and research, liberally aided me during his lifetime, and paved for me the way to the position he so long held at Kew with so great credit to himself, and benefit to our Indian and colonial possessions.[28]

When Joseph Hooker succeeded his father on 1 November 1865, his former post of Assistant Director was abolished, thereby increasing his administrative duties. He complained to Darwin about this unexpected retrenchment, vowing that should scientific research at Kew suffer through inadequate staffing he would seriously contemplate early retirement.[29] The gardens at Kew gave him an excuse to escape from office chores, inspecting them became a daily routine, planning new vistas and paths a therapeutic exercise. When asked to recommend naturalists for tours of overseas duty, he often wistfully longed to join them. 'If I have an ardent wish (which alas is not even tempered by a hope) it is to camp out again for a month or two in a savage country'.[30]

Since 1855 Joseph Hooker had been involved in Kew's activities on behalf of the Colonial Office. Seedlings of commercial crops were raised: West African oil palm for Australia, New Zealand and India; tea for Ceylon; Liberian coffee for India and the West Indies; Queensland nuts (*Macadamia* sp.) for Natal; Brazilian Ipecacuanha for India; the best Manila and Havana tobacco to any colony that wanted it. By 1869 Kew found it difficult to meet the demand for seeds and plants from colonial botanic gardens and plantations. Not all colonial trials were successful; sending cocoa to St Helena was a gesture of misplaced optimism. Though Hooker encouraged the diversification of commercial horticulture on the island, he acknowledged the need to protect St Helena's diminishing native flora. 'It is most desirable also that some of the extremely interesting native plants, which have become very scarce, should be preserved from extinction.'[31] Kew's annual report for 1867 recorded the receipt of 'seeds and plants of species now all but extinct in that interesting island'.

Cinchona, one of the crops introduced to St Helena, was the most successful of all the plant transfers supervised jointly by Sir William and Joseph Hooker. As the source of quinine, the India Office wanted to establish cinchona plantations in India to reduce the cost of treating malaria among British troops stationed there. Consequently, in 1860, Sir William Hooker participated in 'one of the most important horticultural operations in which, as Director of this establishment, it has been my privilege to co-operate'.[32] Kew's crucial role concentrated on germinating cinchona seeds collected in South America in a special glasshouse funded by the India Office, and despatching the seedlings to special nurseries in Ceylon and South India. When he was an old man, Joseph Hooker's godson asked him what commercial transaction had given him the most satisfaction. 'Quite certainly the getting of cinchona into India', was his reply.

28. *Proceedings of Linnean Society*, 1897-98, p. 33.
29. Hooker to Darwin. November 1865. L. Huxley. *Life and Letters ...* , vol. 2, 1918, pp. 48-49.
30. Hooker to D.D. Cunningham. 11 January 1866. L. Huxley. *Life and Letters ...* , vol. 2, 1918, p. 80.
31. *St Helena, Cinchona*, 1868-98, f. 48.
32. *Kew Annual Report*, 1860.

Hand-coloured lithograph of *Fritilleria hookeri* (now *Notholirion macrophyllum*), from a drawing by Hooker's daughter, Harriet Thiselton-Dyer. (*Curtis's Botanical Magazine,* 1878, plate 6385). Found by Hooker in the Lachung valley in Sikkim in 1849. Introduced into cultivation by H.J. Elwes who presented bulbs to Kew.

Chapter 14

Morocco

When Henry John Elwes resigned his commission in the Scots Guards in 1870, he resumed his travels, which up to then had been confined to Europe. Before his death in 1922 he visited India, China, Japan, Russia, North and South America, and the Middle East, indulging at the same time in a passion for birds, insects, plants and big-game hunting. His first expedition in 1870 took him to Sikkim with Hooker's *Himalayan Journals* as his guide. Like Hooker, he, too, illegally slipped across the frontier into Tibet. On his return to England in 1871 he called at Kew Gardens to compliment the Director on the accuracy and comprehensive coverage of his book, just a few days before

PLATE 9.

Watercolour of *Crocus serotinus* subsp. *salzmannii* by George Maw. (Reproduced in his *Monograph of the Genus Crocus*, 1886). He collected it in Tangier in 1870. John Ruskin praised his crocus drawings as 'most exquisite ... and quite beyond criticism'.

Hooker departed for Morocco. This excursion was, Hooker recalled at a Royal Society dinner in 1887, the fulfilment of a 'childish dream of entering Africa by Morocco, crossing the greater Atlas (that had never been ascended) and so penetrating to Timbuctoo'.

At that time little was known about the interior of Morocco, and maps, based largely on hearsay, were unreliable. Captain Washington, who had led the British party to Syria and Palestine in the autumn of 1860, was one of the few Europeans to have reached the slopes of the Atlas Mountains. Besides botanising there, it was Hooker's ambition to be the first to get to the summit. He wanted to discover, too, if its flora had any links with that of Madeira and the Canary Islands. Wanting a companion to share the labour of collecting living plants and herbarium specimens, he invited the botanist George Maw to join him. Maw was an experienced collector and, moreover, his geological expertise would be an asset. When John Ball, an old family friend, asked to be included, Hooker felt he could not refuse the former Under-Secretary of State at the Colonial Office, who had promoted Kew's interests so vigorously. Both men had been to Morocco. Ball had made an abortive attempt in 1851 to climb the Lesser Atlas and Maw had collected in the neighbourhood of Tangier and Tetuan (Tetouan). The young Kew gardener, William Crump, was enlisted as a general factotum. Hooker proposed to allay the suspicions of any xenophobic natives by masquerading as a hakim (or physician) and herbalist on a mission to collect plants for Queen Victoria's garden at Kew. Before his departure he asked Darwin if he had any 'comments'. 'I expect alpine Maroccan botany to be the most novel and interesting of any W. of Central Asia in the Old World'.[1]

On 1 April they boarded a steamer at Southampton for Gibraltar. Crump got off to a bad start by forgetting to pack Hooker's mercurial barometers, an oversight that prejudiced Hooker against him. Fortunately Ball had brought an aneroid barometer to calculate heights. At Gibraltar they transferred to a ship bound for Tangier which they reached on 7 April. There they were the guests of Sir John Drummond, the British Minister Plenipotentiary, who informed them that the Sultan had instructed the governor of the Atlas provinces to provide hospitality and protection. While waiting for the Sultan's written authority, they inspected the local vegetation as far as the headland of Cape Spartel – pink *Erodium*, poppies, the small Star of Bethlehem, a brilliant orange marigold, ericas, irises, masses of broom and the tufted palmetto palm.

On 10 April they set out for Tetuan about forty miles away, with an interpreter and two soldiers. Along the coast *Chrysanthemum coronarium* with florets ranging in colour from orange to pale lemon, and the large purple-flowered *Malcomia littorea* were in bloom. They wasted no time getting through the monotonous belt of cultivated land between the shore and the hills, pausing only to collect *Allium nigrum*. At the end of the valley the

1. Hooker to Darwin.
19 March 1871. L. Huxley.
Life and Letters ... , vol. 2, 1918,
p. 90.

John Ball (1818-1889). Senior civil servant and amateur botanist.

George Maw (1832-1912). Tile manufacturer, Broseley, Staffordshire. Created a notable garden at his home at Benthall Hall.

vegetation became more interesting: many orchids, species of *Smilax* and *Lavendula*, a striking *Cytisus* with silvery leaves and bright yellow flowers, and an elegant *Thymus*. An artichoke (*Cynara humilis*) which grew wild provided food for villagers and fodder for their animals.

Nightfall brought them to the high-walled caravanserai of El Fondak, sheltering a confusion of camels, horses, mules, donkeys, cattle and their owners. Repelled by the accommodation in filthy cells, they slept fitfully on the roof on improvised beds of twigs covered with rugs and waterproofs. At first light they thankfully resumed their journey towards the valley of the Tetuan river beyond which lay the snow-covered Rif mountains. *En route* they passed a stumbling figure, heavily chained, guarded by armed horsemen, the disgraced governor of a distant province who was paying the penalty of having defied the Sultan.

The walled town of Tetuan picturesquely climbed a hill above the river, a labyrinthine-maze of white dwellings, mosques and decorated gateways intersected by narrow lanes, a fusion of Arabic and Spanish styles. Hooker's party lodged comfortably in the Jewish quarter in a small hotel attractively clad with enamelled tiles. Accompanied by an armed escort, they climbed the lime-stone crags of Beni Hosmar, making sure to avoid the vicious thorns of *Calicotome spinosa* and *C. villosa*. Among the alpine flora Maw found *Saxifraga maweana* which he had first collected in 1869. Hooker failed to dislodge the

Hand-coloured lithograph of *Iris tingitana* by Fitch. (*Curtis's Botanical Magazine,* 1872, plate 5981). The iris that Maw admired in Sir John Hay's home, and eventually found about ten miles from Tangier.

Hand-coloured lithograph of *Caralluma europaea* by Fitch. (*Curtis's Botanical Magazine,* 1874, plate 6137). Collected on an island off Mogador by Hooker and his companions who subsequently found it to be common in South Morocco. A French botanist who had discovered it had identified it as a species of *Stapelia*.

roots of *Hemicrambe fruticulosa* firmly clinging to the cliffs. Philip Barker Webb had originally found this genus of Cruciferae in 1827 but his herbarium specimen had been mislaid and no one had ever seen the living plant until its rediscovery by Hooker. At just over 3,000 feet a panorama of the Moroccan and Spanish coasts and distant Gibraltar stretched out before them.

The botanical expertise of his two companions impressed Hooker. Ball, who had an encyclopaedic knowledge of even the most obscure species, quickly and efficiently got together a representative collection. Maw could identify bulbous plants from their leaves alone. They made Hooker aware of his physical limitations. 'I find my eyesight quite fails me as a collector, indeed I

6010

W.Fitch del.et.lith.

Vincent.Brooks Day&Son.Imp.

Hand-coloured lithograph of *Andryala mogadorensis* by Fitch. (*Curtis's Botanical Magazine,* 1873, plate 6010). A handsome species of an otherwise unattractive genus. Formed snow-white masses on a small rocky islet in the bay of Mogador.

have been remarking for two years now that I cannot read the garden labels with my spectacles even, except I stoop down'.[2] Maw dashed to Tangier in order to ship his large collection of living plants on a departing steamer. Hooker and Ball left for Ceuta situated on a narrow promontory opposite Gibraltar, botanising on the way. They blamed their disappointing haul of plants to their being on horseback instead of walking and being able to search more leisurely and intensively.

After a detour to the Spanish port of Algeciras and Gibraltar, they met up with Maw at Tangier three days later. His precious cargo of plants securely stowed on board ship, Maw had spent his time searching for an iris he had admired on Sir John Hay's dinner-table. He failed to find it at his first attempt but his efforts were recompensed by an asparagus with long, spikey foliage and a red-flowered orchid. Given more precise details of the iris's location, he found not one but a dozen near an old ruin. He and his companions decided that its long filiform leaves freckled with purple at the base and its flowers a clear purple with a deep orange spot allied it to *Iris filifolia* and *I. tingitana* of

2. Hooker to D. Oliver. 12 April 1871. *Letters from J.D. Hooker.*

Drawing by John Ball of Tetuan. (Wood engraving in Hooker and Ball. *Journal of a Tour in Marocco*, 1878). Its walls date from the 17th century when the town was rebuilt.

southern Spain. Maw also discovered the British royal fern (*Osmunda regalis*) on sandstone rocks near the shore.

Armed with the Sultan's permit which Sir John Drummond had obtained for them, they boarded the French steamer *Vérité*, their destination the port of Mogador. A few hours ashore at Casablanca added nothing new to their collections. The humidity kept their stock of paper for pressing plants permanently damp, despite draping the sheets in every available spot on the ship – the rigging, the saloon, even the boiler room.

Thanks to the vigilance of a few French residents, the open square and wide straight streets of Mogador were relatively clean. Their letters of introduction were opened in their presence and that of the British Vice-Consul, Mr Carstensen, after the Governor had reverently pressed the royal seal to his forehead. The Sultan had ordered him to convey the English hakim and his friends 'to his slave, the Governor of Morocco' (i.e. Marrakesh) who was to provide an escort to the Atlas Mountains. The Vice-Consul tried to explain the importance of Kew Gardens to the Governor, somewhat bemused by the purpose of their expedition.

They had two free days to botanise locally but a plague of locusts had devoured much of the vegetation. Not even some rocky islets off the coast had escaped, except for a few plants protected by sea spray. The neighbourhood was botanically disappointing. The only worthwhile finds were a *Nerium* in full flower, discovered by Crump, and an *Asphodelus*, collected by Maw, which Hooker recalled having seen on the plains of India.

The Governor laid on a banquet in their honour. Squatting around a carpet they resolutely tried dubious dishes of chicken, lamb, kebabs, radishes sprinkled with sugar, and the inevitable couscous, while four musicians drowned all conversation with an energetic rendering of national songs.

They left Mogador on 29 April an enlarged party: each had been allocated a personal servant, and an obligatory guard of soldiers was in attendance. Camels and mules carried their baggage which included a tent for each of them and also a communal native tent, handsome, large and cumbersome, but deemed a desirable status symbol. Local skirmishing barred their intended route to the south west. A battle, which had been arranged for the previous Sunday, had been postponed out of consideration for one of the leading participants who had fallen ill with smallpox.

They followed the coast for several miles along bridle tracks before turning inland through sand dunes covered with white broom six to ten feet high. Sand eventually gave way to a gravely soil, the domain of the Argan forest. Outlying trees were small and scattered, becoming larger in more compact communities. *Argania spinosa*, sometimes called the Barbary almond, and considered by the three botanists to be the most extraordinary plant in the entire country, is endemic to western Morocco where it covers more than a million acres of flat and undulating ground. This evergreen tree, not unlike an olive, seldom exceeds thirty-five feet in height with branches spreading some sixty or seventy feet. The reticulated scales of its bark suggests the texture of crocodile skin and its fruit resembles small yellow plums, a bountiful source of food for livestock. Hooker's party saw goats agilely climbing branches up to ten feet to get at this delicacy. Villagers produced cooking oil from the kernels.

After hours of riding they reached the eastern extremity of the forest where few flowers bloomed. *Ziziphus lotus*, avoided on account of its vicious thorns, superseded the *Argania* as the dominant plant, its tall thickets frequently smothered by climbing *Ephedra* or *Asparagus*. *Acacia gummifera*, then little known, had neither flower nor fruit to identify it. It was nightfall when they reached the Governor of Shedma's residence. The noise of camels groaning, mules neighing, the ceaseless chatter and singing of their servants, and the brilliant light of a full moon, thwarted their efforts to sleep. Next morning they wandered around the Governor's garden where roses, hollyhocks, masses of tagetes, chrysanthemums and a few vegetables were indiscriminately grown. The view was more pleasing: fields of grazing animals, occasional patches of cultivation, and low hills covered with the ubiquitous *Argania*. They rode for several hours before they saw the last of the Argan trees which, they noticed, varied considerably in foliage and size. Mid-afternoon found them camped near some wells at Ain Oumast. Here they saw the contours of the still distant High Atlas emerging in sharper focus as the sun set, and they speculated whether some patches of lighter colour were snow or limestone rock. An

W.Fitch, del et lith.

Vincent Brooks Day & Son, Imp.

Hand–coloured lithograph of *Sempervivum atlanticum* by Fitch. (*Curtis's Botanical Magazine,* 1873, plate 6055). Discovered by Hooker and his party on rocks in the Ain-Mesan valley in the Great Atlas at about 5,000 feet. Flowered in a rock garden at Kew in 1873.

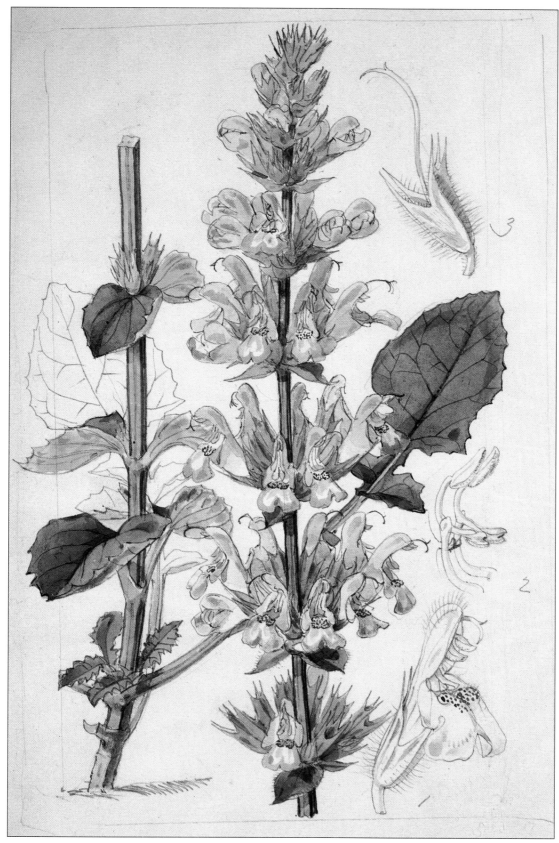

Watercolour of *Salvia taraxacifolia* by Fitch. (Reproduced in *Curtis's Botanical Magazine,* 1872, plate 5991). Found by Hooker and his party growing in rocks and shingle in the beds of rivers along the foot of the Great Atlas, sometimes in great patches.

Drawing by Hooker and Ball of the minaret of the Koutoubia Mosque at Marrakesh. (Wood engraving in Hooker and Ball. *Journal of a Tour in Marocco,* 1878). A superb example of Hispano-Moorish art, the minaret soars to 252 feet.

uncomfortable ride next day took them across a desert plain strewn with fragments of tufa and chalcedony. They managed to find some plants that had survived the heat and the drought: *Peganum harmala, Avena barbata,* two species of *Centaurea* and some other scraps of vegetation were added to their collections. The only dwellings in this uninviting landscape were some low black tents protected by an impenetrable fence of branches of thorny *Ziziphus.* Their route took them over a hill known as the 'Camel's back' where *Frankenia revoluta* grew abundantly. At Sheshaoua they were greeted with a welcome sight: their tents which had preceded them were pitched under the shade of tall fig trees and flowering pomegranates. Hooker and Ball identified over twenty species of British plants in the lush grass around the oasis.

Their trek continued after early breakfast through irrigated fields into another sterile plain, this time littered with fragments of a red basaltic rock. A misunderstanding arose about where they were to rendezvous with the camel baggage train, which as usual, went on ahead of them. In the late afternoon two of their escort went in search of it while they rode on somewhat disconsolately to their night quarters. They paused just once to collect some fine specimens of broom rape (*Cistanthe phelipaea*) with 'sceptre-like spikes of large yellow flowers'. To their great relief the baggage train was waiting for them at Misra Ben Kara, camped in a ploughed field.

The fourth day of their journey brought them to within twenty miles of Marrakesh whose tall, slender minaret was clearly visible. They paused at a stream lined with an impressive floral display of panicles of amethyst-blue flowers of *Limonium ornatum.* At about 1,500 feet they watched cyclonic columns of sand racing across the plain which stretched to the mountain range on the horizon.

They approached the city, very uncertain of the reception they would receive. El Graoui, the Governor of the Atlas Provinces, to whom the Sultan had written, had no jurisdiction over Marrakesh itself whose Governor, Ben Daoud, was reputed to be hostile to travellers and, in particular, to Christians. The only European resident, Mr Hunot, brother of the British Vice-Consul, met them at the city walls. The accommodation reserved for them was

6107

W.Fitch. del et. lith

Vincent Brooks Day & Son, Imp.

Hand-coloured
lithograph of
*Rhodanthemum
catananche* by Fitch.
(*Curtis's Botanical
Magazine,* 1874,
plate 6107). 'One of
the most beautiful
plants of the Greater
Atlas', discovered by
Hooker's expedition
at 7,000–9,000 feet.
Flowered at Kew in
1874.

rejected by Hooker as inadequate. A bigger house, windowless and dirty, also met with his disapproval. He instructed a messenger to tell Ben Daoud that 'my Sultana [Queen Victoria] gives me a large house with a garden to live in; hospitality would require that the Governor of Morocco [Marrakesh] should provide me – the guest of the Sultan – with a better house; but in any case, I shall not live in a worse one'.[3] They were curtly told to find their own accommodation. At this point, El Graoui intervened, and Ben Daoud promised them a house and garden next day.

This unfriendly reception by the Governor of Marrakesh was merely an irritation, a temporary setback, but the co-operation of the Governor of the Atlas Provinces was absolutely vital to the success of the expedition. Before meeting him the trio discussed with Abraham, their interpreter, how best to impress him with the importance of their mission. Abraham felt that El Graoui might not be persuaded that their sole purpose was to collect plants, not even for such a celebrated institution as Kew Gardens. Could they not invoke the authority of Queen Victoria? They wondered whether it would be improper to exploit the undoubted fact that she had a fond regard for Kew; perhaps claim that they had been chosen to collect plants on her behalf. The interpreter was certain that the Governor would never believe that the Queen would ever concern herself with such a trifling affair. He suggested that a quest for plants with medicinal properties might seem more credible. They never discovered what Abraham actually said to the Governor but they became aware that some of their servants were convinced that they were seeking a plant that would confer eternal life on their Queen.

Whatever explanation Abraham concocted, they obtained the Governor's assurance that they could travel on the northern slopes of the mountains but were forbidden to enter the Sous valley. He insisted that they should retain their entire escort and added five of his own soldiers. They had sent the camels back to Mogador when they left Marrakesh on 8 May, a straggling column of thirty-seven men and thirty-three horses and mules. Hooker never anticipated any unfriendliness from the villagers in the mountains but he took a store of presents such as knives, scissors, handkerchiefs, watches, musical boxes, opera glasses, and baubles to smooth the way.

With the intention of getting to the upper reaches of the High Atlas, and remembering Washington's achievement in 1830 in climbing to 7,000 feet from Tasseremout, they made it their objective. After a day's ride and rest they ascended a winding valley. Maw recorded in his diary that 'we have now entered a wonderfully rich flora'. High hedges were a mixture of the familiar and new: dog-roses and *Ephedra altissima* and an unidentified *Coronilla* with large white and lilac-blue flowers. They found a new species of thyme which Ball called *Thymus maroccanus* and a curious milkwort *Polygala balansae*.

3. L. Huxley, *Life and Letters ...*, vol. 2, 1918, p. 130.

Persuaded by a local chief that it was impossible to reach the higher peaks from Tasseremout, they chose an alternative route to the west through the valley of the Ourika river whose vegetation invited closer inspection. A recent introduction to Europe, *Adenocarpus anagyrifolius*, with long racemes of yellow flowers, was conspicuous. Genera belonging to the plant family Leguminosae were especially prolific; Ball named two new species – *Lotononis maroccana* and *Lotus maroccanus*. It was also Ball who found the little stonecrop, *Sedum modestum*, which secreted itself among tree roots or under large stones. 'Ball', wrote Hooker to his wife, was 'the most indefatigable collector I ever met, and nothing escapes his keen eye'.[4] Kaid el Hasbi, the captain in charge of the small contingent of soldiers accompanying them, seemed determined to prevent their ascent. He insisted that the steep track had become too dangerous for heavily laden mules, and indeed, one had missed its footing and fallen into the river. His advice was ignored. He expostulated with Hooker who responded just as vehemently. 'The energy of our interpreter was taxed to the utmost in striving to render the emphatic sentences that were exchanged between Hooker and Kaid el Hasbi, supplemented by pantomimic gestures of the latter'.[5] Kaid el Hasbi had the last word. He announced that tribesmen higher up the valley were in revolt, defiantly refusing to recognise the authority of the Sultan. With no means of verifying this statement, the botanists gave in and reluctantly retraced their steps, but with a foreboding that he would continue to oppose them. They found an unexpected ally in a sheik in the district of Reraya at the base of the mountains when he offered to take them to the snowline. Kaid el Hasbi was silenced when Hooker threatened to report his intransigence to El Graoui and the Viceroy at Marrakesh.

Assured of a handsome present, the sheik of the Ain Mesan valley promised that their next camp would be close to the snows. Before they started, however, Hooker had to dispense medicine and advice to importunate villagers. Ball reckoned that a lone traveller through these regions would be comparatively safe if he had some medical skill and prudently avoided those illnesses with the probability of fatal consequences. Botanists, he judged, were less likely to be molested than geologists who might be suspected of seeking treasure. The three sheiks who joined the party up the valley humoured their guests with a pretence of great excitement whenever a plant caught their attention. They would order their attendants to 'catch him flower' and Hooker, Ball or Maw would make a show of solemnly inspecting it. Villagers crowded around the first Christians they had ever seen and besieged Hooker whose reputation as a hakim had preceded him. Eye complaints and deafness were common; husbands brought wives unable to conceive; supplicants for aphrodisiacs were admonished. Abraham, their interpreter, enterprisingly mixed his own medicine, a sinister black liquid which proved to be a potent laxative.

4. Hooker to his wife.
5 May 1871. *J.D. Hooker. Indian, Moroccan and Syrian Journals*, f. 585.
5. Hooker and Ball. *Tour in Marocco and Great Atlas*, 1878, p. 178.

5983

W. Fitch, del et lith.

Vincent Brooks Day & Son Imp

Hand-coloured lithograph of *Linaria maroccana* by Fitch. (*Curtis's Botanical* Magazine, 1872, plate 5983). Hooker and his friends collected no fewer than twenty species of the genus. Fitch, according to Hooker, had 'failed to attain the rich tint of the native flowers' since, in cultivation, the colour of this species of *Linaria* loses its original depth, sometimes fading to a pale purple or violet tint.

6015

Hand-coloured lithograph of *Bellis coerulescens* by Fitch. (*Curtis's Botanical Magazine*, 1873, plate 6015). A common spring flower in Morocco from Tangier to the valleys of the Atlas mountains up to 11,000 feet.

237

After an early breakfast on 13 May one of the sheiks guided them up the track close to an ancient moraine terminating the valley (no doubt Darwin heard about the moraine in due course). After scrambling to a height of over 8,000 feet they at last walked on snow in the sub-alpine region of the Atlas mountains. Many of the plants were not in flower but Ball discovered a new '*Chrysanthemum*' to which he gave the specific name *catananche* (now *Rhodanthemum catananche*). Much of the ground was covered by *Bupleurum spinosum*. In the fading light they crammed their tin boxes and portfolios with specimens and made a hazardous descent in the dark. Maw fell off his mule and Ball slipped over the edge of the path, his fall broken by a thorny thicket.

During their absence letters had arrived from Carstensen and El Graoui. Their mail unfailingly reached them even with the vaguest of addresses – 'somewhere in the Atlas Mountains'. A letter from the Governor gave them permission to stay in the Mesan valley for as long as they wished. Hooker decided to camp at Arround for a few days, a convenient base for getting up the west flank of the valley by a discernible mule track to the crest of a ridge. The sheik who was to escort them to Arround absolutely refused to let them include several tin trunks, intended for storing plants, in their luggage. He feared that they might be attacked and killed by tribesmen suspecting that they contained money. They, therefore, had to abandon all plans of making a large collection of plants in the High Atlas.

The sheik did not join them on their ascent, but instructed two villagers, selected as guides, that the party must not go beyond a small stone hut, once the dwelling of a saint, at the bottom of the path to the Tagherot (Tagherghout) pass. So when they reached this hut the guides indicated that they had reached the limits of their excursion. But the botanists had already decided that by guile and deception they would continue their climb. They asked the guides to make a fire in the hut while they botanised in the neighbourhood. While they were thus distracted, Hooker, Ball and Maw clambered up the steep path through a drizzle that changed to sleet and then to snow as they neared the ridge above them. A group of traders coming down the path evidently told their guides where they were. The guides hurried up the path anxious that Hooker and his companions should turn back, but were placated with a few silver coins. A wind now rose transforming the falling snow into a blizzard. Despite the intense cold, Maw, his beard a solid block of ice, pressed on ahead and reached the summit of the pass at about 11,500 feet. Visibility was extremely poor as he peered briefly at a steep slope beyond, retraced his steps, and persuaded Hooker and Ball, still toiling up, to abandon their ascent. It had been a frustrating climb: no sign of any alpines, not even the satisfaction of a view. They rested at Arround where Hooker treated the ailments of its inhabitants. A group of wailing women

Drawing by John Ball of the western end of the Atlas mountains seen from the Sektana plain. (Wood engraving in Hooker and Ball. *Journal of a Tour in Marocco,* 1878).

slaughtered a sheep in his honour, thrust a couple of letters in his hand and, through an interpreter, entreated him to petition El Graoui to release their husbands from prison.

When Maw left them on 18 May to return to England, Hooker and Ball were undecided on the route they should take to Mogador. They had had a successful tour. Although they had arrived in the High Atlas rather early in the flowering season and had explored only a few valleys, it was evident that its flora was markedly different from European and West Asian mountains in one respect: no ostentatious display of alpine flowers. It was not until they reached the plateau of Sektana near the foot of the mountains that they enjoyed 'a feast of colour'. The dark crimson flower spikes of *Linaria maroccana*, a new species, gave 'a tone of subdued splendour' to fields of young corn. At Amsmiz (Amizmiz), where the governor was a nephew of El Graoui, they climbed to the top of Djebel Tezah from which they could make out the Anti-Atlas some fifty or so miles away. With little vegetation to examine, they tried to fix the position of peaks and spurs in the mountains around them. On the way down Ball gathered a species of *Monanthes,* previously found only in the Canary and Cape Verde Islands. Local warfare forced them to change their plans, but they botanised whenever they could, making a satisfactory haul of endemic plants at Seksaoua. Carstensen met them at Shedma situated in countryside reminiscent of English parkland with clumps of Argan trees instead of oaks.

Rather than return direct to Mogador, Carstensen recommended a detour via Djebel Hadib or the Iron Mountain. Their clothes were torn and their hands badly scratched collecting *Cistus* and *Helianthemum* among a dense growth of prickly and spiny bushes. They were delighted to collect *Helianthemum canariense* found only in Morocco and the Canary Islands. On 3 June they returned to Mogador and the comfort of furnished rooms, of dining at a table and sitting on chairs. They labelled and packed their dried plants and sent two natives on an urgent mission to Agadir for specimens of *Euphorbia resinifera* which produced the Gum Euphorbium mentioned by Dioscorides and Pliny. An intensification of the war between two neighbouring provinces prevented Hooker going himself. They boarded a British steamer on 7 June. When it docked at Safi their hurried search of the rocky shore was rewarded by the discovery of a plant, *Zygophyllum fontanesii,* thought to grow only in the Canary Islands.

At the outset of the tour Hooker and Ball had fully expected to confirm botanical links between Morocco and these islands nearly 300 miles out in the Atlantic. They only identified fifteen species common to Morocco, Madeira and the Canary Islands, and discounted a former land link between them and the mainland. In his *Spicilegium Florae Maroccanae*[6] – the first attempt to describe the country's plant life – Ball defined its flora as Mediterranean 'which, with local peculiarities, extends from the Indus to the Atlantic Islands'. He was surprised to find so many central European species in the High Atlas.

The labour of writing an account of their tour fell to Ball. Soon after his return Hooker had told him that his work on the *Genera Plantarum*, the flora of India, and ominous developments in the relations between Kew and its parent department made it impossible to collaborate fully in the book. He wrote much of the first two chapters of *Journal of a Tour in Morocco and the Great Atlas* (1878) and contributed three appendices on economic plants and comparisons of the flora of the Canaries and the mountains of tropical Africa with that of Morocco.

Hooker insisted on personally paying all the expenses of the expedition to avoid, it can be assumed, any accusation by the First Commissioner of Works of misappropriation of public funds. Kew Gardens received all the plants he had collected, and in September 1872 he had another small rock garden created for some of his Moroccan introductions. He selected a few of potential interest to British gardeners for illustration in *Curtis's Botanical Magazine* which he edited, dedicating its 1874 volume to George Maw.

He was in his mid-fifties when he went to North Africa. It was to be his final strenuous tour. 'This is the last expedition of the kind I shall ever undertake. At my age one has had too much experience and sees too well how much he leaves undone to enjoy such feats as of yore'.[7]

6. *Journal of Linnean Society, Botany*, vol. 16, 1877, pp. 281-302.
7. Hooker to his wife. 19 May 1872. *Letters from J.D. Hooker.*

Chapter 15

PRESIDENCY OF THE ROYAL SOCIETY AND A KNIGHTHOOD

In May 1872, a few weeks before the end of Hooker's tour in Morocco, the first part of the long overdue *Flora of British India* was published. It dealt with genera in Ranunculaceae, and subsequent parts covered other plant families. Thomas Thomson had been replaced by Thomas Anderson, the former Superintendent of the Royal Botanic Garden at Calcutta, but after only two years as collaborator, he died. Hooker sought other dependable contributors but it was not until 1879 when Charles Barron Clarke was seconded to Kew Gardens by the Government of India for three years that any significant progress was made with the work. An inspector of schools in Bengal, and a dedicated botanist, Clarke had an intimate knowledge of the flora of North East India. Using the resources of Kew and his own extensive collections, he wrote accounts of fifty-three families for the work.

One of the more important distractions that took up so much of Hooker's time was the presidency of the Royal Society. He accepted the honour in 1873 with some reluctance, acutely aware that his own research would suffer as a consequence. 'The dream of my later days is to be let alone, where I am and as I am – I want no higher position, no dignities, nor honors', he told Darwin[1]. He prudently stipulated that his term of office as President should be on a yearly basis and not for an indefinite period. He handled his administrative responsibilities conscientiously, conducted Council meetings efficiently, and contributed his valuable experience as a traveller to the organisation of scientific voyages and expeditions associated with the Society.

Prior to his election as President, Hooker was a member of the Royal Society's Circumnavigation Committee which proposed specific objectives for H.M.S. *Challenger*. The Royal Society had persuaded the Government to equip this ship, a three-masted, square-rigged vessel with steam power, for an intensive investigation of physical and biological conditions in the ocean depths by soundings, trawling and dredging. Captain George Nares commanded it and Professor Charles Wyville Thomson headed a team of scientists who included John Murray and Henry Nottidge Moseley as naturalists. Some of the scheduled stops on the ship's itinerary had been visited by the *Erebus* and *Terror*: Cape Verde Islands, St Paul Rocks, Crozet Islands, Kerguelen's Land, Auckland and Campbell Islands. Captain Nares was to sail 'as near as may be with convenience and safety to the southern Ice-Barrier'

1. Hooker to Darwin.
12 January 1873. L. Huxley.
Life and Letters ... , vol. 2, 1918,
p. 132.

but the ship had not been adequately strengthened for any deep penetration of the ice. Particular attention was to be given to the fauna and flora of oceanic islands. One can detect Hooker's influence in the Circumnavigation Committee's comment that 'these are, in many cases, the last positions held by floras of great antiquity, and, as in the case of St Helena, they are liable to speedily become exterminated, and therefore to pass into irremediable oblivion when the islands become occupied'. It was presumably Hooker, as the country's leading plant geographer, who reminded Moseley that 'facts are also required as to the part played by icebergs in plant distribution ... note any vegetable material which might be found upon their surfaces; also to examine any rock fragments for lichens'.

The *Challenger* left England on 17 December 1872, crossed the Atlantic several times, established 150 observation posts, and in February 1874 became the first steamship to cross the Antarctic Circle, spending a month in the southern polar seas just out of sight of Antarctica itself. Moseley saw yellow stains on ice floes and remembered that Hooker had identified them as the remains of diatoms. On Kerguelen's Land Moseley added seven more flowering plants to Hooker's discoveries. He was the first botanist to land on Marion Island where he found the Kerguelen cabbage and bright green patches of *Azorella selago*. After nearly three and a half years at sea, the *Challenger* returned home in May 1876 with a wealth of scientific data and thousands of specimens. Over the next quarter of a century the scientific reports of this oceanographic voyage were published; on Hooker's recommendation, William Botting Hemsley, a Kew botanist, wrote an account of the insular floras for it.[2]

A government-sponsored expedition to observe the transit of Venus in 1874 presented the Royal Society with another opportunity to study the fauna and flora of isolated islands. It convened a working party consisting of the President, T.H. Huxley and P.L. Sclater to prepare a case for some naturalists to join the astronomers who were to spend several months on Kerguelen's Land and Rodriguez Island. Only one appointment was made, that of Alfred E. Eaton who, during his stay on Kerguelen's Land from October 1874 to February 1875, made the most complete collection of any botanist who had visited the archipelago. He observed nearly all the flowering plants found by Hooker in 1840 and by Moseley early in 1874 and added algae and other cryptogams to the list. In an article published in the *Philosophical Transactions of the Royal Society*,[3] Hooker summarised the history of plant collecting in Kerguelen's Land from the time of Captain Cook in 1776, and enumerated all the plants collected during the *Erebus* and *Terror*, *Challenger* and Transit of Venus expeditions. The remarkable affinities between its flora and that of South America thousands of miles to the west led him to speculate on the means by which this came about: the transportation of seeds by ocean currents and winds or the existence in geological time of land links?

2. *Report on the Scientific Results of the Expedition. Botany*. vol. 1, 1855.

3. 'Observations on the Botanical Collections made in Kerguelen's Land during the Transit of Venus Expedition in the Years 1874-75, with a List of Flowering Plants, Ferns, Lycopods, and Characeae'. *Philosophical Transactions of the Royal Society*, vol. 168, 1879, pp. 9-23.

In 1872 the Royal Geographical Society had proposed an expedition to the north of Greenland to investigate the region's physical geography and natural history. This was supported by the Arctic Committee of the Royal Society. The relationship between the flora of Greenland, Scandinavia and polar North America was, for Hooker, another piece in the jigsaw of plant distribution. Captain Nares left H.M.S. *Challenger* early in 1875 to command H.M.S. *Alert* and *Discovery* on this Arctic voyage; Henry Chichester Hart and Captain Henry W. Feilden were engaged as naturalists after Hooker had been consulted. Hooker recommended that the two ships should be heated by hot water:

> Having served as a Medical Officer on the Antarctic Expedition, when the ships (the 'Erebus' & 'Terror') were heated by hot air & subsequently for many years as Director of this establishment [i.e. Kew Gardens] where structures of all materials have been heated, some by hot air, others by hot water, I am enabled to affirm that the 'Erebus' & 'Terror' could have been heated far more efficiently and economically, & with a great saving of fuel, space & dirt, by a flow & return pipe carried around the ships from the galley-fire, than they were by the hot-air system employed.[4]

The Admiralty rejected this advice in favour of movable stoves. Hooker contributed a botanical appendix to Nares's published account of the voyage.[5]

One compelling reason for the brevity of Hooker's Moroccan excursion was a breakdown in official relations between Kew and the Government department to which it reported. In 1850 the Office of Works had assumed responsibility for the Royal Parks and Kew Gardens. The Minister, or First Commissioner as he was then called, sometimes imposed his preferences and tastes upon a reluctant Director. Sir William Hooker had to submit to Sir Benjamin Hall's demands for more flowerbeds and showy plants. His son's confrontation with Acton Smee Ayrton threatened to destabilise Kew's role as a botanic garden. Ayrton's renowned tactlessness and insensitivity invariably brought him into conflict, and his dislike of 'architects, sculptors and gardeners', proclaimed during an election campaign, boded ill for Kew when Gladstone put him in charge of the Office of Works. Like one of his predecessors, Sir Benjamin Hall, he rated Kew as being little more than a superior public park with no justification for indulging in scientific research. Within months of becoming First Commissioner he set about eroding Hooker's authority. He transferred the responsibility for the heating and ventilation of the glasshouses from Kew to his Office without informing the Director; he did not bother to consult Hooker when he offered his Curator the post of 'Surveyor or Secretary of the Parks'; he constantly questioned Kew's expenditure. Hooker was not a person to take such treatment meekly. He complained direct to the Prime Minister about his minister's 'arbitrary measures'. With no hint of sympathy or understanding from that quarter, he

4. *Voyage of H.M.S.S. Alert & Discovery: Letters, etc.*, f. 37.
5. *Narrative of a Voyage to the Polar Sea during 1875-76 in H.M. Ships 'Alert' and 'Discovery'*, 1878, pp. 301-10.

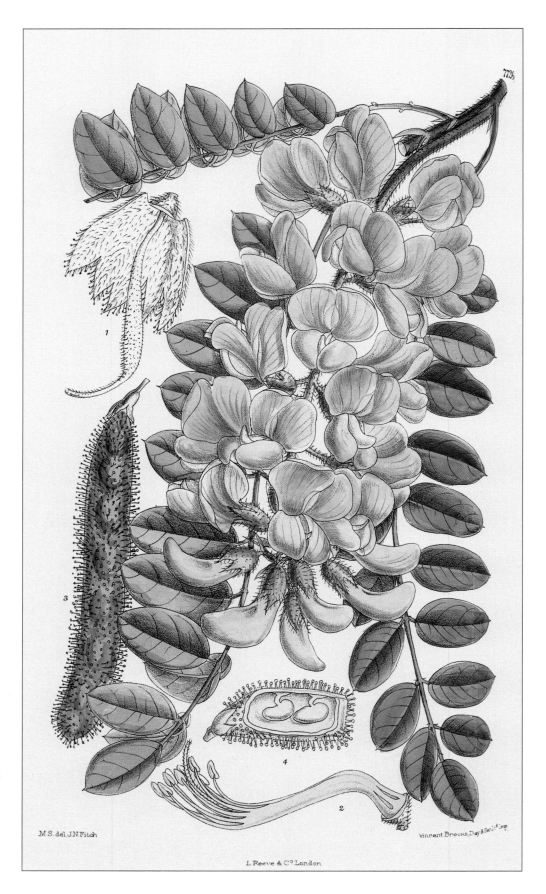

Hand-coloured lithograph of *Robinia neomexicana*, copied from a drawing by Mathilda Smith (*Curtis's Botanical Magazine,* 1900, plate 7726). Collected by Hooker near La Veta Pass.

A B del J.N Fitch lith

Vincent Brooks Day & Son Imp

L.Reeve & Co London

Hand-coloured
lithograph of *Fallugia
paradoxa*, copied from a
drawing by Anne
Barnard. (*Curtis's
Botanical Magazine,*
1882, plate 6660).
Collected by Hooker
on the Sierra Blanca in
southern Colorado.
Flowered at Kew in
July 1877.

told T.H. Huxley that he would resign rather than endure further humiliation, but John Ball advised him 'to make it quite clear that you are not merely or mainly complaining of personal slight but that you are fighting for Kew'.[6] Encouraged by the support of fellow scientists, Hooker vowed to Darwin that 'I am determined that my voice shall not be withered ... I should lose caste altogether if I did not stand up to fight'.[7] When Gladstone remained loyal to Ayrton, he received a memorial in May 1872 from the presidents of the Linnean Society, the Royal Institution, the Royal College of Surgeons, the Royal Geographical Society, the treasurer of the Royal Society, and from Sir Charles Lyell and Charles Darwin deploring Ayrton's 'treating the Director of Kew with personal contumely'. A former Prime Minister, Lord Derby, defended Hooker in a House of Lords debate in July, and the Commons discussed the Kew affair in August. Ayrton, a consummate politician, presented himself as the 'helpless victim of a scientific tyrant'. Sir John Lubbock, Hooker's spokesman, was no match for him. Gladstone wound up the debate with a paternalistic appeal to the two protagonists to forget their differences: 'my right hon. Friend exercising his rule with mildness and Dr Hooker doing his duty in subordination to my right hon. Friend'.

But no matter who his First Commissioner might be Hooker would always resent what he perceived to be bureaucratic interference. He urgently needed an assistant to deal with civil servants, to bring some order into Kew's office procedures, and to relieve him of some of his considerable correspondence with the colonies. The post of Assistant Director had been deleted from the establishment when Hooker became Director in 1865, and when he succeeded in getting it reinstated in 1875, William Thiselton-Dyer was appointed. His new Assistant Director who had been Professor of Botany to the Royal Horticultural Society was just the man Hooker needed – methodical, a stickler for detail, and utterly dependable. He drafted the Director's letters, and took on much of the burden of staff management, leaving Hooker free to welcome important visitors, to carry on with his research, and to undertake his daily inspection of the Gardens. He recast the mandatory annual report which had always received cursory treatment from the two Hookers. Thiselton-Dyer saw it not only as excellent publicity, but also as a source of useful information for botanical institutions and planters in the colonies.

Even Joseph Hooker's attenuated annual reports had conveyed some idea of Kew's involvement with the colonies. It advised the Colonial Office on the introduction of economic plants throughout the Empire, and its report for 1877 boasted that it was now 'the botanical headquarters of the British Empire and its dependencies'. The establishment of a viable rubber industry was one of Kew's most memorable imperial enterprises.

Rubber, now a commercial commodity much in demand, was extracted from three South American trees – *Castilla elastica*, *Hevea brasiliensis* and *Manihot glaziovii*. In 1873 the India Office consulted Hooker about the commercial

6. *Papers relating to Kew, 1861-72. Ayrton Controversy*, f. 45.
7. Hooker to Darwin. 20 October 1871. L. Huxley. *Life and Letters ...* , vol. 2, 1918, p. 167.

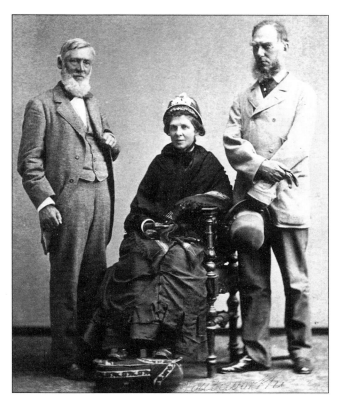

Asa and Mrs Gray and Hooker at San Francisco, September 1877. 'Gray is a man of extraordinary energy and though 5 or 6 years my senior is the younger of the two!' (Hooker to B. Hodgson, 20 October 1877.)

exploitation of India's indigenous rubber tree, *Ficus elastica*, but Hooker favoured the superior latex of *Hevea brasiliensis*. The India Office which decided to establish rubber plantations tempted Hooker with several hundred rubber seeds from Brazil. Six out of a total of twelve seedlings were sent to the Calcutta Botanic Garden. When only one of them survived in India it was agreed that any future consignments of seeds or plants should be despatched to the botanic garden in Ceylon where conditions were believed to be more congenial. Robert Cross, a former Kew gardener who had collected cinchona for the India Office, went to Brazil but few of his seedlings survived. Another collector, H.A. Wickham, had better luck. A restless wanderer, he had earned a living in South America trading in birds' plumage, growing coffee, and occasionally collecting plants. Recommended by Hooker, the India Office engaged him to collect *Hevea* seeds in Brazil. It has been alleged that he smuggled them out of the country, a legend which this rather flamboyant character fostered, embellishing it over the years. On 14 June 1876 he arrived with more than 60,000 Brazilian rubber seeds at Kew Gardens where Thiselton-Dyer took charge of them. They were quickly sown in propagating houses and two months later nearly 2,000 seedlings were shipped to Ceylon. There they were planted in a special nursery to supply the needs of the island, the Indian sub-continent and South East Asia. The rubber industry in Malaya sprang from this successful initiative by the India Office in partnership with Kew Gardens.

Thiselton-Dyer had proved his competence by the efficient way he had handled the rubber transaction, and so Hooker had no doubts that his deputy could look after Kew Gardens while he took leave of absence to tour North America. Asa Gray, Harvard's Professor of Botany, who had been trying to entice him there for some years, was an old family friend and the leading exponent of Darwinism in the United States. Hooker wanted to come not only because he had never been there before, but also because Gray shared his enthusiasm for plant geography. For many years Gray had been identifying floristic relationships between Japan and his own country. Hooker was intrigued by the sharp division between the Arctic flora of America and Greenland. So an invitation to both of them from the geologist in charge of the United States Geological and Geographical Survey to join a surveying party in the Rocky Mountains was irresistible.

6857.

M.S.del J.N.Fitch lith.   Vincent Brooks.Day & Son.Imp.

L.Reeve & C.º London.

Hand-coloured lithograph of *Rosa pisocarpa*, copied from a drawing by Matilda Smith. (*Curtis's Botanical Magazine*, 1886, plate 6857). Collected by Hooker in Upper Sacromento Valley, California at 4,000–6,000 feet.

He sailed for New York on 28 June 1877, leaving Kew in the capable hands of Thiselton-Dyer, now his son-in-law, having just married his daughter Harriet. Thiselton-Dyer obligingly deferred part of his honeymoon to take charge of Kew Gardens during his absence. Hooker was accompanied by his old friend Major-General Richard Strachey, who had served in India and had collected plants and rocks in the Himalayas.

The trip turned out to be much more of a social occasion than he had anticipated. Starting with Boston, he was wined and dined in every city they passed through. Wherever he travelled in the world Hooker found plants that

recalled the English countryside. In the United States it was wild chicory carpeting acres of of ground, and banks covered by ox-eye daisies and mayweed, probably brought to the New World by early settlers. The hills of the Alleghanies reminded him of 'the tamer parts of Wales'. To his surprise he found *Fragaria indica* from India happily at home in the streets of Savannah.

They did not get down to serious botanising until they reached Colorado and entered the Rockies via La Veta Pass. Their first camp site was at 9,000 feet on the fringe of a huge pine forest in the Sangre de Cristo Mountains. Judging by a photograph of their encampment showing them dining at a cloth-covered table with a servant in attendance, they lived in reasonable comfort. The arduous climb of Sierra Blanca, forcing a way through dense aspen shrubbery and conifers to 13,000 feet where they stayed the night, reminded them painfully of their age. They collected on the summit before returning to lonely Fort Garland 'very tired and in rags'. 'This is a very active and indeed hard life', Hooker wrote to his wife. When they left Colorado for Denver he had already harvested about 500 species.

At Salt Lake City he called on Brigham Young who reminded him of 'a stout, elderley and thoroughly respectable butler'. The Mormon leader failed to impress him but California's forests certainly did. The various species of conifers, their enormous size, and the vast areas they covered was 'quite bewildering', he told Brian Hodgson. 'You may travel for weeks in forests of 8 to 10 pines, spruces, silver firs, etc. of which most of the species are never under 150 and often 250 feet high and 20–30 ft in girth'.[8] He was shown two genera described as 'the vegetable wonders of the world', the Coastal Redwood (*Sequoia sempervirens*), and the Sierra Redwood (*Sequoiadendron*

Encampment in the Rockies, La Veta Pass, Colorado at 9,000 feet, 25 July 1877. Asa Gray is squatting on the ground with some specimens of *Abies concolor* beside him; Hooker next to him; Sir Richard Strachey, map in hand, seated at the table.

8. Hooker to Hodgson. 20 October 1877. *Letters from J.D. Hooker.*

249

giganteum). These trees could reach 300 feet or more in height with girths of about thirty feet, and their massive size was matched by their longevity. Ring counts have revealed a life-span of up to 2,000 years for the *Sequoia* and more than 3,000 years for the related genus. In 1878 Hooker told a meeting at the Royal Institution of Great Britain that the 'doom of these noble groves is sealed. No less than five saw-mills have recently been established in the most luxuriant of them, and one of these mills alone cut in 1875 two million feet of big-tree lumber ... before the century is out the two sequoias may be known only as herbarium specimens and garden ornaments', a pessimistic prediction which fortunately has not been entirely realised.

Hooker covered 8,000 miles by train and waggon during his ten weeks' stay and, with the exception of the Yosemite Valley, 'no one place, nor all together, had the interest concentrated in Sikkim, and as to the mountain scenery it is a bagatelle compared with any little bit of the Himalaya or Alps, whether as regards beauty, bulk, grandeur or interest'.[9] Nevertheless it had been a worthwhile trip; about 1,000 specimens for the Kew herbarium and the crystallisation of a viable theory on the migration of plants in North America. He summarised the tour and his preliminary findings in the issue of *Nature* for 25 October 1877, further amplified in his lecture on 'The Distribution of the North American Flora', delivered at the Royal Institution in 1878. Gray had wondered for a long time why the similarities in the floras of North East Asia and the eastern United States were not also replicated in the western United States. He assumed that at some distant time in the past the northern continents had been joined or had been so close as to allow a commingling of their floras. He and Hooker reasoned that prolonged glaciation which had wiped out practically all the Miocene flora in western United States had not afflicted the eastern side so severely. Consequently much of its original flora relating to that of Asia had survived. Gray spent a couple of months at Kew in 1880 when the two men elaborated and developed this proposition in a report which was published by the United States Geological Survey in 1882.[10]

Hooker had started his American trip just a few days after he had learned that he had been gazetted a Knight Commander of the Order of the Star of India (K.C.S.I.), an honour he had long coveted. For years he had nursed a grievance that his services to India had not been officially recognized. Late in 1869 he had accepted the Companion of the Bath (C.B.), but admitted to Sir Charles Lyell that the Star of India would have been more appropriate 'for all I have done for Indian science has been wholly gratuitous. India never gave me a penny'.[11] The Government, he declared, was much indebted to him. He had rescued the disintegrating plant collections of Griffith and other botanists from neglect in the cellars of the East India Company. He had surveyed and mapped Sikkim. 'I was seized, imprisoned, and lost all my instruments, etc. through their [Indian] Government's bad management; and they actually *sold on Government's behalf* the presents the Rajah made me after my release'. His

9. Hooker to Hodgson, 20 October 1877, *Letters from J.D. Hooker.*
10. Gray and Hooker. 'The Vegetation of the Rocky Mountain Region and a Comparison with that of other Parts of the World'. *Bulletin of U.S. Geological Survey*, vol. 6, 1882, 1-62.
11. Hooker to Lyell. 14 October 1869. Ibid.

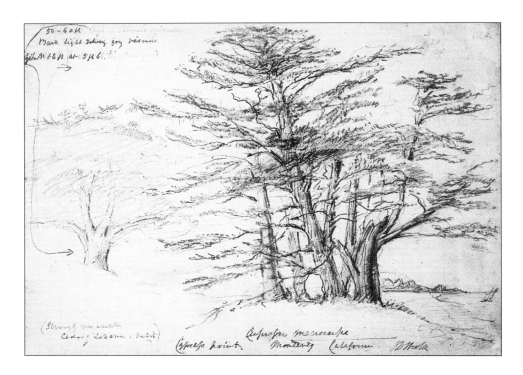

Pencil drawing by Hooker of *Cupressus macrocarpa* in Monteray, California. (*Family of the late R.A. Hooker.*)

sense of injustice led him to make an exaggerated claim: 'they owe the annexation of the province [of Sikkim] and the Government sites of the tea and cinchona cultivation to my misfortune and my energy'. He refused the award of an ordinary knighthood bestowed for duties performed as Director of Kew Gardens: 'they might have offered it in an Order that indicates special service'.[12] Sir Robert Murchison and Sir Charles Lyell had reminded the Secretary of State for India, the Duke of Argyll, that Hooker was a deserving candidate for the K.C.S.I. One can imagine Hooker's irritation when he read in the *Telegraph* that Richard Strachey of the Royal Bengal Engineers had been awarded the K.C.S.I.

> This rather complicates matters for the Duke [of Argyll] could not offer me a lower position in the Order than that R. Strachey will hold! ... Strachey made a similar scientific survey of Kumaon to what I did of Sikkim, but Kumaon was a well-known country, and Sikkim utterly unknown; he spent some 5 months at it – I spent 2 years – and he never published his work, whilst I have mine, and a vast deal more besides. Strachey's Indian career is not distinguished except   in a scientific point of view, and I must confess that much as I should prize the 'Star of India' I would [rather] be left out than be placed in an inferior rank to his; he is already C.S.I. and for the Duke to give me this when Strachey was made K.S.I. would be to offer me his *leavings*.[13]

When, however, Hooker discovered that holders of the K.C.S.I. were limited to twenty-five Europeans, he ceased his agitation and urged Lyell to withdraw a petition he was about to submit. 'I am quite content with C.B., though after all I have now heard and seen, I am not altogether surprised that folk should think it a small affair to give for the Antarctic and India and Kew together'.[14] He expected the C.B., in the fullness of time, to lead to a K.C.B. (Knight Commander of the Order of the Bath). During the Aryton crisis Lyell, with a poor sense of timing, had proposed to Gladstone that Hooker

12. Hooker to Darwin.
14 November 1869. L. Huxley.
Life and Letters ... , vol. 2, 1918,
p. 146.
13. Hooker to Lyell. 1869.
Letters from J.D. Hooker.
14. Hooker to Lyell.
29 November 1869. Ibid.

Hooker saw this fine specimen of a white oak, *Quercus lobata,* at Chico in the United States: 100 feet high, girth of 24 feet and 150 feet spread of branches. Subsequently called 'Sir Joseph Hooker's Oak'.

might be appeased by being made a K.C.B., but there was little likelihood that the Prime Minister would antagonise his minister with such a gesture. Hooker who had heard a rumour that he was to be offered a K.C.M.G. (Knight Commander of the Order of St Michael and St George), firmly believed that the Prime Minister had subsequently blocked it.

The K.C.M.G. was eventually offered to him in March 1874, this time by the Secretary of State for the Colonies, for services rendered to the colonies. Though tempted by the lustre it would add to Kew's reputation, he declined it because, so he told friends, it would be seen as having been given for his presidency of the Royal Society, and the two previous Presidents had received the K.C.B., a superior award. 'The conferring it on me now would therefore be an inadequate recognition of the presidency and not as an ample reward of my services to the colonies'.[15] With Hooker rejecting the K.C.M.G. and with no vacancy for a K.C.B., the Cabinet in 1877 bent the rules that limited the K.C.S.I. to the Indian Service in order to recommend to the Queen Hooker's admission to the Order of the Star of India. As frequently happened, Hooker's persistence eventually won through. Triumphant, he gave Darwin the good news.

> I have always regarded the Star of India as the most honourable of all such distinctions — it is very limited (to K.C.S.I.s) — is never, like K.C.B. given by favor or on personal considerations, and it has a flavor of hard work under difficulties, of obstacles overcome, and of brilliant deeds that is very attractive. Assuredly I would rather go down to posterity as one of the 'Star of India' than as of any other dignity whatever that the Crown can offer.[16]

After all this striving there is a gloss of feigned indifference in his deprecating remark to Brian Hodgson that he 'would infinitely rather be plain J.D.H'.[17]

15. Hooker to Hodgson. 10 April 1874. *Letters from J.D. Hooker.*
16. Hooker to Darwin. 18 June 1877. L. Huxley. Life and Letters ... , vol. 2, 1918, p. 150.
17. Hooker to Hodgson. 2 June 1877. *Letters from J.D. Hooker.*

Chapter 16

A Pioneer Plant Geographer

As well as assessing morphological characters, a taxonomist needs to know the provenance and geographical range of plants in order to identify and classify them. There is an interdisciplinary relationship between the taxonomist, the ecologist and the phytogeographer. Plant geography defines the distribution of the world's vegetation at the taxonomic levels of families, genera and species. Plant ecology, a closely related study, examines plant communities within their environment.

Alexander von Humboldt, the founder of plant geography, was revered by Darwin as 'the greatest scientific traveller who has ever lived'. His achievements and the account of his travels in the Spanish territories of South America during 1799 to 1804 inspired both Darwin and Wallace. He himself had become infected with the urge to explore foreign lands after meeting Georg Forster, a naturalist on Captain Cook's second voyage. He brought to his field studies the skills of a botanist, a zoologist and a geologist; he pioneered climatology and developed techniques of isothermal plotting; he perceived that plants ascended mountains in floristic zones. His classic *Essai sur la Géographie des Plantes* (1807) demonstrated to the aspiring plant geographer the need to seek evidence in geology, palaeontology, meteorology and evolutionary theories. Humboldt, who supported Hooker's candidature for the chair of botany at Edinburgh University in 1845, must have viewed him as an exemplary follower. He admired Hooker's manipulation of data from different disciplines to trace patterns in the spread of plants in the southern hemisphere and in northern India.

Intimations of an awareness of plant distribution appeared early in Hooker's life.

> ... my father used to take me on excursions in the Highlands, where I fished a good deal, but also botanised; and well I remember on one occasion, that, after returning home, I built up by a heap of stones a representation of one of the mountains I had ascended, and stuck upon it specimens of the mosses I had collected on it, at heights relative to those at which I had gathered them. This was the dawn of my love for geographical botany.[1]

Assumptions and theories regarding the geographical distribution of plants gradually emerged and developed during his travels. By the time he came to write the seminal introduction to his *Flora Tasmaniae,* he had reasoned that there

1. Address at the anniversary dinner of the Royal Society, 30 November 1887.

were 'two classes of agents' which 'had a powerful effect in determining the distribution of plants; these are changes of climate, and changes in the relative positions and elevations of land'. In a letter to George Bentham sent from the Falkland Islands in which he confessed that the 'geography of plants is a favorite subject with me',[2] he adds a curious fact about two of Bentham's favourite families – Labiatae and Leguminosae. He had not found a single genus from these families in the Auckland Islands, Kerguelen's Land, Campbell Island, Tierra del Fuego or the Falklands. This 'absence constitutes one of the most remarkable features in the vegetation of those parts of the world'. Equally remarkable was the prevalence of European genera in the southern hemisphere. The similarity between the flora of Tierra del Fuego and isolated islands thousands of miles to the east defied a convincing explanation; 'some of these detached spots are much closer to the African and Australian continents, whose vegetation these do not assume, than to the American'.[3] Were plants dispersed by ocean currents, prevailing winds or some other means? Darwin encouraged him to ponder these and related issues in a mutually informative correspondence begun shortly after Hooker's return to England in 1843.

> This led to me sending him an outline of the conclusions I had formed regarding the distribution of plants in the southern regions, and the necessity of assuming the destruction of considerable areas of land to account for the relations of the flora of the so-called Antarctic Islands. I do not suppose that any of these ideas were new to him, but they led to an animated and lengthy correspondence full of instruction.[4]

Immersed as he was in writing the botany of the Antarctic voyage, Hooker found time to identify the collection of plants Darwin had indiscriminately collected in the Galapagos archipelago some 600 miles off the coast of Ecuador. Supplemented by the collection made by James Macrae in these islands in 1826, Darwin hoped that Hooker would be able to verify that the plants, like the birds and the sea-shells he had collected, displayed South American connections. The Linnean Society published Hooker's enumeration of Galapagos plants in 1851.[5] Of the one hundred and five flowering plants he examined, one hundred were new species, among them many belonging to Compositae. He remarked on the scarcity of monocotyledonous plants. He was astonished by the exclusivity of the flora of several of the islands. He believed that a majority of the plants came from Central and South America; littoral species were probably introduced by ocean currents, others possibly by winds or birds. He told Darwin, who was obsessed by the mechanics of seed dispersal, that he had not found any plants particularly adapted for transmission. 'It is I think high time [to] throw overboard laying too much stress on the subject of migration of seeds', wrote Hooker, 'except in cases of lands we know to have been recently formed, or, from devastating causes, to be recently clothed with vegetation'.[6] When Hooker read a paper to a meeting at the Linnean Society on the plants of the Galapagos in 1846,

2. Hooker to Bentham. 27 November 1842. *J.D. Hooker, Correspondence, 1839-45, from Antarctic Expedition*, f. 140.
3. *Flora Antarctica*, vol. 2, 1847, p. 211.
4. L. Huxley, *Life and Letters ...*, vol. 1, 1918, p. 488.
5. *Transactions of Linnean Society*, vol. 20, 1851, pp. 163-262.
6. Hooker to Darwin. 23 February-6 March 1844. *Correspondence of Charles Darwin*, vol. 3, 1987, p. 13.

Darwin rated it 'the best essay on geogr. distribution in any class'.[7]

Hooker's confidence manifestly grew as he considered his notes, studied his specimens, and talked with colleagues. Now he spoke authoritatively on the need for precise procedures in plant geography:

> ... all seem to dread the making Bot. Geog. too exact a science, they find it far easier to speculate than to employ the inductive process. The first steps to tracing the progress of the creation of vegetation is to know the proportions in which the groups appear in different localities, & more particularly the relation which exists between the floras of the localities, a relation which must be expressed in numbers to be at all tangible.[8]

As the early parts of the *Flora Antarctica* rolled off the printing press, Darwin was delighted to see published so many of the points they had raised in their letters. He kept suggesting new projects for his friend to tackle: a flora of the Sandwich Islands modelled on the Galapagos flora and, more ambitious still, a thorough review of all insular floras – 'what a truly splendid paper you c^d make'.[9]

Hooker's Indian interlude is unquestionably the best-documented of all his travels, consisting of his published letters, his *Himalayan Journals*, the *Flora Indica*, his *Sketch of the Flora of British India* and his *Flora of British India*. All contain observations and conclusions on the distribution of the country's vegetation. Although J.F. Royle had already drawn attention to the prevalence of European genera, Hooker, nevertheless, was still surprised to discover how much of the Indian flora were immigrants from Europe and the East:

> ... sitting at my tent door [at Tallum in Sikkim], I could, without rising from the ground, gather forty-three plants, of which all but two belonged to English genera. In the rich soil about the cottages were crops of dock, shepherd's purse, *Thlaspi arvensi*, *Cynoglossum* of two kinds (one used as a pot-herb), balsams, nettle, *Galeopsis*, mustard radish and turnip. On the neighbouring hills, which I explored up to 15,000 feet, I found many fine plants, partaking more or less of the Siberian type, of which *Corydalis*, *Leguminosae*, *Artemesia*, and *Pedicularis*, are familiar instances. I gathered upwards of 200 species, nearly all belonging to north European genera.[10]

The Himalayan hemlock (*Tsuga brunnoniana*) belonged to a genus found in North America and Japan. The flora of the west, north and east met in the Himalayas which possessed relatively few endemics. He identified 'geographical alliances or affinities' with Australia, the Malay Archipelago, China, Japan, Siberia and Africa. He assumed, for example, 'that the majority of the many plants common to the Himalaya and Java migrated over continuous intervening land, which had been broken up by geological causes, chiefly by subsidence'.[11] While Hooker conceded a role for winds, seas and animals in plant migration, he stuck to the concept of former land masses as a more feasible explanation.

In December 1853 the last issue of the first part of *Flora Novae-Zelandiae*

7. *Correspondence of Charles Darwin*, vol. 3, 1987, p. 13.
8. Ibid., p. 168.
9. Darwin to Hooker. 8 February 1847. *Correspondence of Charles Darwin*, vol. 4, 1988, p. 11.
10. *Himalayan Journals*, 1891, p. 335.
11. *Flora Indica*, 1855, p. 41.

appeared. In addition to a large number of endemics, the country's flora indicated affinities with that of Australia in particular and of South America, the islands of the Antarctic, Tierra del Fuego and Europe. Robert Brown, the naturalist on Captain Flinders's Australasian expedition in 1801-5, had identified 150 European plants in Australia. A microscopic examination of the structure of the seeds of plants common to Europe and New Zealand convinced Hooker that they possessed no special facility for trans-oceanic or aerial transport. He and other progressive botanists did not subscribe to the conventional theory of the double or multiple creation of species. Yet 'how does it happen that *Edwardsia grandiflora* inhabits both New Zealand and South America, or *Oxalis magellanica* both these localities and Tasmania?'[12] The seeds of these particular species could never survive aerial or oceanic currents. During H.M.S. *Erebus*'s voyage in the Antarctic Ocean he had realised the impossibility of such turbulent seas carrying seeds from Tierra del Fuego to Kerguelen's Land. It was then that he began to speculate on 'the possibility of the plants of the Southern Ocean being the remains of a flora that had once spread over a larger and more continuous tract of land than now exists in that ocean; and that the peculiar Antarctic genera and species may be the vestiges of a flora characterized by the predominance of plants which are now scattered throughout the southern islands'.[13] In the *Flora Antarctica*[14] he had already conceded that the Antarctic islands might be the summits of a submerged mountain chain, a line of thought that had been prompted by the geologist Charles Lyell and the botanist Edward Forbes. Lyell had postulated that climate which influenced the migration of plants and animals, was itself dependent on geological changes which might have reshaped existing land surfaces. Forbes believed that plants had migrated overland while Britain was joined to the continent, and that the familial relationship between some Irish and Spanish species suggested the former existence of an Atlantic continent, the mythical Atlantis, perhaps. Hooker did not propose a former continuous land link between South America and New Zealand, but perhaps an intermediate land where the plants now common to both territories once grew. Asa Gray who reviewed the Introductory Essay in the *Flora Novae-Zelandiae* in the *American Journal of Science and Arts*,[15] impressed by such theories on geographical distribution, reprinted it *in toto* in his article.

Another review, this time by Hooker himself, in his father's *Journal of Botany and Kew Garden Miscellany*, was occasioned by the publication in 1856 of Alphonse de Candolle's *Géographie Botanique Raisonée* in two substantial volumes. This comprehensive survey of families, genera and species from a geographical viewpoint demanded serious consideration. Notwithstanding the fact that Hooker deplored 'the vagueness of its principles, the inexactness of its methods, the puzzling complexity of its phenomena', he did not entirely escape its influence. For instance, he endorsed de Candolle's insistence on the

12. *Flora Novae-Zelandiae.* Introductory Essay, p. xix.
13. Ibid., p. xxi.
14. pp. 210, 368.
15. vol. 17, 1854, pp. 241-52, 334-50.

need for statistical analysis in studying plant populations. Darwin also approved such precise methodology regretting that zoologists 'seldom go into strict and disagreeable arithmetic like you botanists so wisely do'. 'De Candolle's great work closed one epoch in the history of the subject,' wrote Asa Gray, 'and Hooker's name is the first that appears in the ensuing one'.

Darwin who thought quite highly of de Candolle's work offered to show Hooker 'the several subjects in which I fancy he is original'. He despaired of Hooker's stubborn refusal to accept the 'accidental means of dispersion of plants', a contentious issue between them. Conscious of the crucial role of plant geography in their respective research, the subject inevitably dominated much of their correspondence. 'It is no exaggeration to assert that the birth of the modern approach to plant geography is documented in the correspondence between these two men' (James Affolter)[16]. Darwin paraded his evidence and views on geographical distribution in two chapters of *The Origin of Species* (1859). He had previously sent a manuscript version of them to Hooker whose wife placed them in a drawer where the children kept their scribbling paper. A quarter of the sheets had disappeared before it was discovered that they had used them for drawing. Fortunately Darwin had retained an earlier draft, 'otherwise the loss would have killed me'. One of the topics discussed by Darwin concerned islands, now submerged, that might have served as stepping stones in the migration of plants by 'accidental means'. He described the experiments he had carried out since 1855 at his home in Kent to determine what those 'means' might have been.

To test whether any seeds were impervious to the harmful effects of seawater, Darwin filled a large tub of salted water with forty or fifty partly opened bottles of different seeds. He germinated sixty-four out of eighty-seven kinds of seeds after an immersion of twenty-eight days; a few survived a soaking of 137 days. Smaller seeds usually sank within a few days; larger ones could remain afloat for a considerable time. He compared the buoyancy of ripe and dried seeds; ripe hazel nuts, for instance, sank immediately, but dried ones floated for ninety days and germinated when planted. His general conclusions were that many seeds could survive twenty-eight days at sea during which time Atlantic currents might carry them over 900 miles. He challenged Hooker to an experiment: to collect seeds of all the European plants growing in the Azores to determine whether they could endure long immersion thereby suggesting that they might have arrived at the archipelago by oceanic currents. 'I believe you are afraid to send me a ripe *Edwardsia* pod', he teased his friend, 'for fear I should float it from New Zealand to Chile'.

Satisfied that oceanic transportation was a possibility, Darwin now considered other agents. Birds, for example. When he found seeds in the droppings of small birds, he wondered whether they would germinate after being voided. Triumphantly he informed Hooker that a seed had germinated

16. 'The "Antarctic" Flora: Researches of Charles Darwin and Joseph Hooker'. *Contributions. University of Michigan Herbarium,* vol. 14, 1980, pp. 1-9.

after twenty-one and a half hours in an owl's stomach. 'This, according to ornithologists' calculation, would carry it God knows how many miles; but I think an owl might go in storm at this time 400 or 500 miles'. Then he remembered seeing dead land birds drifting in the sea. If they had recently eaten seeds, would these germinate when the bodies were washed ashore? A sacrificial pigeon was slaughtered, floated for thirty days in salt water, and, lo and behold, the seeds in its crop had subsequently 'grown splendidly'. He looked at other ways birds could carry seeds. They ate fresh fish which included seeds in their diet. He inserted seeds, therefore, into the stomach of dead fish which he fed to fishing eagles, storks and pelicans at London zoo. He proved that the viability of some seeds was not diminished by this double digestion. When one of the partridges a gamekeeper shot was found to have twenty-two grains of dry earth and a large pebble on one foot, Darwin saw yet another method of transportation. Earth embedded in driftwood might also contain seeds. Sailors reported seeing earth and stones on icebergs, one even had the nest of a land bird on it. He suspected that floes had deposited seeds on Kerguelen's Land, Tierra del Fuego and New Zealand. Seeds were accidentally conveyed in ships' cargoes. All the evidence he had gathered had convinced Darwin that there were many ways by which seeds could be dispersed, and he was not alone in thinking this. Alfred Russel Wallace had seen rafts or floating islands of vegetation in the seas around the Moluccas, home to small animals as well as plants. Even sceptical Hooker conceded that plants had reached the Galapagos archipelago by the 'accidental means' described by Darwin. 'I quite agree that we only differ in *degree* about means of dispersal, & that I think a satisfactory amount of accordance. You put in very striking manner the mutations of our continents, & I quite agree; I doubt only about our oceans',[17] wrote Darwin.

In all his research Darwin sought indisputable facts through observation and experiments. He was reluctant to accept the former existence of land bridges without proof: 'it shocks my philosophy to create land without some other & independent evidence'.[18] 'I cannot gulp down your continent', he protested.[19] In his autobiography he recalled that Hooker 'was almost ... indignant because I had rejected with scorn the notion that a continent had formerly extended between Australia and South America'.[20] They never resolved this difference of opinion but recent research has confirmed that they were both right in some respects. Plants have been distributed over great distances by adventitious means, and movements in the earth's crust could explain peculiarities in the dispersal of species. The presence of fossil remains of the same species of animals in different continents has persuaded scientists that these continents had been physically joined at one time. A Kew botanist, Robert Melville, believed it 'evident that during the Cretaceous the circum-Antarctic land bridge postulated by plant geographers from Hooker to van Steenis actually existed. The reason for such

17. Darwin to Hooker. 29 January 1859. *Correspondence of Charles Darwin*, vol. 7, 1991, p. 236.
18. Darwin to Hooker. 5 June 1855. *Correspondence of Charles Darwin*, vol. 5, 1989, p. 344.
19. Darwin to Hooker. 5 July 1856. *Correspondence of Charles Darwin*, vol. 6, 1990, p. 170.
20. Autobiography, edited by Nora Barlow, 1958, p. 106.

sub-Antarctic distribution as that of *Juncus scheuzerroides* in Kerguelen, Tasmania, New Zealand, Fuegia and the Falklands is now clear'.[21] Continental drift, a theory first propounded by the German meteorologist and astronomer, Alfred Wegener in 1915, envisaged all the continents forming a huge landmass which he called 'Pangaea', the Greek for 'all lands'. This supercontinent began to split about 200 million years ago, according to A.C. du Toit, into two distinct continents: Gondwanaland (comprising what is now South America, Africa, Madagascar, India, Australasia, Antarctica, and fragments such as Kerguelen, the Crozets, Prince Edward and the Marion islands) and Laurasia which eventually separated into North America, Europe and much of Asia. For today's biogeographers it is an hypothesis that offers a plausible explanation for the migration of species of plants and animals.

Darwin and Hooker continued to argue about plant geography, each defending his own point of view but sometimes making small concessions. 'About New Zealand, at last I am coming round, and admit it must have been connected with some terra firma, but I will die rather than admit Australia'.[22] Darwin gloated when he read an article in the *Journal of Linnean Society* [23] that the author, H.H. Travers, had picked up a seed of *Edwardsia* washed ashore on the Chatham Islands in the Pacific. 'I remember your pitching into me with terrible ferocity because I said I thought the seed of *Edwardsia* might have been floated from Chili to New Zealand; now what do you say, my young man, to the three young trees of the same size on one spot alone of the island, and with the cast-up pod on the shore?... The distance I see is 360 miles'.[24] Before Hooker spoke on insular floras at the Nottingham meeting of the British Association for the Advancement of Science in August 1866, Darwin counselled him to 'be honest, and admit how little is known on the subject' of the casual transportation of seeds.[25] Hooker reassured him. 'You must not let me worry you. I am an obstinate pig, but you must not be miserable at my looking at the same thing in a different light from you. I must get to the bottom of this question, and that is all I can do'.[26] The fauna and flora of oceanic islands were key elements in Darwin's theory of evolution. Hooker who had visited many of them during his Antarctic voyage recognised that their very remoteness 'furnish the best materials for a rigid comparison of the effects of geographical position and the various meteorological phaenomena in vegetation, and for acquiring a knowledge of the great laws according to which plants are contributed over the face of the globe'.[27] He formulated some basic tenets regarding them in the essay prefacing his *Flora Tasmaniae* :

> The total number of species they contain seems to be invariably less than an equal continental area possesses and the relative number of species to genera ... is also much less than in similar continental areas. The further an island is from a continent, the smaller is its flora numerically, the more peculiar is its vegetation, and the smaller its proportion of species to genera.[28]

21. *Nature,* vol. 211, 9 July 1916.
22. Darwin to Hooker. 26 September 1863. F. Darwin. *More Letters of Charles Darwin,* vol. 1, 1903, p. 474.
23. 'Notes on the Chatham Islands'. *Journal of Linnean Society,* vol. 9, 1865, pp. 135-44.
24. Darwin to Hooker. 22, 28 October 1865. F. Darwin. *More Letters of Charles Darwin*, vol. 1, 1903, p. 475.
25. Darwin to Hooker. 3 August 1866. F. Darwin. *More Letters of Charles Darwin*, vol. 1, 1903, p. 483.
26. Hooker to Darwin. 7 August 1866. L. Huxley. *Life and Letters ...* , vol. 2, 1918, p. 99.
27. *Flora Antarctica*, vol. 1, 1847, p. xii.
28. pp. xiv-xv.

He told his Nottingham audience that 'those peculiar insular plants which have no affinity with continental ones, are relics of a far more ancient vegetation than now prevails on the mother continent'.[29] He put before them Darwin's 'many powerful arguments in support of trans-oceanic migration', and concluded that 'the great objection to the continental extension hypothesis is, that it may be said to account for everything but to explain nothing; it proves too much: whilst the hypothesis of trans-oceanic migration, though it leaves a multitude of fact unexplained, offers a rational solution of many of the most puzzling phenomena that oceanic plants present'.[30] When Darwin read the lecture in the *Gardeners' Chronicle*, his worse fears allayed, he was delighted: 'you never, in my opinion, wrote anything better'.[31] Still he could not resist telling Hooker about some old notes he had recently unearthed: 'one, that twenty-two species of European birds occasionally arrive as chance wanderers to the Azores; and, secondly, that trunks of American trees have been known to be washed on the shores of the Canary Islands, by the Gulf-stream, which returns southward from the Azores'.[32] To the end of his life Darwin maintained an interest in the geographical dissemination of plant species, but with so many other projects in hand, he never found time to add to the theories propounded in the *Origin of Species*.

Hooker, however, continued to collect data, to evaluate new evidence, and to promulgate the results of his investigations in articles and lectures. When a solitary specimen of *Phylica arborea* was found in Amsterdam Island in the South Indian Ocean it set him wondering how the tree had got there. When the 'Transit of Venus' expedition of 1874-75 brought back new specimens from Kerguelen's Land, Hooker revised his flora of the archipelago but saw no reason to change his opinion that former land between Fuegia and Kerguelen Island, possibly as islands, constituted 'the forlorn hope of the botanical geographer'.[33] In his address as President of the Geographical Section of the British Association for the Advancement of Science's Jubilee meeting at York in 1881, he reviewed the progress of plant geography during the past half century.[34] He concentrated on its pioneers: Humboldt 'the founder', E. Forbes 'its reformer', and Darwin 'its latest and greatest lawyergiver'. Modestly, he said little about his own role. That was put right by the anniversary meeting in May 1883 of the Royal Geographical Society which awarded him its Royal Medal for the Encouragement of Geographical Science and Discovery 'for his eminent services to scientific geography, extending through a long series of years and over a large portion of the globe, ... and more especially for his long continued researches in botanical geography'. George Bentham, a close friend and collaborator, said that the Introductory Essay to the *Flora Tasmaniae* and 'the great memoir [by Hooker] on the *Distribution of Arctic Plants* were only less epoch-making than the *Origin* itself'.[35]

29. 'Lecture on Insular Floras', 1896, p. 26. Also in *Gardeners' Chronicle*, 1867, pp.6-7, 27, 50-51, 75-76 and *Journal of Botany*, 1867, pp. 23-31.
30. Ibid., p. 33.
31. Darwin to Hooker. 9 January 1867. F. Darwin. *More Letters of Charles Darwin*, vol. 1, 1903, p. 492.
32. Darwin to Hooker. 17 March 1867. Ibid., vol. 2, 1903, p.3.
33. *Philosophical Transactions of Royal Society*, vol. 168, 1879, pp. 5-6.
34. *Report of 51st Meeting of B.A.A.S.*, 1882, pp. 727-38.
35. *Journal of Botany*, 1912, p. 4.

Oil painting of Kangchenjunga from Darjeeling by Marianne North who stayed at the hill station in 1878. The mountains 'formed the most graceful snow curves, and no painting could give an idea of its size. The best way seemed to me to be to attempt no middle distance, but merely foreground and blue mistiness of mountain over mountain. The foregrounds were most lovely: ferns, rattans, and trees festooned and covered with creepers, also picturesque villages and huts'. (M. North. *Recollections of a Happy Life,* 1892.) (See also coloured figure on page 10.)

Chapter 17

AN ACTIVE RETIREMENT

Hooker who had never enjoyed administrative chores, had become extremely irritated by them by his early sixties. 'I do wish I could throw off my official duties here', he moaned to Darwin; 'I am getting weary of them'.[1] He claimed he could not afford to retire, but when his salary was increased in 1882 it made retirement on a reasonable pension feasible. In the meanwhile Kew Gardens still demanded his attention. Not all his duties were disagreeable. He was able to negotiate two generous donations to Kew. When the contents of the India Museum, founded by the East India Company, were dispersed by the India Office in 1879/80, Kew got all its ethnobotanical material and over 3,000 flower drawings by Indian artists to add to those Hooker had acquired in 1858. In 1880 a gallery to house Marianne North's paintings was built in the grounds at the artist's expense. A woman of independent means who had gone round the world painting plants in their habitats, she presented over 600 oils to which she added more as she continued her travels. Her Indian tour had taken her to the hill station at Darjeeling where she tried to record the grandeur of the Snowy

1. Hooker to Darwin. 9 September 1881. L. Huxley. *Life and Letters ...* , vol. 2, 1918, p. 227.

Charles Robert Darwin (1809-1882).

Mountains, a view Hooker had admired from Brian Hodgson's cottage.

1882, the year in which Miss North's gallery was opened to the public, was notable for two other events. Hooker had recently decided that the second edition of Steudel's *Nomenclator Botanicus* (1840), the standard work on the names of genera and species, needed drastic revision. Darwin who had experienced the confusion of plant names, offered financial support as a gesture of his appreciation for all the assistance Kew and its Director had given him. Work on the revision started in February 1882, a few months before Darwin died, but his family honoured his intention. When the first volume was published in 1892, Hooker had wanted to call it *Index Darwinianus* or *Nomenclator Darwinaeus* but eventually chose *Index Kewensis*. Still kept up to date by the regular publication of supplements, it is an indispensable reference book for all plant taxonomists.

Charles Darwin died on 19 April 1882 and Hooker was one of the pallbearers at his funeral in Westminster Abbey. Their correspondence over nearly forty years chronicles a mutual indebtedness, each supplying the other with observations and facts, each supportive and encouraging. Such collaboration never obstructed or deflected their independent thought, and similar conclusions were reached through their own research. In some respects Hooker regarded himself a pupil of the older man. Darwin who valued his conversations with such a perceptive protégé confessed that 'he had learned more from Hooker than from any other colleague or friend'. This intimate relationship fostered first by each having experienced a voyage of discovery and by a love of Nature, was strengthened by a recognition of personal integrity and reliability. 'What a candid honest fellow you are, too candid and too honest', wrote Darwin who even found disagreements rewarding: 'fighting a battle with you clears my mind wonderfully'. Hooker's address on the occasion of the unveiling of a statue of Darwin in the University Museum at Oxford in 1899[2] paid tribute to his late friend's industry, his perseverance despite constant illness, and his ability to marshal facts, even 'turning to account the waste observations, failures, and even the blunders of his predecessors in whatever subject of inquiry'.

In 1883 the last volume of the *Genera Plantarum* was published, a model of concise descriptions of families and genera. His co-author, George Bentham, died the following year. Hooker who had relinquished the presidency of the Royal Society in 1878 declined a similar office with the Royal Geographical Society and the Linnean Society of London. Council and Committee meetings had always wearied him and now old age had blunted his interest in such activities. W.W. Graham enthralled an audience at the Royal Geographical

2. *Nature*, 22 June 1899, pp. 187-88.

The Camp, Sunningdale. Hooker's home in retirement, built on a site where troops had been camped, hence its name. A hill within its grounds commanded superb views of a landscape of firs and heather.

Society in June 1884 with an account of his ascent almost to the peak of Kangchenjunga. Was Hooker jealous or resentful when the speaker asserted that he had felt no ill-effects at high altitudes? He got to his feet and told Graham that he himself had never known 'what it was to go a few miles outside his tent without feeling great pressure, or to walk up to 18,000 feet without a feeling of having a pound of lead on each kneecap, two pounds in the pit of his stomach, and a hoop of iron around his heart, and he always returned to camp with nausea'.[3] He was still peeved by his recollection of Graham's exceptional fitness when he wrote to Brian Hodgson about it. 'Curiously enough he did not suffer from difficulty of breathing or discomfort of any sort, as he coolly put all other descriptions of such suffering down to the imagination'.[4]

His Assistant Director, William Thiselton-Dyer, stated that Hooker was not well at this time; he had a heart condition and got 'excited over trifles'. In October 1884 Hooker directed him to take over the entire Gardens except for the Arboretum and the Herbarium. Hooker had a particular fondness for the Arboretum which, he told Harry Bolus in South Africa, he was 'rendering as perfect' as he could. His first positive step towards retirement had been the purchase in 1881 of six acres of ground at Sunningdale in Berkshire to build a house which he christened 'The Camp'. In his sixty-ninth year he reckoned he would have little time or energy left to finish the research he had started. Now that he was 'getting deaf & stiff & no longer fit for active garden duties, but not too old for such work in the Herbarium & supervising publications',[5] he informed Thiselton-Dyer that his retirement was imminent. With the intention of emulating George Bentham who had visited the Herbarium regularly, he retired from Kew, where he had been employed for thirty years, at the end of November 1885. Now the completion of the *Flora of British India* became an urgent priority. C.B. Clarke's three-year secondment to Kew had expired and contributions from other participants were disappointing. He began a routine of visiting the Kew Herbarium at least three times a week.

3. *Proceedings of Royal Geographical Society*, vol. 6, 1884, p. 445.
4. Hooker to Hodgson. 22 June 1884. *Letters from J.D. Hooker*.
5. J.D. Hooker. *Letters to Thiselton-Dyer*, f. 196.

He enjoyed a respite from this intensive research when he selected choice garden plants for featuring in *Curtis's Botanical Magazine* which he had edited since 1865. Naturally he included attractive plants he had seen or collected on his travels and, occasionally, indulged in nostalgic reverie in the accompanying text. *Rhaphidophora decursiva*, a vigorous climber which he figured in an issue in 1893 was especially evocative.

> I shall never forget the first occasion on which I saw this noble aroid. I was skirting the edge of the magnificent forest that then clothed the base of the Sikkim Himalaya (now, I believe, replaced by tea plantations); twilight had just commenced, and I had hardly realised the scene, when the cicadas burst into full cry (it is impossible to call it song), with startling effect, sound and scene combining to herald my advance into, to me, a new world of interest and botanical excitement.[6]

Before he resigned as editor in 1904, he had directed the attention of British gardeners to nearly 300 plants from India, Ceylon, Burma, Morocco and the United States.

His public response to the award of the Copley Medal at the anniversary dinner of the Royal Society on 30 November 1887 provided another opportunity to reminisce. He recalled that as a small boy and as a youth his determination to travel had been nurtured by books on exploration and by actually meeting some of his heroes who visited his father's home in Glasgow. Among all his friends and acquaintances, Charles Darwin was pre-eminent – 'The Pole Star and Lode Stone of my scientific life'.

Himalayan rhododendrons flourishing in a Cornish garden during a holiday in 1889 poignantly recalled his collecting days. 'Tell Brian [Hodgson] with my love that I saw, in Cornwall, *many, many* plants of *Rhod. Hodgsoni* in the open, 6 feet across and more, and with leaves a foot long – they were past flower unfortunately. They were planted in the woods and throve luxuriantly. There were also noble plants of *Falconeri, Aucklandii, argenteum, barbatum* and others – together with *Hodgsoni* forming regular shrubberies, as if natives of the soil'.[7]

He read with immense pleasure an article by G.A. Gammie, an assistant on a cinchona plantation, of a botanical trip to the Sikkim-Tibetan frontier in 1892.[8] Gammie who had followed in Hooker's footsteps, so to speak, also admired the same view from the top of Donkia Pass that Hooker had lyrically described in his *Himalayan Journals*. His report amply endorsed his predecessor's assertion that the country was one of the richest botanical regions in the world.

Rhododendrons, orchids and balsams were high on the list of Hooker's favourite plants. Two hundred plates in Hooker's *Icones Plantarum* for 1892-94 reproduced drawings of Indian orchids.[9] He chose a hundred more from the official collection of drawings in the Royal Botanic Garden, Calcutta for publication in 1895.[10]

6. *Curtis's Botanical Magazine*, 1893, plate 7282.
7. Hooker to Mrs Hodgson. 30 June 1889. *Letters from J.D. Hooker.*
8. *Kew Bulletin,* 1893, 297-314.
9. *Hooker's Icones Plantarum*, vols. 21 and 22, 1892-94.
10. 'A Century of Indian Orchids'. *Annals of Royal Botanic Garden, Calcutta*, vol. 5, 1895.

As an agreeable diversion from botanical publications, he edited Sir Joseph Banks's journal of Captain Cook's *Endeavour* voyage, its first appearance in print. Banks was his exemplar of the traveller/naturalist, an acute observer who collected diligently and kept records with the assistance of a botanist and an artist. With the original manuscript in Australia, Hooker had to make do with a transcription made for Dawson Turner by members of his family. Hooker's version, published in 1896, incomplete and partly rewritten, is not a reliable text.

When Henry Trimen, Director of the Botanic Garden at Peradeniya in Ceylon, died in 1896, he left his *Handbook to the Flora of Ceylon* incomplete at the third volume. Hooker, now an octogenarian, unhesitatingly agreed to a request from the island's government to finish the work, believing it not to be a formidable task since he had described most of Ceylon's plants in the *Flora of British India*. His confident prediction that it should be finished within eighteen months to two years turned out to be over-optimistic. The fourth volume emerged in 1898 and the concluding one in 1900.

Presumably he never gave much attention to Trimen's work until he had completed the *Flora of British India*. The grass family (Gramineae), the last to be finished, proved troublesome. 'The grasses have never been worked up and species have been made here, there and everywhere upon insufficient data, with incomplete characters. The synonymy is pretentious in consequence'.[11] The index and introduction, published in December 1897, brought to a close a work which ran to 6,000 pages in seven volumes. During its compilation he had the services of at least thirteen collaborators and consulted a vast network of knowledgeable correspondents. He constantly moaned about shoddy fieldwork such as imprecise observation and inadequate records. Conscious of its limitations, he told J.S. Gamble, one of his regular Indian correspondents, that it was 'past praying for in the matter of errors in detail, from bad identifications, bad specimens and bad examinations'. He was equally self-critical to another confidant, J.F. Duthie. 'That work is a hurried sweeping up of nearly a century of undigested materials, and is in no sense a flora like Bentham's Australian [*Flora Australiensis*]. It had to be carried out in a reasonable time, and except myself and Clarke, none of my coadjutors was really well up in Indian botany, or authorities, or works, or climate, or geography. It is merely a crude guide to the extent and variety of the native vegetation of India'.[12] He had lived with the work for so long that he was unable to view it dispassionately. He adopted a defensive stance in his preface, as if anticipating criticism. He presented it as a pioneering work with three objectives: to facilitate the identification of plants, to encourage the compilation of local floras and monographs of genera, and to assist the phytogeographer in his understanding of its cosmopolitan vegetation. Whatever his own misgivings about its imperfections, others saw it as an

11. Hooker to W. La Touche. 9 April 1894. *Letters from J.D. Hooker.*
12. Hooker to Duthie. 24 January 1901. L. Huxley. *Life and Letters ...* , vol. 2, 1918, p. 387.

Arthur Balfour, First Lord of the Treasury, meeting a delegation of the National Antarctic Expedition (which included Hooker) on 22 June 1899. (*Daily Graphic* 23 June 1899.)

impressive achievement. 'No other living botanist could have accomplished this', wrote Thiselton-Dyer; 'none other possesses so vast a knowledge of the vegetable kingdom, or so intimate an acquaintance with India and its natural productions'.[13] The Government showed its appreciation of his devotion to Indian botany by elevating him to Knight Grand Commander of the Star of India. The Linnean Society chose its completion to strike a special gold medal in 1898 in recognition of his services to science over sixty years. *The Flora of British India*, now urgently needing revision, is still the only flora to attempt to cover the sub-continent, a classic among tropical floras.

He took time off to see the ships of the Royal Navy lit up at Spithead during Queen Victoria's jubilee celebrations in 1897. An impressive sight, he conceded, but for him it did not compare with 'the view of the glacier-clothed and berg-imprisoned mountain chain of South Victoria Land, with Mount Erebus blazing in the front ... [or] the first view of the Himalaya, as seen from Darjeeling, covering perhaps 100° (of one of the horizons with perpetual snow, with Kinchinjunga 28,000 feet towering over all'.[14]

Outliving all the officers on Ross's Antarctic expedition, Hooker had become the doyen of polar exploration. Little interest had been shown in Antarctica since that epic voyage. H.M.S. *Challenger* had briefly crossed the Antarctic Circle but sealers and whalers no longer found it profitable to hunt there. In 1885 the British Association for the Advancement of Science formed an Antarctic Committee which recommended a resumption of exploration in its report in 1887 to which Hooker contributed. The colony of Victoria in Australia offered to participate provided British authorities subscribed £5,000, but the Government, seeing no commercial advantage in such a venture,

13. Thiselton-Dyer to India Office. 13 February 1897. *Kew Bulletin*, 1905, p. 35.
14. Hooker to Mrs K. Lyell. 2 July 1897. *Letters from J.D. Hooker.*

declined. John Murray of the *Challenger* expedition urged a meeting at the Royal Geographical Society in November 1893 to petition for another expedition to Antarctica. 'Is there a sixth continent within the Antarctic Circle, or is the land nucleus, on which the massive ice-cap rests, merely a group of lofty volcanic hills?'[15] Hooker participated in the discussion that followed. He reminded the audience that the earlier successes of Weddell and Ross had been accidental. 'Had Ross not followed a course dictated by other circumstances than those of geography and discovery he might have spent his first two seasons, as he did his third, in unavailing struggles with pack-ice.'[16] He advised the expedition now being proposed to spend its first year in locating the main areas of sea ice, and finding soft places in the pack, charting open water, taking deep-sea soundings and temperature readings. Following this meeting, Sir Clements Markham, the Society's energetic President, convened an Antarctic Committee and invited Hooker, whom he had known since the cinchona and rubber transfers, to serve on it. Hooker's attention was again being focused on that part of the world that had launched his career. The International Geographical Congress which met in London in 1895 passed a resolution that 'the exploration of the Antarctic regions is the greatest piece of geographical exploration still to be undertaken'. Markham lobbied tirelessly, eventually persuading a luke-warm Royal Society to support the project. At a gathering in the Royal Society in 1898 John Murray commended the 'scientific advantages of an Antarctic expedition'.[17] This was the occasion when Hooker urged the use of a captive balloon to establish whether land lay beyond the high wall of the great ice barrier. He was a member of the Antarctic Committee formed jointly by the Royal Society and the Royal Geographical Society in 1898; in 1899 he chaired its Biological Sub-Committee. A deputation of the National Antarctic Expedition, as it was now called, which included Hooker, saw the First Lord of the Treasury in June 1899. 'I shall end my active life as I began it, in the interest of Antarctic discovery', he told Mrs Sabina Paisley.[18]

With Government backing and financial support, preparations for the expedition at last went ahead. Robert Falcon Scott, a young lieutenant in the Royal Navy, was chosen by Markham to command the *Discovery*, specially built for the purpose. Hooker complained to Markham when he learned that no provision had been made for an observation balloon. Apart from its primary role in surveying, wrote Hooker, 'suppose a party exploring the surface of the barrier comes to grief, & has to be searched for, a balloon would be invaluable in aid'.[19]

Scott, too, thought it was a splendid idea but had difficulty in convincing the War Office. Eventually he got two balloons and, on 4 February 1902, tethered by a wire rope, ascended in one of them to 800 feet, the Antarctic's first aviator. He saw that Ross's ice shelf was not flat, as he had imagined, but

15. J. Murray. 'The Renewal of Antarctic Exploration'. *Geographical Journal*, vol. 3, 1894, p. 10.
16. Ibid., p. 29.
17. *Proceedings of Royal Society*, vol. 62, 1898, pp. 424-51.
18. Hooker to Mrs S. Paisley. 12 December 1897. *Letters from J.D. Hooker*.
19. Hooker to Markham. 21 December 1900. *Letters from J.D. Hooker*.

Scott's *Discovery* passing Mount Erebus, named by Captain J.C. Ross. The first attempt to climb this active volcano was made by E. Shackleton's expedition in 1908. The United States MacMurdo Base is now situated near it. (*Royal Geographical Society, London.*)

Observation balloon being deflated by R.F. Scott's men in Antarctica. (*Royal Geographical Society, London.*)

'continued in a series of long undulations'.

Hooker was reminded of his time in New Zealand when T.F. Cheeseman wrote to him in April 1899 seeking his advice on the compilation of a new flora, based on an incomplete manuscript by the late T. Kirk. They corresponded for some years but Hooker did not live to see the publication of Cheeseman's *Illustrations of the New Zealand Flora* (1914).

A couple of days before a meeting with Scott who had returned from a successful mission, Colonel F.E. Younghusband, a member of the 1903 Sikkim–Tibet Boundary Commission, paid Hooker a visit. He was flattered to see, framed and hanging on the dining-room wall, the congratulatory telegram which he and other members of the Boundary Commission had sent Hooker.

'And Thee' at Lamteng in Sikkim. 'There was an old man there who remembers you extremely well, and even where you camped. He is still very hardy and active, and I send you a snapshot I took of him. He also sends you his best salaams. His name he pronounced "And Thee"'. (Letter from C.E. Simmonds to Hooker. 12 June 1908.)

Major Prain, Colonel Younghusband and officers of Tibet Mission desire to send you their felicitations by telegraph from Khambajong and express their high admiration of that zeal displayed by you fifty-five years ago, which has enabled them to follow in your steps and has inspired them to emulate your devotion to science and your country.

In December 1903 Hooker received a copy of Douglas Freshfield's *Road to Kangchenjunga*, dedicated to him as 'the pioneer of mountain travel in the eastern Himalaya'. The object of Freshfield's trek in Sikkim in 1899 was to explore a blank space on Hooker's map, 'to link the recent routes of Mr [Claude] White, the Political President in Independent Sikkim, east of Kangchenjunga, with those of Sir Joseph Hooker in Nepal on the other side of the mountain in 1848'.[20] Hooker, seduced by the dedication, read the book 'with pleasure that I cannot express in words...You have brought to me visions of my happiest early days that I never hoped to see: for your descriptions are as happy as they are truthful; so much so that they have set me dreaming by night of the Teesta, Zemu, Jongri, and above all, Jannu'.[21]

Travellers in India like Elwes, Younghusband and Freshfield either visited or wrote to him; botanists there sent him specimens or sought his advice. He had never severed his connections with the sub-continent. When the Calcutta Botanic Garden was severely damaged by a cyclone in 1867, he had written to

20. D. Freshfield. 'The Sikkim Himalaya'. *Scottish Geographical Magazine*, vol. 21, 1905, p. 177.
21. Hooker to Freshfield. 16 December 1903. L. Huxley. *Life and Letters ...* , vol. 2, 1918, pp. 452-53.

Hooker at his desk in his home at Sunningdale, 16 October 1906.

influential people in India pointing out that this disaster presented an opportunity to move the Garden nearer to Calcutta and its citizens and to the students of the Medical College. He had complained to M.E. Grant Duff, Under-Secretary of State for India, that botany in India was in 'an utterly chaotic and disgraceful state'.[22] due to the absence of any centralised research policy. When George King and J.F. Duthie, superintendents respectively of the Calcutta and Saharanpur Botanic Gardens, were in London in 1884, he had joined them on an official visit to the India Office to discuss an efficient co-ordination of botanical research in the country. He had already succeeded in 1883 in getting the Indian Government to post a liaison botanist to Kew. Even after retirement he monitored progress – or rather the lack of it – in India. 'The fact is, that except at Calcutta the botanists of India have been asleep since the days of Wight, Beddome, Law, Stocks, Dalzell and a few others'.[23] He contrasted botanical activity elsewhere in the Empire with lethargy in India. 'Excuse my growl', he wrote to A.T. Gage at the Calcutta Botanic Garden, 'I so love Indian botany'.[24]

Because of this genuine affection for India, he succumbed to an invitation from the Government of India in 1901 to contribute a succinct account of Indian botany to the new edition of the *Imperial Gazetteer of India*. When he finished it, he had more than doubled the twenty pages allocated to it, and had taken six instead of the agreed three months. Even then he had found it 'desperately hard work' to condense a life-time's knowledge of the subject into a short article. His geographical limits embraced countries on the periphery of the sub-continent: Nepal, Sikkim, Bhutan, Burma, Ceylon and the Malay Peninsula. He increased his original estimate of species of flowering plants to 17,000, identified the principal elements in the flora as Malayan, European-Oriental, African, Tibetan-Siberian, and Sino-Japanese, named ten dominant plant families, and divided British India into nine phytogeographical provinces.

22. Hooker to Grant Duff. 6 February 1869. *Letters from J.D. Hooker.*
23. Hooker to Gamble. 11 November 1903. *Letters from J.D. Hooker.*
24. Hooker to Gage. 12 July 1906. *Letters from J.D. Hooker.*

A watercolour and pencil sketch of a species of *Impatiens* by Hooker. His interest in this genus began during his expedition to India.

As endemics were rare, he doubted whether 'there is any Indian type flora, pure and simple, at all! and that India is a geographical, not a botanical expression'.[25] His essay appeared as *A Sketch of the Flora of British India* in 1904 before its inclusion in the first volume of the *Gazetteer* in 1907. It was a masterly summary; in the words of F.O. Bower, 'the natural close to the most remarkable study of a vast and varied flora that has ever been carried through by one ruling mind'.[26]

As he now rarely went to functions in London or dined at his favourite club, the Athenaeum, people came to Sunningdale. In the summer of 1907 he entertained to lunch the Rajah of Sikkim, the grandson of his former enemy.

The secret of his impressive productivity in retirement lay not only in reasonable health and stamina for his age, but also in a disciplined daily routine. A friend, who had lived at The Camp from 1895 to 1899, reported that Hooker always worked for an hour before breakfast and continued to lunchtime. He dispensed with afternoon tea, paused briefly for a light supper and went to bed at eleven. His eyes remained good enough for him to use a microscope and his fingers sufficiently steady and nimble to dissect flowers, fruits and seeds, 'a life-long passion'. Like his father who had studied ferns right up to his death, his son also had a group of plants that engrossed him entirely.

Species of *Impatiens*, known as balsams, presented a taxonomic challenge he could not resist. They form a large population whose subtle differences in floral structure make identification difficult, especially dried specimens. 'As I am the only one who understands them (they are so difficult to diagnose), they gravitate to me for naming and describing', he joked with one of Darwin's sons.[27] Specimens came from herbaria in India and elsewhere, and drawings of living ones were specially executed for him. Since he had doubts about the accuracy of descriptions of them in the *Flora of British India,* often due to inadequate, damaged or badly mounted specimens, he obtained fresh material from India. He published a list of the balsams in Wallich's herbarium, then housed in the Linnean Society,[28] and compiled an epitome of Indian species for the *Records of the Botanical Survey of India.*[29] Their study became an all-consuming passion, and tapping the resources of continental herbaria, he

25. Hooker to Gamble. 2 March 1902. L. Huxley. *Life and Letters ... ,* vol. 2, 1918, p. 390.
26. F.O. Bower, *Sir Joseph Hooker: an Ovation,* 1912, p. 20.
27. Hooker to W. Darwin. 3 December 1904. *Letters from J.D. Hooker.*
28. 'On the Species of Impatiens in the Wallichian Herbarium of the Linnean Society'. *Journal of Linnean Society.* Botany, vol. 37, 1904, pp. 22-32.
29. 'An Epitome of the British Indian species of *Impatiens'. Records of the Botanical Survey of India,* vol. 4, 1904-06, pp. 1-58.

extended his survey to Chinese and Malayan species. A letter he wrote to Frank Darwin in 1907 gives some idea of the monotonous labour, and the meticulous preparation involved in this obsession.

> I have been for years working at *Impatiens*, an enormous genus in Asia and Africa. The analysis of the dried flowers is most tedious and difficult; single flowers often taking two hours and some even a whole day to lay out for description – reagents have failed to help me, they either harden the tissues so as to prevent their being laid out, or soften them, so that a touch of the needle tears them. Herbarium specimens without accompanying drawings of every organ are perfectly useless. I defy the sharpest botanist to describe a single floral organ until the flower is dismembered (and this must be done under water) and the wrinkles of every organ spread out. These organs I preserve on gummed papers, as evidence of the accuracy of the drawings. I have full descriptions of 3-4,000 Asiatic species. The segregation of the species is most furious, the W. Himalaya differ from the E. Himalaya, and both (with few exceptions) from the Burmese and all those from the Malay Peninsula and Malabar. Only three species cross the Bay of Bengal! I am now at the Chinese species, some 130 – only 4 or 5 are common to India! The genus has been studiously shunned by all Indian botanists but the Malabarian and Cingalese.[30]

In 1909 he told Gage that he had written full descriptions of almost 300 Indian species. Right to the end he was still patiently dissecting and drawing the flowers, his spectacles characteristically pushed up on his forehead. In 1911, the year in which he died, the *Kew Bulletin* published two of his papers on balsams.[31] He had begun his career as a plant taxonomist in 1837 with a description of three species of Himalayan mosses; and with symmetrical neatness it ended with Indian plants.

On 29 May 1910 Captain Scott wrote to Hooker with the news of the departure of his ship, *Terra Nova*, to Antarctica. 'On Tuesday she will hoist the white ensign under Admiralty warrant. I wonder if there is any possibility that you could hoist our flag on that occasion'.[32] Hooker's frailty compelled him to decline 'an honour which would have been the crowning one of my long life could I have accepted it'.[33] He died at midnight on 10 December 1911 in his ninety-fifth year. An offer by the Dean of Westminster to place his ashes next to those of Darwin and Lyell in the Abbey was declined in order to respect Hooker's wish to be buried next to his father in the churchyard of St Anne's on Kew Green.[34]

Apart from occasional ailments like the bout of 'rheumatic fever' at the time of his father's death, Hooker was extraordinarily fit for much of his life. Just under six feet tall, lean and sinewy ('Don't let all the flesh be worried off your bones', T.H. Huxley once cautioned him, 'there is not much as it is'), he had immense reserves of nervous energy. He claimed that as a youth he had thought little of walking twenty miles, and once did sixty miles in a day. As a student he had mastered the technique of needing little sleep, a habit which gave him a bonus of extra hours for study and research. His general well-being and powers of

30. Hooker to F. Darwin. 14 December 1907. *Letters from J.D. Hooker.*
31. 'On some species of *Impatiens* from the Malayan Peninsula. II'. *Kew Bulletin,* 1911, pp. 249-50. 'Indian Species of *Impatiens*. On some Western Peninsular Indian Balsamineae collected by Mr A. Meebold'. *Kew Bulletin,* 1911, pp. 353-56.
32. *Antarctic Expeditions,* 1842-1901, f. 109A.
33. Hooker to Scott. 1 June 1910. Ibid., f. 213.
34. A medallion of Hooker was added to the memorials of scientists in the nave of Westminster Abbey.

Sir Joseph and Lady Hooker in their drawing room, 1911. His first wife died on 13 November 1874. He married Hyacinth, daughter of Rev. W.S. Symonds, two years later.

endurance were severely tested during exhausting climbs in the Himalayas; only altitude sickness appeared to trouble him. Even at ninety he still maintained an upright posture, with a halo of white hair the most striking sign of old age.

His friends admitted that he could be 'testy', 'hot-tempered', 'over-critical', and 'very impulsive', and he himself confessed to being 'short of temper ... in trifles'. His complex personality was full of contradictions. Shyness had afflicted him as a young man, and despite presiding over societies and chairing meetings, he could never rid himself of nervous apprehension when he spoke in public. Though modest, he was shrewdly aware of his own worth and proud of his achievements. In his dealings with senior civil servants Sir William had always been cautious and diplomatic, but his son often behaved impetuously and inflexibly. An official closely involved in his notorious conflict with his Commissioner of Works, agreed that 'Ayrton had an evil tongue, but I confess I thought him the more reasonable of the two'. Hooker defiantly ignored public clamour for an extension of the opening hours at Kew Gardens until the Government intervened. One can sympathise with his impatience with Thomas Thomson's perverse procrastination but deplore his insensitive, even brutal, way of getting rid of him, a friend of many years who had used his inheritance to finance the publication of the *Flora Indica*. The artist W.H. Fitch, who had so brilliantly illustrated his books, incurred his wrath through claiming ownership of his drawings in *Curtis's Botanical Magazine*; the bitterness of the quarrel severed a relationship of nearly fifty years. But it was Hooker who eventually got him a Civil List pension. Behind a brusque manner, he was fundamentally kind, one of the qualities that endeared him to so many people. The friendship he enjoyed with Charles Darwin was the catalyst in both their lives. His letters written home during his travels reveal strong family bonds and an over-riding love and admiration for his father.

Wedgwood plaque commemorating Sir Joseph Hooker in St Anne's church, Kew Green. Portrait in white relief on green ground by Frank Bowcher. The surrounding plants representing some of his botanical interests were modelled by Matilda Smith, his cousin and botanical artist at Kew.

Clockwise from upper right panel: *Nepenthes albo-marginata* (pitcher plants and Malayan flora); *Rhododendron thomsonii* (Indian flora); *Celmisia vernicosa* (Antarctic flora); *Cinchona calisaya* (Introduction of cinchona into India); *Aristolochia mannii* (African flora).

His father had shaped his destiny by encouraging him to observe the natural world about him, by creating opportunities for him to travel, by getting him an appointment at Kew. It was through travel that Joseph Hooker gained an unrivalled knowledge of the world's flora which he collected and recorded. He used geology and palaeontology to support his theories on the global distribution of plants. F.O. Bower described him as 'a philosophical botanist'. His son-in-law, Sir William Thiselton-Dyer, believed that his enduring reputation could rest solely on his work as a plant geographer. His achievements as an observant and well-informed traveller, explorer and discriminating collector also deserve to be remembered.

Bibliography

Books and Periodical Articles

Books and Periodical Articles

Affolter, J. 'The "Antarctic" Flora: Researches of Charles Darwin and Joseph Hooker'.*Contributions. University of Michigan Herbarium,* vol. 14, 1980, pp. 1-9.

Allan, M. *The Hookers of Kew, 1785-1911.* London, 1967.

Ball, J. 'Spicilegium Florae Maroccanae'. *Journal of Linnean Society. Botany,* vol. 16, 1877, pp. 281-302.

Barlow, N., editor. *Charles Darwin's Diary of the Voyage of H.M.S. Beagle.* Cambridge, 1933.

Beaglehole, J.C., editor. *The* Endeavour *Journal of Joseph Banks, 1768-1771.* Sydney, 1962. 2 vols.

Beaglehole, J.C., editor. *The Journals of Captain James Cook: the Voyage of the* Resolution *and* Adventure, *1772-1775.* London, 1969.

Boulger, G.S. 'Sir Joseph Dalton Hooker (1817-1911)'. *Journal of Botany,* 1912, pp. 1-9, 33-43.

Bower, F.O. 'Sir Joseph Dalton Hooker, 1817-1911'. In F.O. Oliver, editor. *Makers of British Botany.* Cambridge, 1913, pp. 302-33.

Bower, F.O. *Joseph Dalton Hooker.* London, 1919.

Bramwell, D., editor. *Plants and Islands.* London, 1979.

Browne, J. *The Secular Ark: Studies in the History of Biogeography.* Yale, 1983.

Browne, J. *Charles Darwin: Voyaging.* London, 1995.

Cameron, I. *Antarctica: the Last Continent.* London, 1974.

Darwin, C. *Journal of Researches into the Geology and Natural History of the various Countries visited by H.M.S.* Beagle. London, 1839.

Darwin, C. *On the Origin of Species by means of Natural Selection.* London, 1859.

Darwin, C. *Correspondence,* vol. 2 to date. Cambridge, 1986.

Darwin, F., editor. *Life and Letters of Charles Darwin.* London, 1887. 3 vols.

Darwin, F., editor. *More Letters of Charles Darwin.* London, 1903. 2 vols.

Desmond, R. 'Walter Hood Fitch, 1817-1892, Botanical Artist'. *Medical & Biological Illustration,* vol. 19, 1969, pp. 255-59.

Desmond, R. *The European Discovery of the Indian Flora.* Oxford, 1992.

Desmond, R. 'Sir Joseph Hooker and India'. *The Linnean,* vol. 9, 1993, pp. 27-49.

Desmond, R. *Dictionary of British and Irish Botanists and Horticulturists.* Basingstoke, 1994.

Desmond, R. *A Celebration of Flowers.* London, 1994.

Desmond, R. *Kew: the History of the Royal Botanic Gardens.* London, 1995.

Dodge, E.S. *The Polar Rosses: John and James Clark Ross and their Explorations.* London, 1973.

Fitzroy, R. *Narrative of the Surveying Voyages of His Majesty's Ships* Adventure *and* Beagle *between the Years 1826 and 1836 ...* London 1839. 2 vols.

Freshfield, D.W. 'Glaciers of Kangchenjung'. *Geographical Journal,* vol. 19, 1902, pp. 453-74.

Freshfield, D.W. *Round Kangchenjunga: a Narrative of Mountain Travel and Exploration.* London, 1903.

Gammie, G.A. 'Botanical Exploration of Sikkim-Tibet Frontier'. *Kew Bulletin,* 1893, pp. 297-315.

Hooker, J.D. See separate sequence in Bibliography.

Hooker, W.J. 'Notes on the Botany of the Antarctic Voyage conducted by Captain James Clark Ross ... in Her Majesty's Discovery Ships *Erebus* and *Terror;* with Observations on the Tussac Grass of the Falkland Islands'. *Hooker's London Journal of Botany,* vol. 2, 1843, pp. 247-329. Also published separately as a pamphlet.

Hunter, W.W. *Life of Brian Houghton Hodgson.* London, 1896.

Huxley, L. *Life and Letters of Sir Joseph Dalton Hooker. Based on Materials collected and arranged by Lady Hooker.* London, 1918 ... 2 vols.

Lewis, J. *Walter Hood Fitch: a Celebration.* London, 1992.

Linklater, E. *The Voyage of the* Challenger. London, 1972.

McCormick, R. *Voyages of Discovery in the Arctic and Antarctic Seas and round the World.* London, 1884. 2 vols.

Oliver, F.W. 'Sir Joseph Dalton Hooker'. *Proceedings of Linnean Society,* 1912, pp. 47-62.

Prain, D. 'Sir Joseph Dalton Hooker'. *Smithsonian Report,* 1911, pp. 659-711.

Risley, H.H. *The Gazetteer of Sikhim.* Calcutta, 1894.

Ross, J.C. 'Antarctic Discoveries'. *Tasmanian Journal of Natural Science,* vol. 1, 1842, pp. 409-14.

Ross, J.C. *A Voyage of Discovery and Research in the Southern and Antarctic Regions, during the Years 1839-43.* London, 1847. 2 vols.

Ross, M.J. *Ross of the Antarctic: the Voyages of James Clark Ross in Her Majesty's Ships* Erebus *and* Terror, *1839-1843.* Whitby, 1982.

Ross, M.J. *Polar Pioneers: John Ross and James Clark Ross.* London, 1995.

Stafleu, F.A. and Cowan, R.S. *Taxonomic Literature.* vol. 2, 1979, pp. 267-83.

Stapf, O. and Jackson, B.D. 'Joseph Dalton Hooker'. *Proceedings of Linnean Society,* 1912, pp. 47-62.

Turrill, W.B. *Pioneer Plant Geography: the Phytogeographical Researches of Sir Joseph Dalton Hooker.* The Hague, 1953.

Turrill, W.B. 'Joseph Dalton Hooker (1817-1911)'. *Notes and Records of the Royal Society of London,* vol. 4, 1959, pp. 109-20.

Turrill, W.B. *Joseph Dalton Hooker: Botanist, Explorer and Administrator.* London, 1963.

Thiselton-Dyer, W.T. 'Sir Joseph Dalton Hooker'. *Proceedings of the Royal Society of London,* vol. 85, 1912, pp. i-xxxv.

Watson, M. *A Botanical Gazetteer for Sikkim-Darjeeling.* Edinburgh, 1992.

Williamson, M. 'Sir Joseph Hooker's lecture on Insular Floras'. *Biological Journal of Linnean Society,* vol. 22, 1984, pp. 55-77.

Publications of Sir J.D. Hooker

'Contributions towards a Flora of Van Diemen's Land, chiefly from the collections of Ronald Gunn, Esq., and the late Mr Lawrence'. *Hooker's Journal of Botany,* vol. 2, 1840, pp. 1-21.

'On the Examination of some Fossil Wood from Macquarie Plains, Tasmania'. *Tasmanian Journal of Natural Science,* vol. 1, 1842, p. 24.

The Botany of the Antarctic Voyage of H.M. Discovery Ships Erebus *and* Terror *in the Years 1839-1843:*

　　Part 1. *Flora Antarctica.* London, 1844-47. 2 vols.

　　Part 2. *Flora Novae-Zelandiae.* London, 1852-55. 2 vols.

　　Part 3. *Flora Tasmaniae.* London, 1855-59. 2 vols.

'Some Account of a New *Elaeodendron* from New Zealand'. *Hooker's London Journal of Botany,* vol. 3, 1844, pp. 228-30.

'Catalogue of the Names of a Collection of Plants made by Mr Wm. Stephenson in New Zealand'. *Hooker's London Journal of Botany,* vol. 3, 1844, pp. 411-18.

'Hepaticae Antarcticae' (with T. Taylor). *Hooker's London Journal of Botany,* vol. 3, 1844, pp. 454-80.

'Notes on the Cider Tree (*Eucalyptus gunnii*). *Hooker's London Journal of Botany,* vol. 3, 1844, pp. 496-501.

'Musci Antarcticae' (with W. Wilson). *Hooker's London Journal of Botany,* vol. 3, 1844, pp. 533-56.

'Hepaticae Novae Zelandiae et Tasmaniae' (with T. Taylor). *Hooker's London Journal of Botany,* vol. 3, 1844, pp. 556-82.

'Lichenes Antarctici' (with T. Taylor). *Hooker's London Journal of Botany,* vol. 3, 1844, pp. 634-58.

'Hepaticae Antarcticae, Supplementum' (with T. Taylor). *Hooker's London Journal of Botany,* vol. 4, 1845, 1844, pp. 79-97.

'On the Huon Pine, and on *Microcachrys,* a new genus of Coniferae from Tasmania; together with Remarks upon the Geographical Distribution of that Order in the Southern Hemisphere'. *Hooker's London Journal of Botany,* vol. 4, 1845, pp. 137-57.

'Algae Antarcticae' (with W.H. Harvey). *Hooker's London Journal of Botany,* vol. 4, 1845, pp. 249-76, 293-98.

'Algae Novae Zelandiae' (with W.H. Harvey). *Hooker's London Journal of Botany,* vol. 4, 1845, pp. 521-51; vol. 7, 1848, pp. 443-45.

'On *Fitchia,* a New Genus of Arborescent Compositae ... from Elizabeth Island ... in the South Pacific'. *Hooker's London Journal of Botany,* vol. 4, 1845, pp. 640-43.

'Note on some Marine Animals, brought up by Deep-sea Dredging, during the Antarctic Voyage of Captain Sir James Ross'. *Annals of the Natural History,* vol. 16, 1845, pp. 238-39.

'Note on a Fossil Plant from the Fish River, South Africa'. *Transactions of the Geological Society,* vol. 7, 1846, p. 227.

'Description of *Pleuropetalum,* a New Genus of Portulaceae from the Galapagos Islands'. *Hooker's London Journal of Botany,* vol. 5, 1846, pp. 108-09.

'Description of a New Genus of Compositae [*Scleroleima*] and a New Species of *Plantago* from the Mountains of Tasmania'. *Hooker's London Journal of Botany,* vol. 5, 1846, pp. 444-47.

Botanical contributions to J.C. Ross. *A Voyage of Discovery and Research in the Southern and Antarctic Regions ... 1839-43.* London, 1847. vol. 1, pp. 83-87, 144-49, 158-63; vol. 2, pp. 5-8, 261-77, 288-302.

'Flora Tasmaniae Spicilegium'. *Hooker's London Journal of Botany,* vol. 6, 1847, pp. 106-25, 265-86, 461-79.

'Algae Tasmanicae' (with W.H. Harvey). *Hooker's London Journal of Botany,* vol. 6, 1847, pp. 397-417.

'On the Diatomaceous Vegetation of the Antarctic Ocean'. *British Association for the Advancement of Science Report,* 1847, pp. 83-85.

'Extracts from the Private Letters of J.D. Hooker, written during a Botanical Mission to India'. *Hooker's London Journal of Botany,* vol. 7, 1848, pp. 237-68, 297-321; *Hooker's London Journal of Botany and Kew Garden Miscellany,* vol. 1, 1849, pp. 1-14, 41-56, 81-89, 113-20, 129-36, 161-75, 226-33, 274-82, 301-08, 331-36, 337-44, 361-70; vol. 2, 1850, pp. 11-23, 52-59, 88-91, 112-18, 145-51, 161-73, 213-18, 244-49.

'Observations made when following the Grand Trunk Road across the Hills of Upper Bengal, Paras Nath, etc. in the Soane Valley; and on the Kymaor Branch of the Vindhya Hills'. *Journal of the Asiatic Society of Bengal,* vol. 17, 1848, pp. 355-411.

'Notes, chiefly Botanical, made during an Excursion from Darjeeling to Tonglo, a Lofty Mountain on the confines of Sikkim and Nepal'. *Journal of the Asiatic Society of Bengal*, vol. 18, 1849, pp. 419-46; *Journal of the Horticultural Society of London*, vol. 7, 1852, pp. 1-23.

The Rhododendrons of Sikkim-Himalaya. London, 1849-51. 3 parts.

'Letter from Chuvra Poonji, Khasiah Hills'. *Gardeners' Chronicle*, 1850, pp. 694, 710.

'A Fourth Excursion to the Passes into Tibet by the Donkiah La'. *Journal of the Geographical Society*, vol. 20, 1851, pp. 49-52.

'Enumeration of the Plants of the Galapagos Islands, with Descriptions of the New Species'. *Transactions of the Linnean Society*, vol. 20, 1851, pp. 163-234.

'On the Vegetation of the Galapagos Archipelago, as compared with that of some other Tropical Islands and of the Continent of America'. *Transactions of the Linnean Society*, vol. 20, 1851, pp. 235-62.

'On the Physical Character of Sikkim-Himalaya; a Letter to A. von Humboldt, 1850'. *Hooker's Journal of Botany and Kew Garden Miscellany*, vol. 3, 1851, 21-31.

'On the Climate and Vegetation of the Temperate and Cold Regions of East Nepal and the Sikhim Himalaya Mountains'. *Journal of the Horticultural Society of London*, vol. 7, 1852, pp. 69-131.

'On a New Genus [*Milligania*] and some New Species of Tasmanian Plants'. *Hooker's Journal of Botany and Kew Garden Miscellany*, vol. 5, 1853, pp. 296-300.

Himalayan Journals; or, Notes of a Naturalist in Bengal, the Sikkim and Nepal Himalayas, the Khasia Mountains, etc. London, 1854. 2 vols. 'A new edition, carefully revised and condensed', 1855. Reprinted in 1891.

'On *Maddenia* and *Diplarche*, New Genera of Himalayan Plants' (with T. Thomson). *Hooker's Journal of Botany and Kew Garden Miscellany*, vol. 6, 1854, pp. 380-84.

Flora Indica (with T. Thomson). London, 1855.

Illustrations of Himalayan Plants chiefly selected from the Drawings made for the Late J.F. Cathcart. London, 1855.

'On *Hodgsonia* ... a New and Remarkable Genus of Cucurbitaceae'. *Proceedings of the Linnean Society*, vol. 2, 1855, pp. 257-59.

'On *Decaisnea*, a Remarkable New Genus of the Tribe Lardizabaleae' (with T. Thomson). *Proceedings of the Linnean Society*, vol. 2, 1855, pp. 349-51.

'On *Enhyanthus himalaicus* and *Cassiope selaginoides*, two New Species of Himalayan Ericaceae' (with T. Thomson). *Hooker's Journal of Botany and Kew Garden Miscellany*, vol. 7, 1855, pp. 124-26.

'Géographie Botanique Raisonnée ... par M.A. de Candolle' Reviewed by J.D. Hooker. *Hooker's Journal of Botany and Kew Garden Miscellany*, vol. 8, 1856, pp. 55-64, 82-88, 112-21, 151-57, 181-91, 214-19, 248-56.

'On *Notospartium*, a New Genus of Leguminosae from New Zealand. *Hooker's Journal of Botany and Kew Garden Miscellany*, vol. 9, 1857, pp. 176-77.

'On *Bryocarpum*, a New Genus of Himalayan Primulaceae' (with T. Thomson). *Hooker's Journal of Botany and Kew Garden Miscellany*, vol. 9, 1857, pp. 199-200.

'On three New Indian Scrophylarineae' (with T. Thomson). *Hooker's Journal of Botany and Kew Garden Miscellany*, vol. 9, 1857, pp. 243-46.

'On a New Species of *Diapensia* from the Eastern Himalaya'. *Hooker's Journal of Botany and Kew Garden Miscellany*, vol. 9, 1857, pp. 272-73.

Assistance given to G.H.K. Thwaites's *Enumeratio Plantarum Zeylaniae*. London, 1858-64.

'Praecursores ad Florum Indicum: being Sketches of the Natural Families of Indian Plants, with Remarks on their Distribution, Structure and Affinities' (with T. Thomson). *Journal of the Linnean Society*, vol. 2, 1858, pp. 1-29, 54-103, 163-80; vol. 4, 860, pp. 106-57; vol. 5, 1861, pp. 128-81.

'On a New Genus of Balanophoreae *(Dactylanthus taylori)* from New Zealand and two New Species of *Balanophora*'. *Transactions of the Linnean Society*, vol. 22, 1859, pp. 425-27.

'Outlines of the Distribution of Arctic Plants'. *Transactions of the Linnean Society*, vol. 23, 1862, pp. 251-348.

'On three Oaks of Palestine'. *Transactions of the Linnean Society*, vol. 23, 1862, pp. 381-87.

'On the Cedars of Lebanon, Taurus, Algeria, and India'. *Natural History Review*, 1862, pp. 11-18.

'The Botany of Syria and Palestine'. W. Smith. *Dictionary of the Bible*. vol. 2, 1863.

Handbook of the New Zealand Flora. London, 1864-67.

'On the Genus *Euptelea*' (with T. Thomson). *Journal of the Linnean Society. Botany*, vol. 7, 1864, 240-43.

Catalogue of the Plants distributed at the Royal Gardens, Kew ... from the Herbaria of Griffith, Falconer, and Helfer. London, 1865.

'Description of a New Genus *(Brandisia)* of Scrophylarineae from Martaban'. (with T. Thomson). *Journal of the Linnean Society, Botany*, vol. 8, 1865, pp. 11-12.

'On the identity of *Pinus pence* ... of Macedonia, with the *P. excelsa* of the Himalaya Mountains. *Journal of Linnean Society. Botany*, vol. 8, 1865, pp. 145-47.

'Lecture on Insular Floras, delivered before the British Association for the Advancement of Science at Nottingham, August 27, 1866. *Gardeners' Chronicle*, 1867, pp. 6-7, 27, 50-51, 75-76; *Journal of Botany*, 1866, 23-31; *Biological Journal of the Linnean Society*, vol. 22, 1984, pp. 55-77.

Presidential address to British Association for the Advancement of Science at Norwich, 1868. *Report of British Association*, 1868, pp. 58-75.

'Letters from J.D. Hooker to Sir Roderick Murchison, giving an Account of his Ascent of the Atlas'. *Proceedings of Royal Geographical Society*, vol. 15, 1871, 212-21.

Flora of British India. London, 1872-97. 7 vols.

'On the Discovery of *Phylica arborea*, a Tree of Tristan d'Acunha, in Amsterdam Island in the S. Indian Ocean; with an Enumeration of the Phanerogams and Vascular Cryptogams of that Island and St Paul'. *Journal of the Linnean Society. Botany*, vol. 14, 1875, pp. 474-80.

'Notes on the Botany of the Rocky Mountains'. *Nature*, vol. 16, 1877, pp. 539-40; *American Journal of Science*, vol. 14, 1877, pp. 505-09.

Journal of a Tour in Marocco and the Great Atlas (with J. Ball). London, 1878.

Botanical appendix to G.S. Nares. *Narrative of a Voyage to the Polar Sea during 1875-76 in H.M. Ships 'Alert' and 'Discovery'*, London, 1878, vol. 2, pp. 301-10.

'The Distribution of the North American Flora. A Lecture ... delivered on April 12, 1878 before ... the Royal Institution of Great Britain'. *Proceedings of Royal Institution*, vol. 8, 1879, pp. 568-80; *Gardeners' Chronicle*, 1878, pp. 140-42, 216-17.

'Observations on the Botanical Collections made in Kerguelen's Land during the Transit of Venus Expedition in the Years 1874-75 with a List of Flowering Plants, Ferns, Lycopods, and Characeae'. *Philosophical Transactions of the Royal Society*, vol. 168, 1879, pp. 1-15.

'On the Discovery of a Variety of Cedar of Lebanon on the Mountains of Cyprus'. *Journal of the Linnean Society. Botany*, vol. 17, 1880, pp. 517-19.

Presidential Address on Geographical Distribution given on 1 September 1881 at the British Association for Advancement of Science Annual Meeting at York. *British Association Report*, 1881, pp. 727-38; Nature, vol. 24, 1881, pp. 443-48.

'The Vegetation of the Rocky Mountain Region and a Comparison with that of other Parts of the World' (with A. Gray). *Bulletin of U.S. Geological and Geographical Survey*, vol. 6, 1880, pp. 1-62.

'The Himalayan Larch'. *Gardeners' Chronicle*, 1886, p. 718.

'The Himalayan Silver Fir'. Ibid., p. 788.

'The Himalayan Hemlock'. Ibid., p. 72.

Review of J.M. Coulter. Manual of the Botany of The Rocky Mountain Region. *Nature*, vol. 33, 1886, pp. 433-35.

'A Century of Indian orchids'. *Annals of Botanic Garden*, Calcutta, vol. 5, 1895, pp. 1-68.

Edited *Journal of ... Sir Joseph Banks during Captain Cook's First Voyage*. London, 1896.

Continuation of H. Trimen. *Handbook to the Flora of Ceylon*. London, 1898-1900.

'Reminiscences of Darwin'. *Nature*, 27 June 1899, pp. 187-88.

A Sketch of the Flora of British India. London, 1904. Reprinted in *Imperial Gazetteer of India*, vol. 1, 1907, pp. 157-212.

'An Epitome of the British Indian Species of *Impatiens*. *Records of Botanical Survey of India*', vol. 4, 1904-06, pp. 1-58.

'On the Species of *Impatiens* in the Wallichian Herbarium of the Linnean Society'. *Journal of the Linnean Society. Botany*, vol. 37, 1904, pp. 22-32.

'Asiatic Species of *Impatiens*'. *Hooker's Icones Plantarum*, vol. 29, 1908, plates 2851-75, vol. 30, 1910, plates 2301-25; 1911, plates 2951-75.

'On some species of *Impatiens* from Indo-China and the Malayan Peninsula'. *Kew Bulletin*, 1909, pp. 1-12.

'A Review of the known Philippine Islands Species of *Impatiens*'. *Kew Bulletin*, 1909, pp. 282-89.

'New *Impatiens* from China'. *Kew Bulletin*, 1910, pp. 269-75.

'Indian Species of *Impatiens*'. *Kew Bulletin*, 1910, pp. 291-300.

'On the Balsaminaceae of the State of Chitral'. *Kew Bulletin*, 1911, pp. 209-11.

'On some Species of *Impatiens* from the Malayan Peninsula'. *Kew Bulletin*, 1911, pp. 249-50.

'Indian Species of *Impatiens*. On some Western Peninsular Indian Balsamineae collected by Mr A. Meebold'. *Kew Bulletin*, 1911, pp. 353-56.

Sir J.D. Hooker manuscripts at Kew Gardens

Letters from Hooker, 1839-87.

Hooker. Letters and Journal, 1839-43.

Hooker. Correspondence, 1839-45, from Antarctic Expedition.

Hooker. Antarctic Journal (typescript).

Hooker. Correspondence received.

Hooker. Letters received from his father during voyage.

Hooker. Indian Letters, 1847-51.

Hooker. Indian Journal.

Hooker. Record of Seeds, Plants, and Museum Specimens sent to the Garden by Dr Hooker from India, 1847-51.

Hooker. Indian, Moroccan and Syrian Journals.

Hooker. Journey to America, 1877.

Hooker. Notebooks, 1840-77.

Voyage of H.M.S. *Challenger*. Letters, etc.

Transit of Venus Expedition, 1874-75. Letters, etc.

Voyage of H.M.S. *Alert* and *Discovery*. Letters, etc.

G. Maw. Journal of a Visit to Morocco and Account of the Great Atlas, 1871.

Page numbers in **bold** refer to illustrations